Using Corpora to Explore Linguistic Variation

Edited by

Randi Reppen
Susan M. Fitzmaurice
Douglas Biber
Northern Arizona University

John Benjamins Publishing Company
Amsterdam/Philadelphia

™ The paper used in this publication meets the minimum requirements of American National Standard for Information Sciences – Permanence of Paper for Printed Library Materials, ANSI z39.48-1984.

Cover design: Françoise Berserik
Cover illustration from original painting *Random Order* by Lorenzo Pezzatini, Florence, 1996.

Library of Congress Cataloging-in-Publication Data

Using corpora to explore linguistic variation   / edited by Randi Reppen, Susan M. Fitzmaurice, Douglas Biber.
     p.   cm. (Studies in Corpus Linguistics, ISSN 1388–0373 ; v. 9)
    Includes bibliographical references and indexes.
      1. Language and languages--Variation--Data processing. I. Reppen, Randi. II. Fitzmaurice, Susan M. III. Biber, Douglas. IV. Series.

   P120 V37 U84 2002
   410'.285--dc21   2002026160

ISBN 90 272 2279 7 (Eur.) / 1 58811 283 7 (US) (Hb; alk. paper)

John Benjamins Publishing Co. · P.O. Box 36224 · 1020 ME Amsterdam · The Netherlands
John Benjamins North America · P.O. Box 27519 · Philadelphia PA 19118-0519 · USA

Table of contents

Introduction

Broadly speaking, linguistics as a discipline approaches the study of language from two main perspectives: studies of structure and studies of use. Traditionally, linguistic analyses have emphasized structure. However, there has been an increasing interest in language use over the past three decades, investigating the systematic ways in which speakers and writers exploit the resources of their language.

Linguistic variation is central to the study of language use. In fact, it is impossible to study the language forms used in natural texts without being confronted with the issue of linguistic variability. Variability is inherent in human language: a single speaker will use different linguistic forms on different occasions, and different speakers of a language will express the same meanings using different forms. Most of this variation is highly systematic: speakers of a language make choices in pronunciation, morphology, word choice, and grammar depending on a number of non-linguistic factors. These factors include the speaker's purpose in communication, the relationship between speaker and hearer, the production circumstances, and various demographic affiliations that a speaker can have.

Analyzing the influence of contextual factors on linguistic variation presents difficult methodological challenges. Analyses of language structure have relied primarily on linguists' intuitions to distinguish between grammatical and ungrammatical forms in a language. However, these methods are not appropriate for studies of language use. While linguists might have strong intuitions about use, such intuitions often turn out to be incorrect, in part because we notice unusual occurrences more than typical occurrences (e.g., Biber and Reppen, 2002). Instead, adequate descriptions of variation and use must be based on empirical analyses of natural texts. Further, such analyses should be based on multiple texts collected from many speakers, so that conclusions are not influenced by a few speakers' idiosyncrasies. Finally, such analyses must simultaneously consider the influence of a range of contextual factors on linguistic variability.

Because of these difficulties, many large-scale investigations of linguistic variation are unfeasible using traditional analytical approaches. Corpus-based analysis, however, provides a means of handling large amounts of language and keeping track of many contextual factors at the same time. It therefore has opened the way to a multitude of new investigations of language variation and use.

Using Corpora to Explore Linguistic Variation is a collection of papers that illustrates the ways in which linguistic variation can be explored through corpus-based investigation. Most of the authors of these papers were present at the Second North American Conference on Corpus Linguistics and Language Teaching held at Northern Arizona University in Flagstaff, Arizona in the spring of 2000.

Following the approach developed in Biber, Conrad, and Reppen (1998), we have organized the chapters of the present book according to their primary research questions. There are two main kinds of research questions that can be investigated through corpus analysis. The first type of research question focuses on the use of a particular linguistic feature: a single word, a set of related words, a grammatical construction, or the interaction between particular words and grammatical structures. In contrast, the second kind of research question focuses on the overall characteristics of language varieties, either a single dialect or register, or the similarities and differences among a range of dialects/registers. Although some studies combine the two types of research issues, we have found this to be a useful organizing principle for the studies included in the present book: Part 1 focuses on variation in the use of particular linguistic features, while Part 2 focuses more on the overall characteristics of dialects and registers.

Part 1 of the book — 'Exploring variation in the use of linguistic features' — focuses on the study of specific words, expressions, or grammatical constructions. In many cases, these papers also adopt a register/dialect perspective, considering how related forms are used in different ways in different varieties. However, the main research goal of these papers is to study variation in the use of a particular linguistic feature, rather than to describe the overall linguistic characteristics of a language variety.

For example, the first paper in Part 1 — by Deanna Poos and Rita Simpson — focuses on two specific expressions used as hedges: *sort of* and *kind of*. This study compares the hedging functions of these forms in spoken academic English, focusing especially on variation associated with speaker gender and academic discipline, based on analysis of the Michigan Corpus of Spoken English (MICASE). Poos and Simpson conclude that these forms perform multiple functions, making it difficult to categorize them consistently as markers of tentativeness, understatement or mitigating tool in interaction.

Fiona Farr and Anne O'Keeffe are similarly interested in the use of a single word — the modal verb *would* — as a hedging device. This study contrasts variation in the use of this form between two institutional Irish English settings: the radio phone-in and post-observation teacher training interactions. Farr and O'Keeffe document how prevailing socio-cultural norms tend to shape the ways in which speakers interact in institutional settings, and how socio-cultural norms and institutional settings interact to shape the nature of the hedging that marks different registers. The following three papers extend the study of particular words to entire word classes. Michael McCarthy studies a set of words with related functions: non-minimal responses (like *wow, absolutely*, and *sure*). McCarthy compares the use of these forms in British and American English, concluding that in both varieties, 'good listenership' demands more than mere acknowledgment and transactional efficiency in interactions.

Graeme Kennedy's study of modal verbs in the British National Corpus shows how register differences interact with grammatical context to influence the choice among particular verb forms. In particular, Kennedy provides detailed descriptions of (1) the distribution of modal verbs across the register ('genre') categories of the BNC; (2) the distribution of modal verbs across different grammatical contexts (depending on the type of verb phrase); and (3) the interaction of these two factors in predicting variability in the choice of specific modal verb. Ferdinand de Haan's study similarly investigates the expression of modality, but focuses on these forms in Russian rather than English. In particular, de Haan focuses on the interaction of strong modality (expressed by impersonal verbs) and negation in Russian. The study shows how the modality of obligation and necessity combines with negative constructions to create indeterminacy and ambiguity, and how speakers resolve this structural ambiguity in practice.

Corpus-based techniques have also been used to study variation in the use of extended lexical expressions, including the study of idioms, formulaic language, and lexical bundles. The following two papers in Part 1 illustrate studies of this type. David Oakey focuses on the use of specific formulaic lexical phrases, like *it is/has been (often) been asserted/believed/noted that*. By contrasting the use of these expressions in different professional disciplines of academic writing — the social sciences, medicine and technology — Oakey is able to document how the same expression can serve distinctive discourse functions in different registers. In contrast, Viviana Cortes investigates the whole class of lexical expressions that occur with high frequencies in academic writing, what she refers to as 'lexical bundles'. Specifically, Cortes focuses on the use of lexical bundles in freshman composition essays, contrasting these patterns of use with those found in published academic writing and in conversation. Interestingly, Cortes finds that freshman composition texts often use the same structural lexical bundles found in academic prose, but that they are often used with different functions.

Finally, the study of variation in the use of linguistic features can be extended to grammatical constructions. The papers by Meyer and Hunston illustrate studies of this type. Chuck Meyer focuses on variation in the use of pseudo-titles, comparing the patterns of use in newspapers from the different subcorpora of the International Corpus of English (ICE). Despite the British-based stigma associated with the use of pseudo-titles in the press, Meyer finds that their use appears to be increasing in frequency as well as becoming increasingly formulaic, both in Britain and the US and in the journalistic discourse of English in East Africa, New Zealand, the Philippines and Jamaica. Susan Hunston takes a broader lexico-grammatical perspective, referred to as 'pattern grammar', which studies the transitivity and complementation characteristics of particular verbs. In addition, Hunston discusses how corpus-driven analyses can be applied for pedagogical purposes in language teaching, especially for illustrating both the patterns and the range of variation that students will encounter in natural language.

The two papers in Part 2 of the book — 'Exploring dialect and register variation' — were carried out to describe salient characteristics of dialects or registers. These papers also focus on particular linguistic features, but the primary research goal is to identify salient characteristics of the dialect/register, rather than description of the linguistic feature itself.

The paper by Chandrika Rogers is an example of a dialect study. Rogers examines a range of linguistic features in written Indian English registers to investigate the extent to which Indian English differs from British and American English in its syntax as well as its lexis and phonology. Her corpus findings indicate that written Indian English does not appear to differ markedly from other standard varieties in its syntax, but concludes that this research needs to be extended to spoken Indian English to investigate the issue further.

In contrast, the paper by Eniko Csomay illustrates a corpus-based study of register variation. Csomay focuses on the linguistic description of academic lectures, a hybrid register with a marked informational function coupled with the restrictions of real-time production circumstances. Csomay considers a broad array of linguistic features to document systematic patterns of variation among lectures, depending on factors such as the degree to which they occur in interactive as opposed to non-reciprocal settings and the level of instruction they are designed to satisfy.

Finally, the two papers in Part 3 of the book — 'Exploring historical variation' — show how these same two major perspectives on variation can be applied to historical issues as well as synchronic descriptions. The paper by Susan Fitzmaurice illustrates a historical study with a primary research focus on a specific linguistic feature: negation. In contrast, the paper by Christer Geisler illustrates a historical study carried out to study the general patterns of register variation.

Specifically, Susan Fitzmaurice interrogates the language of a network of men and women writing in late seventeenth- and early eighteenth-century England to discover the extent to which they exhibit the use of early modern and late modern English patterns of phrasal and clausal negation. In contrast, Christer Geisler looks at suites of linguistic features to explore patterns of variation in registers of nineteenth-century British English. Both papers show that linguistic variation is conditioned by social factors; Fitzmaurice concludes that age influences the choice of negation pattern, and Geisler shows how different registers demonstrate different patterns of variation with respect to a wide array of features.

One recurring theme of the papers in this volume is the extent to which linguistic variation depends on register differences, reflecting the importance of register as a key methodological and thematic concern in current corpus linguistic research. The papers collected here indicate some of the different ways in which the study of this interaction can be developed and expanded, from the study of linguistic variation in native speaker dialects, both contemporary and historical, to the preparation of diverse materials for teaching the registers of English to ESL and EFL students.

References

Biber, D., Conrad, S. & Reppen, R. 1998. *Corpus linguistics: Exploring language structure and use.* Cambridge: Cambridge University Press.
Biber, D. & Reppen, R. 2002. What does frequency have to do with grammar teaching? *Studies in Second Language Acquisition, 24,* 2 199–208.

PART I

Exploring variation in the use of linguistic features

CHAPTER 1

Cross-disciplinary comparisons of hedging

Some findings from the Michigan Corpus of Academic Spoken English

Deanna Poos and Rita Simpson
The University of Michigan

1. Introduction

The linguistic strategy known as hedging has received a good deal of attention over the past twenty-five years, especially by scholars interested in language and gender. In her 1975 work *Language and Woman's Place*, which started a boom in research on language and gender, Robin Lakoff listed hedges as one of nine qualities particular to feminine speech, viewing them as expressions of deference. In this tradition, Holmes (1986, 1998) has successfully challenged the association of hedging with powerlessness, focusing instead on its politeness functions, but she has nevertheless continued to find support for the notion that hedging is more characteristic of women's language then men's. In experimental studies, however, Meyerhoff (1992) and Dixon and Foster (1996) failed to find significant gender differences in hedge usage, leading the latter to claim that "if they do exist, gender differences in hedging are subtle and subject to marked variation across speakers and contexts of use" (1996, 90). Our data, taken from a corpus of natural interaction, support this claim. Like that of Dixon and Foster, our research is in part a reaction against the "wanton frequency counts and generalizations about women's subordination in conversation" that have plagued the field (p. 95).

In addition to the gender-related research, there have also been numerous studies of hedging in written discourse from English for Academic Purposes scholars (Crompton 1997, 1998; Hyland 1996, 1998a, 1998b, 2000; Kreutz and Harres 1997; Markkanen and Schröder 1997; Salager-Meyer 1994; Varttala 1999; Vassileva 1997). Hyland in particular has written extensively on the distribution and pragmatic functions of various hedging devices in scientific research articles. He has argued that hedging devices constitute an important pragmatic feature of effective scientific writing, as writers need to present their claims cautiously, accurately, and modestly in order to negotiate a balance between authority and concession. We have found the same to be true for academic speech across the disciplines, particularly in humanities and social science fields.

Our research links the study of gender and hedging with that of hedging in written academic discourse by analyzing the occurrence and function of hedges in an emerging corpus of academic spoken English. English has a wealth of lexical resources for expressing uncertainty, lack of commitment to a proposition, and vagueness, and it is beyond the scope of this paper to consider a wide variety of these terms. Rather, we have taken two prototypical examples of hedging, *kind of* and *sort of*, and analyzed the relationship of speaker gender and academic disciplinary context with respect to the frequency and functions of these terms. After preliminary forays into the data, we hypothesized that the frequency of *kind of*/*sort of* hedges would correlate more strongly with academic division than with speaker gender, with a higher rate of hedges in the humanities and social sciences than in the so-called hard, or natural, sciences.

In this paper, we first present the results of our quantitative analysis of the frequencies of the hedges in two subcorpora of MICASE. Then, like Aijmer in her 1986 corpus-based study of hedges, we analyze the complex pragmatic functions of *kind of* and *sort of* that we found in this academic corpus, many of which are similar to her findings. Additionally, we examine one speaker's use of these hedges in detail in order to further explicate their pragmatic functions. We analyzed this transcript, as much as possible, with respect to aspects of context such as academic discipline, speech event, interlocutor, and topic of discussion. We found that the hedges, taken in context, cannot be defined with a single meaning, but are better considered as pragmatic tools for managing speakers' relations to one another and to the topic being discussed. Uses of *kind of* and *sort of* do not only occur as markers of a speaker's tentativeness or insecurity, but also as markers of that person's relationship to interlocutors, training in a particular field, and views about knowledge and how to talk about knowledge. Hedging in a spoken academic context appears to have less to do with gender and more to do with academic discipline, type of interaction, and the speaker's additional needs and obligations within the institutional system. We aim to demonstrate that corpus-based research can provide insightful as qualitative well as quantitative information about language use.

2. The Corpus

The data for this analysis come from the Michigan Corpus of Academic Spoken English (MICASE) (Simpson, et al. 1999). This corpus has been under development at the University of Michigan's English Language Institute for the past two years, and at the time of this research consisted of almost 900,000 words and over 100 hours of recordings — a little over half the target size of 1.5 million words. Some of those transcripts are currently available on a searchable Web site (http://www.hti.umich.edu/m/micase), and by mid-2002, all the transcripts from the corpus will become publicly available at that location. The approximately 90 transcripts currently transcribed in MICASE include both classroom speech events, such as lectures, discussion sections, seminars, and labs, as well as non-classroom speech events, such as office hours, research group meetings, and advising sessions, to name a few. With the exception of those speech events that are not related to a specific discipline, such as undergraduate advising or staff meetings, all of the speech events are classified according to one of the graduate school's four academic divisions; that is, biological and health sciences, physical sciences and engineering, social sciences and education, and humanities and arts.[1]

For this study, we relied primarily on those transcripts that were classified into one of these four academic divisions, omitting non-discipline-specific speech events. That subcorpus consisted of 64 speech events, totaling 722,423 words. Table 1 shows the distribution of speech event types for all four divisions. Because the corpus is still under development, at this stage the four academic divisions do not contain equal numbers of each speech event type or equal numbers of total words. Looking at the total word counts for each division, we see that the biological and health sciences division is significantly smaller, and thus presumably not as representative, with only 122,762 words, compared to the other three, each with close to, or over, 200,000 words. In addition, the social sciences division contains more large lectures or colloquia than any of the other three divisions.

However, the breakdown by speech event is not an entirely reliable indicator of comparability of the speech, since some lectures can be quite interactive compared to others and some discussion sections and seminars can be largely monologic. A better indicator of comparability for these four subcorpora of academic divisions is a category assigned to each event in MICASE called the 'primary discourse mode'. There are four discourse mode categories, which for our purposes can be condensed into three: monologic, interactive, and mixed.

Table 1. Breakdown of Speech Events and Word Counts, Subcorpus 1: 64 speech events across four academic divisions

Speech Event Type	HUM/ARTS		SOCIAL SCI		BIO/ HEALTH SCI		PHYS SCI/ ENGIN	
	S	W	S	W	S	W	S	W
Large Lecture or Colloquium	3	30,688	9	88,368	2	23,444	4	34,015
Small Lecture	3	36,028	1	14,726	4	36,501	4	39,765
Discussion Section	1	8,129	1	8,463	1	8,019		
Student Presentations	3	48,442	1	12,344			1	6,684
Seminar	2	44,787	1	23,570			1	12,431
Lab					4	32,670	2	15,870
Defense	1	14,397	1	11,629			1	20,442
Office Hours			1	28,978			2	28,902
Tutorial	1	3,215					2	18,696
Advising	1	8,010						
Museum Tour	1	8,769						
Meeting					2	17,259	1	16,475
Study Group							1	15,838
Interview					1	4,869		
Total	16	202,465	15	188,078	14	122,762	19	209,118

S = Speech Events, W = Words

(This classification corresponds roughly to the scheme adopted by Biber et al. (2001) in their T2K-SWAL corpus, which classifies speech events as either low, high, or medium interaction.)

Table 2 shows the breakdown by discourse mode for each academic division in subcorpus 1. A few points of interest emerge from this breakdown. First, the social science division has a much higher percentage (52%) of monologic speech than the other three categories. Conversely, the two hard science

Table 2. Percentage of Monologic, Interactive, and Mixed Speech, Subcorpus 1

Primary	HUM/ARTS			SOCIAL SCI			BIO/ HEALTH SCI			PHYS SCI/ ENGIN		
Discourse Mode	S	W	%	S	W	%	S	W	%	S	W	%
Monologic	4	43,207	22%	10	99,239	52%	4	40,364	33%	6	56,544	27%
Interactive	5	73,511	36%	2	40,607	22%	7	54,798	45%	10	106,176	51%
Mixed	7	85,747	42%	3	48,232	26%	3	27,600	22%	3	46,398	22%

S = Speech events, W = Words

divisions have higher percentages of interactive speech than the other two (51% and 45%, compared to 36% and 22%). In spite of the unequal distribution of speech types, this corpus is still useful for preliminary research into the primary research questions, as long as these imbalances are kept in mind. So, for example, if we assume that the hedges *kind of* and *sort of* are likely to be more prevalent in interactive speech,[2] then we would expect to see more hedges in the biological and physical sciences and fewer in the social sciences. As we will see below, however, these trends are exactly the opposite.

To investigate the gender variable, we had to use a smaller subcorpus. Because we cannot at this point automatically identify the speaker of each token in the quantitative analysis unless there is only one speaker in the transcript or all the speakers are of a single sex, we limited the gender comparison to primarily single-speaker monologic speech events such as lectures, including some non-discipline-specific events. Unfortunately, the corpus at present does not yet contain enough monologic speech events in all of the four academic divisions to compare male versus female speakers within each division. As shown in Table 3, the subcorpus of male speakers includes five speech events from the physical sciences, two from the biological sciences, four from the social sciences, four from the humanities, and one non-disciplinary event. The subcorpus of female speakers includes two from the physical sciences, two from biology, six from the social sciences, one from the humanities, and two non-disciplinary events. In sum, we have investigated gender differences by comparing a subcorpus of 13 female speech events (146,738 words) with a subcorpus of 16 male speech events (160,077 words).

Table 3. Breakdown of speech events and word counts, subcorpus 2: 13 female and 16 male speech events

	HUM/ARTS		SOCIAL SCI		BIO/ HEALTH SCI		PHYS SCI/ ENGIN		NON-DISCI- PLINARY		TOTAL	
Gender	S	W	S	W	S	W	S	W	S	W	S	W
Female	1	17,968	6	56,875	2	24,366	2	19,525	2	27,999	13	146,733
Male	4	43,216	4	41,572	2	15,998	5	49,993	1	9,298	16	160,077

S = Speech events, W = Words

3.   Quantitative findings

In the following section, we present the results of the quantitative portion of the study. In calculating the frequency of *kind of* and *sort of* tokens, we did not include tokens that are synonymous with *type of*, editing out clear non-hedging examples such as:

> that's not the *kind of* mall that people socialize in
> you can find them by the *sort of* reasoning I've been doing

Instances of *kind of* and *sort of* that are ambiguously synonymous with *type of*, but are part of a noun phrase that conveys inexactitude, remain in the data set. Thus examples such as:

> any real coherent *sort of* way
> that *kind of* thing
> this *kinda* stuff
> I need some *sort of* verb (to govern the infinitive)

are counted as hedges. Although weeding out the non-hedging sense of the words seems like an obvious first step for this kind of study, none of the previous researchers in the studies we found mentions doing this, which is further evidence of the problem of "wanton frequency counts" mentioned earlier.

Figure 1 summarizes the results comparing male and female speakers. The points in the graph represent the overall frequencies of *kind of* and *sort of* for males versus females in subcorpus two, calculated as a rate per 1,000 words. These results show little or no difference in the *kind of/sort of* frequencies for the total subcorpus of males versus females, and for the social science and physical science divisions. Of those two divisions, the social science division has the most balanced number of words and transcripts for both genders, therefore providing

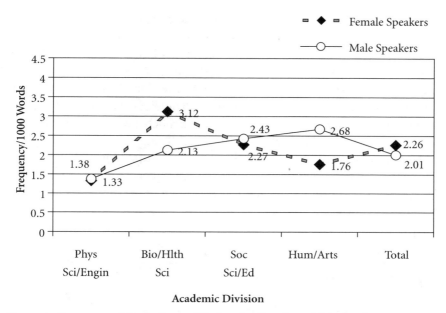

Figure 1. Frequency of *kind of/sort of* Hedges for Female vs. Male Speakers

a more reliable basis for comparing gendered use of the phrases than the physical sciences. That is to say, if female speakers are underrepresented, the frequency of hedging is more likely to be attributable to individual speaker variation. The other two divisions — biological science and humanities/arts — show opposite tendencies; i.e., female speakers have a higher hedging frequency in the biological sciences, and male speakers have a higher frequency in the humanities. These numbers cannot necessarily be interpreted as strong evidence for those trends, because of the relatively small word counts and number of speakers being compared. However, based on the minimal differences in both the overall hedging frequencies (2.26 for males versus 2.01 for females), and the frequencies in the more balanced social sciences subset (1.38 versus 1.33), this limited data set for gender comparisons definitely does not show a correlation between gender and frequency of hedging in academic speech.

Now we turn to the frequency counts for subcorpus one comparing the four academic divisions. As illustrated in Figure 2-a, these results show a clear trend: hedging frequencies are lowest in the physical sciences, slightly higher in the biological sciences, highest in the social sciences and second highest in the humanities. The only surprising finding here is that the average frequency for the social sciences is higher than for the humanities. However, we note here that the social science subcorpus is anomalous in one respect: one speaker from the longest transcript, an anthropology office hours session, uses an extremely high number of *sort of/kind of* tokens — 12.01/1,000. (In order to speculate on interactive motivations for *sort of/kind of* use, we look more closely at this speaker's hedging strategies in Section 5.) Therefore, we recalculated the numbers without that transcript, resulting in a much lower average frequency for the social sciences, 2.66/1,000, which is slightly higher than the average for the biological sciences, as shown in Figure 2-b. Omitting this outlier from the picture, we see a definite increase in hedging frequencies going from left to right, along the continuum of hard to soft disciplines, with the humanities disciplines at the top.

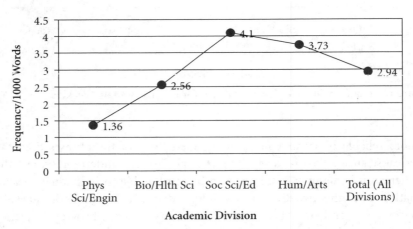

Figure 2a. Frequency of *kind of/sort of* Hedges Across Academic Divisions

Figure 3 shows the range of hedging frequencies for each individual speech event across the disciplines. This graph illustrates at least two important trends that further support the above findings. First, the highest and lowest frequencies for the physical sciences category are lower than the highest and lowest frequencies for all three other divisions. Second, the average frequencies for all the humanities transcripts going from lowest to highest are consistently higher than the corresponding averages for all other divisions — with the exception of the highest frequency transcript, which is surpassed by the aforementioned outlier in the social sciences, and one in the biological sciences.

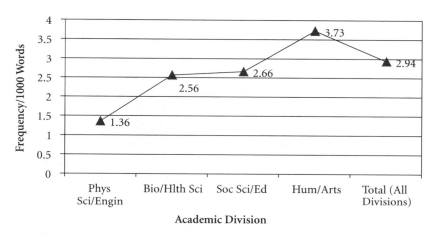

Figure 2b. Frequency of *kind of/sort of* Hedges Across Academic Divisions, without outlying speaker/transcript in Social Sciences

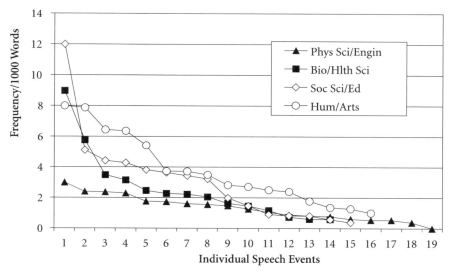

Figure 3. Range of Frequencies of *kind of/sort of* Across Academic Divisions, from Highest to Lowest

Although the preceding comparisons of average hedging frequencies are convincing, one further set of quantitative comparisons provides an even clearer picture of the trend we see emerging here. A wordlist frequency count of two-word phrases in each of the four disciplinary sub-corpora produced the results shown in Table 4.

In the humanities, *kind of* was the seventh most frequent two-word phrase, comprising .19% of that subcorpus, and *sort of* was the eighth most common phrase, at .18%. Similarly, in the social sciences, *sort of* was seventh (.20%) and *kind of* was eighth (.18%). In contrast, in the biological sciences subcorpus, *sort of* was 16th (.14%) and *kind of* was 18th (.12%). Finally, in the physical sciences and engineering subcorpus, *kind of* was only the 42nd most common two-word phrase, comprising .08% of the total, and *sort of* was ranked 126th, at .05%. Furthermore, a keyword comparison[3] of these two-word phrases generated with WordSmith Tools (Scott 1999) comparing the physical sciences with both the humanities and the social sciences reveals the results shown in Table 5. When the wordlist of two-word phrases from the humanities is compared against the physical sciences, the number one ranked keyword phrase for the humanities corpus is *sort of*, and *kind of* is ranked fourth. In comparing the social sciences with the physical sciences, *sort of* is the second highest keyword phrase (after *you know*) and *kind of* is the tenth highest. Neither *kind of* nor *sort of* showed up as keyword phrases for the physical sciences.[4] Furthermore, although the present study has focused only on the hedges *kind of* and *sort of*, it is worth noting that several other hedging-type phrases appear in the keyword lists for the soft disciplines. In the humanities subcorpus, *it seems* is ranked fifth, and *you know, I mean,* and *I think* are all in the top five for the social sciences, whereas none of these or any similar phrases emerge as key word phrases in the physical sciences.

To summarize the quantitative findings, from the preceding analyses, there is a wealth of evidence in support of our hypothesis that academic discipline, broadly defined, is a stronger predictor of frequency of hedges with *kind of* and *sort of* than is gender in this corpus. Naturally this finding begs the question of why these correlations exist, so we consider here some possible explanations for this trend. Is it possible that humanists are by nature more tentative, less

Table 4. Frequency of *kind of/sort of* as 2-word phrases

	HUM/ARTS	SOCIAL SCI	BIO/ HEALTH SCI	PHYS SCI/ ENGIN
kind of	7th (.19%)	8th (.18%)	18th (.12%)	42nd (.08%)
sort of	8th (.18%)	7th (.20%)	16th (.14%)	126th (.05%)

Table 5. Keyword Comparisons

HUM/ARTS	SOCIAL SCI	PHYS SCI/ ENGIN
1. **sort of**	1. you know	1. the probability
2. the building	2. **sort of**	2. probability of
3. the word	3. I mean	3. equal to
4. **kind of**	4. think that	4. you have
5. it seems	5. I think	5. travel time
6. the Spanish	6. the U.S.	6. the rack
7. the story	7. the target	7. real time
8. that he	8. growth rate	8. one and
9. the studio	9. the growth	9. is equal
10. native speakers	10. **kind of**	10. minus one

confident people, while scientists are more assertive and sure of themselves? In other words, one might propose as an explanation that it is the personalities of people who are drawn to the humanities and to the sciences that predisposes them to be "hedgers" or "non-hedgers." In response to this proposal, we cite evidence from an experimental study by psychologists Schachter et al. (1991, 1994), which showed that disciplinary differences in the filled pauses *um* and *uh* were not a result of individual speaking styles, but rather of the subject matter being discussed.[5] Filled pauses are related to hedging in that at least some hedges appear to function primarily as another kind of filled pause. In fact, this finding is corroborated by frequency counts of these two filled pauses in the four disciplinary subcorpora of MICASE; like *kind of* and *sort of*, these filled pauses occur most frequently in the humanities and least frequently in the physical sciences.

A more plausible explanation that may account for some of the differences in frequencies is one put forth by Schachter et al., which attributes the differences in frequency of filled pauses to the vocabulary range available to the hard versus the soft disciplines. They argue that speech about a humanities subject is more likely to be punctuated with filled pauses than that on a scientific subject because vocabulary in humanities fields is less standardized and speakers must choose the best possible word from a field of possibilities. For example, they write, "there are no synonyms for *molecule* or *atom* or *ion*... In contrast, consider the alternatives for *love, beauty, group structure, prejudice,* or *style*" (Schachter 1994: 37). Their point is that language in the social sciences or humanities is characterized by richer vocabularies than in the sciences, and is therefore more likely to include pauses and filled pauses uttered by speakers searching for the right word among many possibilities. Because *sort of* and *kind of* can also act as filled pauses for a speaker searching for the precise expression (as we discuss further in Section 5), this explanation may help account for some of the disciplinary frequency differences.

A closely related explanation is that content in the humanities and social sciences is by nature more open to multiple interpretations than content in the hard sciences, which deals more with discrete, observable data, facts, and processes. Simply put, there is more to hedge about in the softer disciplines than in the sciences. Norms of interaction in the humanities and social sciences call for presenting alternate points of view, stating and eliciting opinions, carefully crafting arguments, and allowing for multiple possibilities — all of which can and do involve the use of various hedging strategies. Finally, it must also be considered that there are other hedging devices that occur more commonly in the sciences, particular those having to do with imprecise numerical expressions, such as *about, around, approximately,* etc.

4. Pragmatic analysis

At this point, we present an analysis of the pragmatic functions of *kind of* and *sort of,* preceded by a brief summary of their grammatical distribution.

Grammatically, the hedges occur freely in front of any word class. Most commonly, they occur as part of noun phrases such as example (a), or preceding simple nouns as in (b). They also occur quite frequently before verbs, as in (c), less frequently before plain adjectives (d), and only occasionally do they modify a prepositional phrase, as in (e). A quantitative examination of grammatical categories across the four academic divisions did not reveal any significant trends or differences in these frequencies.

a. *kind of* an informal gathering type space
b. it's *kind of* a cycle
c. repetition can *sort of* devalue things
d. planning is *kind of* irrelevant
e. then *sort of* just beyond the mailbox

As Dixon and Foster likewise note (1997: 103), too often researchers assume a one-to-one relationship between tokens of hedging and expressions of tentativeness. Hedges have in fact been defined as words that convey inexactitude, uncertainty or tentativeness — or, to quote George Lakoff (1973) in his classic account of hedges, "words whose meaning implicitly involves fuzziness." Our data suggest that these linguistic elements often also perform rather complex functions in discourse, such as metpragmatically marking the speaker's relationship to the interlocutor — a function that may be especially salient in academic or other institutional settings. A closer examination of typical hedges in the MICASE data reveals diverse functions and strategic uses, and our premise here is that these subtle interactional functions are worth further investigation.

The following examples illustrate the multiplicity of discursive or pragmatic functions a typical hedge can serve. The most obvious function of *sort of* or *kind of* is the expression of inexactitude. Take, for example, the following:

f. This *sort of* reddish brownish object twentyish feetish from me (HA: philosophy discussion section)

g. yeah it had *sort of* a... r- rusty or not rusty but, yellowish... (BS: biology lab)

h. because Bley is also a *kind of* chameleon-like figure. (HA: dissertation defense)

Note that in this decontextualized setting, the utterance of these phrases does not seem to reflect the speaker's self-confidence or even expertise, but is rather used, particularly in the first two examples, to describe a state of inexactitude. In examples (f) and (g), *sort of* seems to function in parallel with the suffix — *ish*.

Closely related to the prototypical function of conveying inexactitude, *sort of* and *kind of* can be used in an effort to soften the force of a stance or opinion, as in the following examples. In these contexts — i.e. making an assertion or stating an opinion — the semantic fuzziness conveyed through the use of hedges begins to serve the pragmatic function of politeness, in that speakers mitigate the force of their opinions or assertions.

i. okay, so, the fact that those people don't consider planning is *kind of* irrelevant right? (PS: dissertation defense)

j. well, I *sort of* a- I I *sort of* agree more with Paul on that (BS: graduate student meeting)

k. well we *kind of* uh are reasonably sure of that (PS: engineering seminar)

l. in, the journal-equilibrium approach, um the *kind of* the ideal situation is to end up with a competetive equilibrium... (PS: graduate student meeting)

Similarly, speakers often use *sort of* and *kind of* to mitigate a criticism or request, as in examples (m) through (p). These types of examples are found with some frequency in speech events that by definition involve a high degree of feedback, such as office hours, dissertation defenses, or tutorials.

m/ I was just *kinda* hoping you'd read over this and say this has to be changed,
or you know whatever (SS: student, anthropology office hours)

n. I mean I've told you this before the way you write is *sort of* chatty... you
can't let your argument *kind of* disappear as you *kind of* tell me this little
story (SS: graduate student instructor, anthropology office hours)

o. but somehow I feel that surface needs to be broken up. And one way would
be doing with big roof and you notice this could extend down somehow
maybe to *kind of* acknowledge, the exterior of the building (HA: architecture critique)

p/ ...ask us in office hours to see how much we'll tell you and then, *kind of* just
write a paragraph that says (PS: office hours)

The above examples, demonstrating *sort of* and *kind of* in the contexts of
displaying inexactitude, softening a bald assertion and mitigating a remark that
could potentially threaten the interlocutor's positive or negative face, support
Lakoff's description of hedges as indicating "fuzziness." The following uses of
kind of and *sort of* might be invoking "fuzziness," but they also seem to serve a
more important interactional function.

We found that *kind of* and *sort of* frequently precede the use of particularly
sophisticated vocabulary or jargon words, as in (q) through (u).

q. I didn't look carefully enough at *sort of* the iconography of the jewelry or
anything (SS: instructor, anthropology office hours)

r. where I was talking about, um, folk music and how to *sort of* nuance that
view (HA: advising / tutoring)

s. along with that success has come *kind of* a Faustian bargain (BS: natural
resources colloquium)

t. and how they're *sort of* situated in this political and economic context (SS:
instructor, anthropology office hours)

u. wood gets a variety of uses, *sort of* the artis- ar- ar- artisanal uses of wood
(BS: natural resources colloquium)

In the above examples, *kind of* and *sort of* modify "the iconography of the
jewelry," "to nuance that view," "Faustian bargain," "situated in this political
and economic context," and "the artisanal uses of wood." It is true that *kind of*
and *sort of* hedges are here mitigating the force of the phrases they precede, but
they seem to do so not to modify the semantic meanings or force of the terms
(as in examples (f)–(h) of "typical" inexactitude hedges), but rather to modify
their pragmatic effects. The speakers seem to use *kind of* and *sort of* in these

instances as a device to position themselves in relation to the material, and in particular, in relation to the interlocutor. For example, "the iconography of the jewelry" and "situated in this political and economic context" are uttered by an anthropology graduate student instructor in an office hours meeting. Throughout the meeting, she kept a friendly rapport with the visiting under-graduates. She often used *kind of* or *sort of* before uttering a phrase from the register of anthropology or even general academic jargon, as if to distance herself from the technical vocabulary in an effort to display more solidarity with her less academically indoctrinated interlocutors. The speaker in example (r) above uses *nuance* as a verb rather than a noun — certainly a more marked usage and therefore one the speaker might feel obliged to flag. Example (s) precedes a phrase unlikely to be heard in a biological sciences colloquium (*Faustian bargain*). More importantly, a reference to a *Faustian bargain* in any context implies a certain degree of academic and literary sophistication on the part of the interlocutors, therefore, by flagging the phrase with the hedge *kind of*, the speaker subtly acknowledges the potential face-threatening nature of this allusion.

Example (t) is another instance of a fairly unpretentious noun (artisan) being used in a marked word class, the adjective *artisanal*. The speaker's false starts preceding the full pronunciation of the word are most likely a result of uncertainty about the stress pattern, and are further evidence of the markedness of this word form.

Similarly, *kind of* and *sort of* often precede metaphors.

v. my *sort of* semisolid definition of life, would be anything that can… (BS: biology lecture)
w. so just to give you *kind of* a map of where we are going (SS: sociology lecture)
x. that promoter is *sort of* the on-off switch for the expression of your gene of interest (BS: genetics lecture)
y. it's like this *sort of* underbelly that has some, figural characteristics (HA: architecture critiques)
z. there're some questions which *sort of* straddle, the reading as a whole (SS: sociology lecture)

Like the hedges preceding sophisticated vocabulary, these hedges also seem to function as metapragmatic markers — drawing the listeners' attention to the non-literal terminology, and attesting to the speakers' self-consciousness about using an overt metaphor.

Of course, each of these categories of meaning is much fuzzier than we have so far described. Most instances of *sort of* and *kind of* in any given text are difficult to place definitively in any one of these categories, a fact likewise noted by Dixon and Foster (1997, 97). Many are tied up with connotations of politeness, accommodation, vagueness, and understatement, among other possibilities of interpretation. Many belong in multiple categories, as in example (o) above from an architecture critique, in which the speaker — a professor and juror — suggested that a big roof could "extend down somehow maybe to *kind of* acknowledge, the exterior of the building." The speaker uses *kind of* in a long string of other hedges as a tool for mitigating her critique, while also using it to invoke a field-specific metaphor (the roof acknowledges the exterior). Additionally, as mentioned earlier (and exemplified in Section 5 below), there is the possibility that *kind of* and *sort of* function as filled pauses in some speaker's personal styles.

From the perspective of interpretation, it is impossible to say with certainty what a speaker "means" by using *kind of* or *sort of*. It is certain, however, that each hedge could simultaneously serve several of the functions described above. This provides further support for our argument that speakers should not uniformly be described as tentative or lacking confidence based on the number of times they use so-called hedge words, as these words clearly perform many discoursal and interactional functions.

5.   A Closer Analysis of One Speaker

As mentioned earlier, our corpus included a clear outlier in the social sciences. This anthropology teaching assistant used *kind of* and *sort of* hedges an average of 12 times per thousand words during an office hours interaction (compared with the social science division average of 2.66/1,000, excluding her file). This office hours interaction, a discussion of term paper progress shortly before the end of the semester, provides an especially rich setting for the use of hedges; young students tentatively explain their ideas and solicit feedback and the teacher diplomatically offers her suggestions. The consequently high number of hedges in this transcript allows us to examine the main interactional functions *kind of* and *sort of* may have in the context of a series of one-to-one encounters with one speaker remaining constant. Additionally, the authors' own familiarity with the field of anthropology, and more importantly, with the conversational norms for making assertions in the context of that discipline, aided their interpretation of the interactional functions of hedging. In this speech event, the primary speaker, a young teacher, uses *sort of* and *kind of* to mitigate her criticisms of the students' work, and also as part of a discourse style often used when dealing with problematic concepts in this discipline.

To investigate how her stance might change as she interacts with a variety of students and subjects, we broke her office hours transcript down into subsections divided by the change in conversation partner. When discussing a student's term paper on the social dynamics of midwestern American malls, she hedges using *kind of* and *sort of* 8.37/1,000 times. Alternatively, when she discusses a paper on displays of collective identity at an African-American cultural festival, this white teacher hedges using *kind of* and *sort of* 19.81/1,000 times. When discussing an Indian-American student's research on self-perception of Indian-Americans, she hedges using *kind of* and *sort of* a similarly exorbitant 18.94/1000 times. These numbers could be interpreted as revealing her relative lack of information on these subjects or her status as an outsider, and therefore marking her reticence to speak decisively. The simplistic conclusion is that this speaker is insecure or at best tentative in her assertions. We would like to offer an alternative explanation, however.

Rejecting the assumption that this speaker lacks confidence in her assertions, we want to reframe her language as intellectually sophisticated. She uses hedges pervasively to mark her disciplinary stance and to make the meta-linguistic claim that the best way to talk about cultural issues is in these indefinite terms. The speaker herself gives the disclaimer that underlies many instances of her use of *sort of / kind of* when, in a typical example, she states that

> we're talking about *sort of* racial cultures I mean there exists an African-American culture //[S4]right// um, which isn't singular which is multiple la-de-da we can't draw boundaries around a culture…

In anthropology, whose disciplinary standards she is presently teaching, it is a very complex endeavor to make a statement about "racial cultures." Since she nevertheless wants to talk about the phenomenon of collective identity, she hedges her assertion and discusses "*sort of* racial cultures." This *sort of* hedge abbreviates the following disclaimer that "culture … isn't singular … [but] is multiple" and allows her to succinctly reiterate or remind her addressees of the fluidity of concepts like community, race, and culture. Her linguistic choices thus reflect her disciplinary epistemology.

The filled pause function is also especially evident with this speaker. For example, consider the following typical example:

"but um, also especially the Friends and um, the, housing activist ones are *kind of,* um, none of those are organizations that are actually centered in the African-American community…"

The speaker has used *kind of* here to keep control of the floor as she determines the conclusion of her utterance. It is clear that this apparent hedge functions as a filled pause because the speaker in fact changes the direction of the utterance in order to make her point — *kind of* never modifies an adjective, as the beginning of the utterance leads one to expect.

Perhaps this outlying speaker uses *kind of* and *sort of* frequently because she speaks in a "feminine" way. This could be, but it seems equally likely that her distinctive use of this form is due to other factors such as her role as social scientist, her disciplinary convictions, and her position as a young person in a teaching position — as well as personal style. In other words, she isn't just "doing" gender — she's doing a lot of other things having to do with the presentation of her identity. The central concern should not be negotiation of gender role, because in this situation she has several other roles that supercede her position as a woman — in particular, anthropology teacher.

6.   Conclusion

This study has offered clear evidence that in the domain of academic speech, there is no significant gender-related effect on speakers' hedging frequencies, but rather that there is a noticeable difference in hedging frequencies depending on the academic division. In particular, looking at the two ends of the academic division continuum, the physical sciences versus the humanities, there is a conspicuous difference in *kind of/sort of* uses. Further, we have posited some possible explanations for the finding that hedging frequencies are lowest in the physical sciences and highest in the humanities.

These findings are significant not only for their implications in the study of variation across registers of spoken English, but also because they offer food for thought to EAP practitioners, who until now have had a wealth of information available on the nature of hedging in academic writing, but no comparable data about hedging strategies and distributions in academic speech. Learning to express and interpret hedges appropriately is important for advanced learners of English, because of the important interactional and social functions they perform in addition to their role in conveying shades of certainty or commitment.

Because of the relatively small corpus used for this study, there are of course limitations to the generalizability of the data, and we realize the need for additional research in this area. Beside replicating the current study with a larger corpus and more tightly controlled subcorpora, other possible avenues for further investigation include the effects of speech event type as well as speaker age and/or academic position on the use of hedging devices. There is also, of course, a need for studies examining a wider range of hedging devices in speech, comparable to Hyland's (1998) work on scientific research articles.

In this paper we have also shown that the phrases *kind of* and *sort of*, while identified primarily as hedges, are multifunctional and serve a variety of often overlapping sociopragmatic purposes in spoken interaction. They can be used to reduce the force of an utterance or to convey inexactitude; they can be used to mitigate criticisms, requests, and directives for the sake of politeness, minimizing threats to the listener's face; they can also be used as a subtle form of accommodation to interlocutors who may not be familiar with technical jargon or metaphorical references used by the speaker; finally, these phrases can function as filled pauses, or floor-holding devices, in some speakers' styles.

The two essential aspects of our argument are, first, that hedging is not necessarily — or not always, at any rate — a gender-based phenomenon, and second, that so-called hedge words like *kind of* and *sort of* are not merely, and indeed not always, indicators of tentativeness. The argument that hedging is not necessarily an indicator of gender is not new, nor is the argument that hedging is not necessarily an indicator of linguistic tentativeness. However, we want to reiterate these arguments together with a plea for context in the investigation of language difference and for an understanding of speaker identity as multiplex and not reducible, however convenient, to check-marked boxes. Even when working with data that necessarily appear as essentialized categories, such as the divisions organizationally necessary in a corpus such as MICASE, it is possible to pursue a more nuanced understanding of the individual speaker and why he or she might speak in a particular way. An attention to the most basic elements of context demonstrates that use of particular linguistic forms does not index a single element of identity. When thinking about gender and its construction through language, one must look well beyond use of a single word, and beyond that word's supposed semantic meaning.

Notes

1. Although this division of academic fields of study into larger groupings is not universal and there are a number of departments and courses within certain departments that are interdisciplinary by design, we believe that on a macro level, the categories are useful — especially when viewed as a continuum. Furthermore, the number of disciplines — like English, philosophy, sociology, physics, chemistry, or biology — that fall clearly into one category or another are more numerous than those whose boundaries are less discrete, such as linguistics, history, women's studies, or biopsychology.

2. A frequency count comparing hedging rates in the interactive transcripts to those in the monologic ones in each division (omitting events in the mixed category) indicates that this assumption holds true for all four divisions.

3. Key words are those whose frequencies are unusually high in comparison to another text, and thus characterize the text in question. The key word function of WordSmith Tools works by comparing two existing word lists, calculating the frequencies of every word in both corpora, and using a log likelihood test to determine the statistical significance of the difference in frequencies, and to rank the words in order of *keyness*.

4. The keyword list for the physical sciences is consolidated from the two lists comparing the physical sciences once against the humanities and once against the social sciences. There were few substantive differences in the two lists.

5. They determined this by collecting and analyzing speech samples from professors both in disciplinary lectures and in one-on-one interviews on a topic of equal familiarity to all of them; they found significant differences for the disciplines only in the lecture speech.

References

Aijmer, K. 1986. "Discourse variation and hedging." *Corpus Linguistics II: New Studies in the Analysis and Exploitation of Computer Corpora*, J. Aarts and W. Meijs (eds) 2–18. Amsterdam: Rodopi.

Biber, D., Reppen, R., Clark, V., and Walter, J. 2001. "Representing spoken language in university settings: The design and construction of the spoken component of the T2K-SWAL Corpus." In *Corpus Linguistics in North America: Selections from the 1999 Symposium*, R.C. Simpson and J.M. Swales (eds), Ann Arbor: University of Michigan Press.

Crompton, P. 1998. "Identifying hedges: definitions or divination." *English for Specific Purposes* 17(3): 303–313.

Crompton, P. 1997. "Hedging in academic writing: some theoretical aspects." *English for Specific Purposes* 16(4): 271–289.

Dixon, J.A., and Foster, D.H. 1997. "Gender and Hedging: From Sex Differences to Situated Practice." *Journal of Psycholinguistic Research* 26(1): 89–107.

Holmes, J. 1998. "Signaling gender identity through speech." *Moderna Sprêak* 92(2): 122–128.

Holmes, J. 1986. "Functions of *you know* in women's and men's speech." *Language in Society*, 15(1): 1–22.

Hyland, K. 2000. *Disciplinary Discourses: Social Interactions in Academic Writing.* Harlow, England: Pearson Education Limited.

Hyland, K. 1998a. *Hedging in Scientific Research Articles.* Amsterdam: John Benjamins Publishing Company.

Hyland, K. 1998b. "Boosting, hedging and the negotiation of academic knowledge." *Text*, 18(3): 349–382.

Hyland, K. 1996. "Nurturing hedges in the ESP curriculum." *System*, 24: 4, pp. 477–490.

Kreutz, H. and Harres, A. 1997. "Some observations on the distribution and function of hedging in German and English academic writing." In *Culture and Styles of Academic Discourse*, A. Duszak (ed), 181–203. Berlin: Mouton de Gruyter.

Lakoff, G. 1973. "Hedges: A study of meaning criteria and the logic of fuzzy concepts." *Journal of Philosophical Logic* 2: 458–508.

Lakoff, R. 1975. *Language and Woman's Place.* New York: Harper and Row.

Markkanen, R. and Schröder, H. 1997. *Hedging and Discourse. Approaches to the Analysis of a Pragmatic Phenomenon in Academic Texts.* Berlin: Walter de Gruyter.

Meyerhoff, M. 1992. "A sort of something — hedging strategies on nouns." *Working Papers on Language, Gender and Sexism* 2(1): 59–73.

Salager-Meyer, F. 1994. "Hedges and textual communicative function in medical English written discourse." *English for Specific Purposes* 13(2): 149–170.

Schachter, S., Rauscher, F., Christenfeld, N., and Crone, K. T. 1994. "The vocabularies of academia." *Psychological Science* 5(1) : 37–41.

Schachter, S., Christenfeld, N., Ravina, B., and Bilous, F. 1991. "Speech disfluency and the structure of knowledge." *Journal of Personality and Social Psychology* 60(3): 362–367.

Scott, M. 1999. *WordSmith Tools, Version 3.0.* Oxford: Oxford University Press.

Simpson, R. C., Briggs, S. L., Ovens, J., and Swales, J. M. 1999. *The Michigan Corpus of Academic Spoken English.* Ann Arbor, MI: The Regents of the University of Michigan. http://www.hti.umich.edu/micase

Varttala, T. 1999. "Remarks on the communicative functions of hedging in popular scientific and specialist research articles on medicine." *English for Specific Purposes* 18(2): 177–200.

Vassileva, I., 1997. "Hedging in English and Bulgarian academic writing." In *Culture and Styles of Academic Discourse*, A. Duszak (ed), 203–221. Berlin: Mouton de Gruyter.

CHAPTER 2

Would as a hedging device in an Irish context

An intra-varietal comparison of institutionalised spoken interaction

Fiona Farr and Anne O'Keeffe
University of Limerick, Ireland

1. Introduction

Hedging is an interactional strategy that speakers and writers avail of in communication, and they do so in a variety of ways and for different reasons. Hedging is born out of its conditions of use, which extend beyond the immediate context to the socio-cultural setting of the interaction. The purpose of this study is to look at one hedging device in two institutional face-to-face interactions in an Irish setting. We have chosen to look at the modal verb *would* as a hedging device in the following institutionalised settings in Irish society: (1) radio phone-in on national Irish radio (henceforth RPI), and (2) post-observation teacher training interaction in an Irish university as part of an MA teacher training programme (hereafter POTTI). For the purposes of our analysis, we will use two corpora of transcribed spoken data from these settings. In doing so, we aim to build on the work of Clemen (1997:235) to show that hedging is achieved primarily by setting an utterance in context rather than by straightforward statement. Furthermore, it is our contention that 'context' should be extended to levels that allow for the inclusion of the sociocultural norms prevalent in the setting from which the data has emerged.

1.1 Hedging: Existing research

Much has been published on hedges and hedging from theoretical, empirical and applied perspectives. In a thirty-year period, so much has been published on this interactional language feature that it has warranted review articles and volumes (e.g., Clemen 1997, and Schröder and Zimmer 1997). Inevitably, with such publication density comes diversity and conflict and this will become more evident as our discussion unfolds. For present purposes, we have decided to review hedging in terms of definition, gender, culture, genre, psycho-affective aspects, and pedagogic application.

Throughout the research literature, hedges have eluded any widely-accepted definition. Fundamental to the problem of definition is the divergence in approach to the nature and realisation of hedging. Traditionally, hedges were considered to be semantic modifiers or approximators in the spirit of the original definition by Lakoff (1972:195), who coined the term 'hedge' to describe a word or phrase 'whose job it is to make things fuzzier or less fuzzy'. Lakoff is concerned with hedges in terms of the semantic contribution they make to the statements in which they occur (Loewenberg 1982:196), in that hedges can weaken or strengthen category membership. This is in keeping with Rosch (1978) who developed the prototype theory and views hedges as linguistic devices that modify prototypical category membership e.g. A penguin is *a kind of* bird. Such an approach is rooted in cognitive science where "semantic grasp" has preceded analysis at the level of discourse, and therefore discounts language function (Clemen 1997:235).

Concurrent with this is the emergence of research which focuses on the pragmatic aspect of hedges in discourse. Within this approach, research questions focus more on *why* hedges are used and offer reasons such as politeness, indirectness, vagueness and understatement — to name but a few. The work of Brown and Levinson (1978) on politeness strategies has provided a framework for investigating the role of hedging in domains such as mitigation and indirectness. In this approach, hedges are context- dependent and are integral to face saving strategies. Channell (1990), Clemen (1997), and Markannen and Schröder (1997) examine pragmatic strategies and their linguistic components in terms of hedges from various perspectives.

In addition to these approaches, many researchers have attempted to reclassify and subcategorise what have traditionally been collectively called hedges. Prince et al. (1982), for example, suggest that hedges should be divided into *shields* (those performing a pragmatic function) and *approximators* (those performing a semantic function) and Rounds (1982) adds *diffusers* to this. Hübler (1983) proposes *understatements* and *hedges* while Fraser (1975) examines in some detail *hedged performatives*, and subsequently differentiates between hedging and *mitigation* (Farser 1980). Not surprisingly then, in the words of Markannen and Schröder (1997:15), "through extension the concept has lost some of its clarity and sometimes seems to have reached a state of definitional chaos, as it overlaps with several other concepts".

Gender has long been considered integral to the nature and use of hedges. Preisler (1986), following in the Lakoff (1975) tradition, maintains that women hedge more than men because their speech is more tentative and less assertive. However this viewpoint has become contentious and much research based on naturally occurring speech data has failed to support such conjecture (see Bradac et al. 1995, Dixon and Foster 1997, and Holmes 1986, 1990, 1993). Lakoff's original proposals, based primarily on hypothesis and personal observation, have not only been challenged, but many findings now suggest that the contrary may in fact be true. As with many areas of inquiry, evidence remains inconclusive on the effect of gender on the use of hedges. On the other hand, more recent work expands the sphere of investigation into the cultural constraints on the use of hedges, for example, Crismore et al. (1993) cross sociocultural boarders by comparing the American and Finnish contexts. Hinkel's (1995) innovative study examines the use of modals on a comparative and contrastive basis between native and non-native users of English in a written context and finds that there are considerable sociocultural constraints on the pragmatics associated with modality. Cultural values and norms also form a central tenet of our present study.

Several researchers have examined the effects that the use of hedges and intensifiers have on the listener in terms of features such as attractiveness, authority, credibility etc. Results are conflicting and not easy to compare due to dissimilarities in empirical procedures adopted by researchers such as Bradac et al (1995), Holmes (1990) and Hosman (1989). Furthermore, specific language domains have formed test-beds for how and why native speakers employ hedges. There has been considerable research into the use of hedges in academic texts (Myers 1989, 1992; Fahnestock 1986, Hyland 1994, 1996, Salager-Meyer 1994, and Rounds 1982). Another significant corpus-based study into the use of hedging in a professional spoken context is that of Prince et al. (1982). In their corpus of 12 hours of physician to physician talk, they note that the most salient linguistic feature, in terms of frequency, is that of hedges. Using Lakoff's (1972:195) definition of a 'hedge' as a word or phrase 'whose job it is to make things fuzzier', they identified between 150 and 450 hedges per hour, more than one every fifteen seconds.

Some researchers address the practical application that their findings may have in pedagogic terms (Hinkel 1995, Holmes 1988, Markannen and Schröder 1997,

Table 1.

Item	LC (Ir)	CANCODE (Br)	CIC (Am)
I would say	266	164	105
I'd say	177	159	100

and Skelton 1988). However, most of the research in this area engages at either a theoretical or descriptive level exclusively and it appears that much territory remains unexplored in relation to pedagogic implications and applications in foreign language teaching.

2.   Data for this study

For the purposes of our analysis, we have isolated two sub-corpora of spoken data from the Limerick Corpus of Irish English (L-CIE). The datasets were selected primarily on the basis of comparability, in that both comprise asymmetrical dyadic interactions in institutional settings.

Sub-corpus A (RPI): 55,000 words of radio phone-in conversations from *Liveline*, a national Irish radio programme on Radio Telifís Éireann.

Sub-corpus B (POTTI): 52,000 words of post-observation teacher trainee interaction — feedback on teaching practice which took place as part of the Master of Arts in Teaching English as a Foreign Language programme at the University of Limerick, Ireland.

3.   Variation at the Level of Dialect

A striking feature of both the RPI and POTTI data is the pervasive use of the modal verb *would* as a hedging device. Table 1 profiles the frequency of a commonly occurring cluster: *I would say*, and its contracted form *I'd say*, is compared across three Irish, British and American English: the Limerick Corpus of Irish English[1], the Cambridge and Nottingham Corpus of Discourse in English (CANCODE) and a corpus of American spoken data from the Cambridge International Corpus.[2]

This very superficial level of comparison merely served to verify that on a basic quantitative analysis, at a dialectal level, the structures *I would say* and *I'd say* as hedges are used more frequently by Irish speakers than by British or American speakers. In fact, on the basis of the above results, Irish speakers seem to be twice as tentative, or *hedgy*, as American speakers. An inter-varietal exploration of one exponent of the interactional strategy of hedging, at what Biber et al. (1999) call a dialectal level, is restrictive in its insightfulness. The question of language variety is much more complex than that presented within a quantitative and geographically-constrained framework. This should by no means preclude looking at variation across geographical boarders, but for our present purpose of examining the hedging device *would*, numerical results such as these, do not further our understanding of how or why it is used in face-to-face interaction. At a broader level, it could be argued that corpus-based research into how varieties of a language differ need to go beyond the level of lexis and syntax, and naturally-occurring language has much to offer by way of comparison at the level of discourse across language varieties.

3.1 Variation at the Level of Register

If we are to characterise the use of *would* in our data, we need to examine its situational distribution, that is to say, variation in spoken language is not only a by-product of place and history, it is also integral to context. We have chosen to adopt the term *register* for what Halliday (1978: 31–32) refers to as the "very simple and very powerful … fact that the language we speak or write varies according to the type of situation". This term is strongly associated with Biber's research over the years (see especially: Biber 1988, 1995). In Table 2, we use the matrix for the major distinctions between the situational characteristics which distinguish registers from each other as outlined in Biber et al (1999: 15–17). We have added *spoken genre range*, which refers to the Bakhtinian notion of relatively stable units of talk where "each separate utterance is individual … but each sphere in which language is used develops its own *relatively stable types* of utterances" (Bakhtin 1986: 60) (italics from original source). We use the term *spoken genre range* within the framework of Biber et al (1999: 16) to refer to the finite range of expected generic talk units within each register. RPI and POTTI may be compared thus in Table 2.

With this comparison in mind, we can now move to quantify the occurrence and distribution of *would* in the corpora.

Table 2.

RADIO PHONE-IN	POST OBSERVATION TT INTERACTION
Register	**Register**
– *Mode*: Spoken: voice only	– *Mode*: Spoken: face to face
– *Interactive online production* – with a degree of advanced planning	– *Interactive online production* – with a degree of advanced planning
– *Shared immediate situation* – no – (shared society)	– *Shared immediate situation* – a university office
Main communicative purpose/content: good radio disclosure, entertainment	– *Main communicative purpose*: instructive/directive
– *Audience*: public within broadcast range, mainly Irish	– *Audience*: individual, mainly Irish.
– *Dialect domain*: local	– *Dialect domain*: local
– *Spoken Genre Range*: (diverse but finite) – narrative, argumentative, expository, directive, opinion-giving/seeking.	*Spoken Genre Range*: (less diverse than RPI) directive, observation-comment, expository, reflection/self-direction, motivational.

4.   A Quantitative Analysis

An initial search of *would* in the RPI and POTTI registers yielded the results illustrated in Table 3 below. The distribution of *would* from a quantitative perspective is strikingly similar, with RPI data producing 3930 occurrences, and POTTI data 3942 occurrences per million words. At this level of analysis, it seems that there may be nothing of significance or interest to note about the use of *would* as a hedge between these registers.

Table 3.

RPI		POTTI	
Total no. of words	54.707	Total no. of words	51.754
Total hits for *would* per million words	3.930	Total hits for *would* per million words	3.942

Subsequent to this surface-level analysis, independent concordances were generated for each register. Repeated patterns, left and right of the node word *would,* which occurred more than twice in either register were isolated. Idiosyncratic repetitions and non-hedge uses of *would* were excluded at this stage. Negative and contracted forms were further investigated, and all results were converted into 'words per million'. Where negatives or contractions are excluded from the tables below, there were no occurrences in either register. Three significant patterns emerged: (1) pronoun plus *would,* (2) questions with *would* (inverted and "wh-") and (3) *would* in verb phrase constructions.

4.1 Pronoun + *Would*

The overall pronoun distribution for the two registers was quantified and the results are shown in Figure 1 below.

The results in Figure 1 are in line with the register characteristics as outlined in Table 2. The 'on-lineness' and level of personal involvement is represented in the high results in the *I* and *you* domains, where the main communicative goals are achieved collaboratively within the dyads and within the respective spoken genre ranges. These results are very similar to the distribution of pronouns in conversation in general as represented in the findings of Biber et al (1999: 334). Table 4 below shows the results for the distribution of pronoun plus *would* in our data.

Proportionally, we find the first person singular most frequently co-occuring with the hedge *would,* this is in line with expectation within the speech

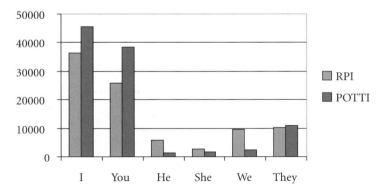

Figure 1.

Table 4.

Item	RPI	POTTI
I would	1151	1024
You would (sing.)	73	213
You would (pl.)	0	0
You would (generic)	55	174
He would	91	0
She would	39	39
We would	91	77
They would	219	270

genre range of these registers (expository, directive, and so on), that is to say, the speaker habitually seeks to downtone or make fuzzy when explaining, directing etc. in the first person. The nil result for the pronoun *he* in POTTI is explained by the female gender bias among the trainer and student cohorts. The result for impersonal *you*, especially in the POTTI data, and the result for *we*, are linked to the strategic use of 'other attribution' which we will return to at a later stage. Table 5 offers a breakdown of other nominal colligates.

These results again relate to how speakers distance themselves from the content of their utterance, for example:

Extract 1 (POTTI)
Trainer: Am is that what you meant by **this**?
Trainee: Am yes.
Trainer: Well now you see **that is that would not be clear to me** when I look at this as a lesson plan+
Trainee: Right.
Trainer: +and see it as an aim **I thought** that you were going to look at **maybe** differences in eating in various cultures.

Table 5.

Item	RPI	POTTI
People would	54	77
It would	475	502
There would	91	0
This would	54	19
That would	128	231

We see that the trainer has chosen to change the pronoun from *this* to *that* between her first and second turn. *That* can be used as a means of referring in a non-central, marginalised manner (McCarthy 1994), in other words, by using *that* the speaker seeks to put the criticism at a safe distance. In the speech genre of argumentation (see Extract 2 below), the caller uses *that would* as a subtle means of raising opposition or scepticism as if from a distance, whereas the direct implication of the caller's utterance is: *I don't agree with what you have said.*

> **Extract 2** (RPI)
> Presenter: ...I mean people are still getting married and they're getting married for all best of reasons and they're mad about one another and they want to live happily ever after.
> Caller: Yes. That **would** be the that **would** be the the pretty picture that's painted but as time goes on it's cool these days ah and pardon me for using that word because it's a slang word I don't like. But as they say it's cool to say "I'm separated". It's attractive.

Similarly in Extract 3, the trainer is trying to bring the trainee around to self-direction. Her attempt at elicitation fails and consequently her utterance *that would be* offers a palatable front for the implication that the trainee's answer was wrong. The more direct, face-threatening version would be: *No, that's at the correction stage.*

> **Extract 3** (POTTI)
> Trainer: ...if you're not sure which words they're not going to know and which words they are going to know?
> Trainee: Ask them well like ask concept questions or something?
> Trainer: That **would** be at the correction stage but before they start to do the activity so you might not know for example that am oh excuse me that "cook" and "cooker" are going to be+

It is also worth noting that the high results for *I, they* and *it* plus *would,* in both registers, is in keeping with the findings of Luukka and Markkanen (1997), who say that this is representative of spoken interaction where levels of involvement with oneself, the audience and what is being talked about are high.

4.2 "Would" in Questions

Typical of institutional spoken registers is a high density of questions (Harris 1995). In our data, we note the frequency of second person singular questions which are hedged using *would*. Table 6 illustrates the results for concordance searches of *would* + pronoun in questions.

Table 6.

Item	RPI	POTTI
Would you	292	541
Signifiant reoccurence within this:		
Would you say	73	19
Would you have	37	19
Would you not get	37	0
Would you prefer	0	58
Would you talk	0	173
Would you use	0	58
Would they	18	19
Would we	18	0

From the above table, *you, they* and *we* represent the pronoun domains which are hedged using *would* and they are reflective of the results for Pronoun + *would* in Table 4 (apart from the obvious lack of *I* in questioning). Table 7 shows the results for *Wh-* questions.

These results characterise the marked contrast in the communicative goals of each register. In all cases, the POTTI data shows much higher frequencies. The use of *what would* underpins the importance of reasoning and rationalising in POTTI and *how would* indicates the essential place of methodological issues involved. *When* and *which would* suggest that temporality, precision and decisiveness are vital and clearly illustrate the necessity to make hard and fast choices.

> **Extract 4** (POTTI)
> Here the trainer is trying to bring about trainee reflection.
> Trainer: Okay now if you had to change some general aspects of not necessarily of the lesson because I'm not sure how much of that you could change+
> Trainee: Mm.
> Trainer: +of either the lesson or your planning **what would** it be?
> Trainee: Am+

On the other hand the narrative speech genre within the RPI speech genre range does no involve hedged questioning using *what, when, how* and *which* — if such a question type is used, it functions to seek clarification, rather than validation or self-direction, and so on, from the story teller, and so it does not need to be hedged. Also, it is more incremental in RPI to use declarative questions, which function as formulations to be accepted or rejected, and these are frequently hedges, for example.

Table 7.

Item	RPI	POTTI
What would	37	155
How would	18	39
When would	0	39
Which would	0	59

Extract 5 (RPI)
In an opinion-giving unit, the presenter offers the following formulation:
Presenter: And **you would think** not all for the better?

Extract 6 (RPI)
Presenter: **There would be** the smallest little bit of prejudice in that no?

4.3 Would in verb phrase structures

The following results were found in our investigation of how *would,* as a hedging device, co-selects certain verbs. Table 8 lists the most frequent structures (using a cut-off point of 50 occurrences per million words). When a collocation was found in either corpus above the cut-off point, its frequency in the second corpus was also generated even if it was below this point. Each item was also profiled in the contracted and negative forms.

Notable here in the *would + VERB* pattern is the absence of performative verbs relating to the modes of speaking within the range of the respective registers, especially, *advise, disagree, explain, argue.* The absence of these patterns is indicative of a non-directive stance taken up by the presenter in *Liveline,* where advice or explanation is sought from the listeners rather than from the presenter. Equally, arguments in RPI are very genial and *I'd argue* does not occur within an argumentative unit in the RPI corpus. In the case of POTTI, the absence of these hedged performatives is evidence of a desire to encourage rather than dictate reflection and self-direction.

At this point, we have explored to some degree the colligational and collocational patterns (after Sinclair 1996), of *would* as a hedge, and now we need to go beyond the numerical evidence to look at the wider context in pursuit of a global characterisation of how and why *would* is used so frequently as a hedging device in our data. Several integral factors will be considered.

Table 8.

Item	RPI	POTTI
Would be	749	676
'd be	311	97
Would not be	37	39
Wouldn't be	73	77
TOTAL	1170	889
Would do	37	58
'd do	0	19
Wouldn't do	110	0
TOTAL	147	77
Would go	37	77
'd go	0	58
TOTAL	37	135
Would have	439	618
'd have	146	77
Wouldn't have	73	97
TOTAL	658	792
Would think	91	19
Wouldn't think	0	19
TOTAL	91	38
Would like	91	77
'd like	165	231
Wouldn't like	18	0
TOTAL	274	308
Would say	183	425
'd say	238	97
Wouldn't say	110	58
TOTAL	531	580
Would see	54	77
Wouldn't see	54	19
TOTAL	108	96
Would agree	91	19
TOTAL	91	19

5.   Institutional Setting and Hedging

The Irish national broadcasting station, *Radio Telefís Éireann*, and an Irish university are the institutional settings from where the RPI and POTTI data originate respectively. These interactions are set within institutionally defining parameters. As is the case in any conversation, participants enter into a 'conversational contract' (after Fraser 1980:343) where each party brings an understanding of some set of rights and obligations vis à vis the other (for example, Clark and Carlson 1982 refer to *the Principle of Responsibility* at a sociocultural level, and Thomas 1983 talks about pragmatic *ground rules*). Within institutional settings these rights, obligations and norms are fixed to a greater degree than in everyday conversation, and this is largely due to the institutionalised roles of the participants. Specific to this study are the roles of presenter and caller, and trainer and trainee. These exogenous roles are not symmetrical in terms of rights, obligations, and power. The presenter and the trainer, by virtue of role, are bestowed more power in the interaction. In the case of the presenter, the power semantic is, to a degree, less asymmetrical than in the case of the trainer-trainee dyad, because it is mitigated by the caller being the 'primary knower' (term adapted from Berry 1981) of his or her own experience, problem or opinion (O'Keeffe 1999). The trainer, on the other hand, is both the power role holder and the 'primary knower' in terms of professional expertise.

Would is used strategically within these institutional conditions on a relational or interpersonal level to redress the asymmetry of the power semantic within the dyads, and on an transactional level to mitigate or downtone the perlocutionary force of the utterances in 'difficult' or threatening speech genre units, and to frame the focus of the talk into a safe hypothetical band. These strategies are dealt with in greater detail in the following discussions.

5.1 Maintaining a Solidarity-based Persona

In both of these dyads, the power holders are very aware of establishing and maintaining their professional personas within a solidarity base rather than a power base. The radio presenter wishes to be perceived as the nation's friend and facilitator, and the trainer needs to ensure that she is perceived as someone who is collaborative, motivating and facilitative rather than someone who has the power to pass of fail a student on the basis of teaching performance. We can say, therefore, that both the presenter and the trainer are very aware of mitigating their role-related power for relational reasons. *Would* can function as a hedge at an interpersonal level to downtone at moments when the presenter or trainer feel their power needs to be played down. Typically, in the case of RPI, this occurs in questioning, where the presenter has superior role-related power to ask the questions and in POTTI, it frequently occurs in criticism/directive units. We reintroduce Extract 1 to see how *would* is used by the trainer to downtone the force of her criticism. It is well within her conversational right, and within the expected speech genre range, to give criticism, but for reasons thus elaborated, she uses various hedging devices to mitigate the perlocutionary force of the criticism and so plays down the institutionalised power associated with her role.

> **Extract 1** (POTTI)
> Trainer: Am is that what you meant by **this**?
> Trainee: Am yes.
> Trainer: **Well now you see that is that would not be clear to me** when I look at this as a lesson plan+
> Trainee: Right.
> Trainer: +and see it as an aim **I thought** that you were going to look at **maybe** differences in eating in various cultures.

In Extract 7 we see *would* used in questioning. This call involves a distressed mother calling the show to seek advice on her son's new tattoo, which she strongly disapproves of. The presenter knows the caller's answer to this question will be negative and we see how she re-frames it grammatically so as to reduce the face threat and to allow for a less direct answer from the caller. In this way she realigns the power asymmetry.

> **Extract 7** (RPI)
> Presenter: And **will you would you** like to go **sort of** on a sun and sea holiday with him this year?
> Caller: Not particularly he's involved in a lot of water sports and am I suppose that's where ⟨sigh⟩ people will see this tattoo and I just wonder what they'll think about it.

In both 1 and 7, one notices the abrupt, or online, change of grammatical construction (anacoluthon) from *that is (not clear to me)* to *that would not be clear to me (POTTI)* and *will you would you (RPI)*. We also find clustering of other hedging devices: *Well now, you see, maybe,* also attribution is to the first person singular *to me, when I look, I thought* which provide a subjective cushion or possibility that *I could be wrong, it's only what I perceive.* As mentioned earlier, we find the use of the pronoun *that (that would not be clear to me)* which again serves to attribute responsibility for the problem away from the trainee (see *other attribution* — Halliday and Hasan 1976, McCarthy 1994). *That* functions similarly in Extract 8 below (***that's what the theory tells us***). *Here* we see a further strategic use of *would* by the power role holder.

5.2 Downtoning Knowledge-based Power

There are frequent examples where the trainer downplays knowledge-related power, for instance in Extract 8 below. The trainer alludes to what pedagogical theory tells *us* (solidarity alignment with the trainee — *us = all teachers*) rather than asserting what she knows as part of her professional expertise.

> **Extract 8** (POTTI)
> Trainee: Yeah but **d'you think that** was **kind of** that was appropriate?
> Trainer: Yeah yeah **I would think so** I I mean tha= **that's what the theory tells us that's what we spoke about yesterday in class**+
> Trainer: (6 turns later) **I would say so** yeah yeah I think so am yeah the just the organisation and the way you set up that activity wasn't quite as clear-cut as as it might have been+

Interesting to note here that the trainee is also hedging, using appropriate devices marked in the above extract, such as *kind of*. We see that the trainee is being self-directive and the inversion of advice-giver role accounts for the hedging in this utterance, which could have been asserted as a statement: *I think that was appropriate*. We see therefore that the trainee attends to the negative face of the trainer, since advice normally comes from the trainer, the power-role holder.

5.3 Downtoning Threatening Speech Units

Another systematic use of *would*, at a transactional level, is found in the following extract from RPI. In this argumentative unit, *would* is used by the caller to downtone the force of her assertions. *Would* is also used by the presenter to pose opposition to these assertions. This is a very genial form of augurmentation, typical of *Liveline*, where directness in opposition is generally avoided. Consistent with this is the use of other-attribution *they, most people worldwide, one million people in Northern Ireland* and so on.

> **Extract 9** (RPI)
> Caller: In a subtle yes I know but within Article Two we're always said that our national territory was the whole island **I would think**

most+

Presenter: Yeah but but it wasn't
Caller: +but I think **most people worldwide would** when **they would** say
              Ireland **they would** see see the whole island right? Now I think
              everybody be wo= **would** be aware that there's been a conflict on
              our island for a hell of a long time. But as as its territory I think
              most people **would would** define that the island as being the
              whole island.
Presenter: Well **one million people in Northern Ireland wouldn't**.
Caller: Oh yes I know isn't **that** the ongoing conflict?

The equivalent 'difficult' moments in POTTI are where direction is given, in
other words, trainees are told what *should* be done, or indeed what *should have
been done* in the classroom. Systematically, the trainer uses *would* where *should* is
substitutable. We can say that in these instances, *should* is downtoned to *would*.

Extract 10 (POTTI)
Trainer: Now they are they are actually discussing things for purposes of
            fluency+
Trainee: Umhum.
Trainer: +so you **wouldn't** correct them+
Trainee: Right.
Trainer: +that normally **you'd** note the things that+

Extract 11 (POTTI)
Notice the use of *I* by the trainer to further mitigate the implied criticism (also
in 12).
Trainee: +it a good idea to leave them where they are?
Trainer: It depends on what you're doing like ah for this oh if had finished this
            exercise **I would have have told them** they could go+

Extract 12 (POTTI)
Trainee: But what way **would** I have like quickened up the correction and
            that?
Trainer: No **I wouldn't** am ⟨$E⟩ pause two seconds ⟨/$E⟩ the I mean you went
            through it word line by line+
Trainee: Yeah.
Trainer: +by you know and you asked the same question each time "have
            we"+
Trainee: Yeah.
Trainer: +"are there any mistakes in this line" but you just said "okay" **you
            would** start perhaps start the class by saying "okay we'll we'll go
            through this quite quickly because I have the="+

5.4 Transposing face threat into a hypothetical 'Safe Band'

Many of the extracts hitherto cited could be interpreted as hypothetical. The power holder very often moves the topic into a hypothetical band, where face threat is removed, as such the speaker chooses the least threatening option on the pragmatic continuum (Givón 1984). We refer to this strategy as *transposing*. In the example below, the presenter is talking to a well known Irish barrister, she could ask a prototypical question: *Do you knowingly take spurious cases?*, but she transposes this to the opposite end of the pragmatic continuum and asks *if you think a case is spurious would you take it?* This allows room for the caller to decide if he will elect to answer the question directly, from a personal stance, or from a professional or hypothetical stance. He chooses the latter (*every barrister, a lot of barristers*) and interprets the *you* in the presenter's question as generic.

> **Extract 12** RPI
>
> Presenter: +if you think a a case is spurious **would** you take it?
>
> Caller: Well I mean ah **the answer is yes every barrister** is obliged to take a case in an area in which he professes to be competent and he's not supposed to be say "I just don't like the look of my client ah I won't take the case". But am if I'd I I think a **a lot of barristers** if they thought there was a genuine try on they **would** say well no foal no fee doesn't apply in this case.

Conversely, in the following extract, the caller (a bishop) takes up a personal stance though he is given the option to give a general answer.

> **Extract 14** (RPI)
>
> Presenter: Right. Ah uh **if you take the society that you would have grown up** in+
>
> Caller: Um.
>
> Presenter: +and **you take where we are now I mean there are quite remarkable differences.**
>
> Caller: Yes oh absolutely yeah absolutely.
>
> Presenter: And you **would** think not all for the better?
>
> Caller: No **I think** it's always mixed **I think** it as you know in in one way it a very it's impossible to compare one one ah period with another because there are good points and bad points in what's happened but **I think** it's it's it's certainly different

This strategy frequently occurs in POTTI when the trainer seeks to initiate reflection on the part of the trainee, and self-criticism is safely transposed to the hypothetical band. Here is a typical example.

Extract 15 (POTTI)
Trainer: Yeah now what other instruction **would** you need ah?
Trainee: I should have told them that there were four words that **wouldn't**
           have been used that **would** not necessarily fit into the…

Hedging to downtown advice/direction seems to be a typical politeness strategy
in this register. It lends a theoretical and global significance to the advice. The
unspecified human agent implies a wider application of the direction being
given (see Extract 16).

Extract 16 (POTTI)
Trainer: Am the whole all the time they were discussing ah again because we
           discussed this the you didn't have space to really monitor them but
           normally you'd be able to monitor and+
Trainee: Umhum.
Trainer: +**more closely and ah it would be needed** a variety of good dis=
           good discussions don't just occur teacher stands back as far as
           possible but the teacher is still+

6. Sociocultural norms and hedging

The main data for this paper are not only defined by respective institutional
settings and register issues, they are also rooted in a sociocultural context, that
is to say, both sets of data are from institutional settings *within* Irish society. It
is accepted by many researchers that the linguistic manifestations of hedging are
not only complex but that the functions they express cannot be identified in 'a
social and textual vacuum' (Holmes 1990:186). In order to fully understand
hedging, we feel that sociocultural context needs to be considered as one of
critical factors in explaining why speakers hedge in discourse. In Irish society,
directness is very often avoided and this is attested throughout our data. We
suggest that 'forwardness', which ranges from being direct to being self-pro-
moting is not valued within Irish society. That Irish society does not place a
high value on powerful or direct speech is borne out by some of the above
results for the use of *would* as a means of downtoning assertiveness and
directness in asymmetrical interactions. In the extracts below, a notable feature
is indirectness in answering polar questions. Irish people will rarely answer a
polar question with a single word answer (yes or no), it is considered too direct
and impolite (Asián and McCullough 1998:49). This is consistent with the
sociocultural norm of avoiding over-assertiveness.

Extract 17 (POTTI)

Here the trainer is giving advice to the trainee on how a particular exercise should have been conducted based on the trainee's performance in the classroom

Trainer: **Do you think it would have been possible at all** to **just** leave them work through them all? ⟨pause: two seconds⟩ like it w= it was always going to be a better idea to split up the sentences **was it?**

Trainee: **I would say so.**

Trainer: Mm.

Trainee: Given your time **I would say so.**

Trainer: Umhum.

Trainee: Yeah **maybe** not into such small sections maybe into just three different groups "can you work on the first two can you work on the fourth to the eighth can you work on the eighth to the twelfth"+

Extract 18 (RPI)

Here the topic is boarding schools. The caller phones the programme to talk about his memories of being at a boarding school.

Presenter: Did you find it wo= girls very alien beings when you came up in contact with them?

Caller: Well yeah I **would.** Ah yeah there was that sorry for the noise there there was that ah there was that element am I mean when I came to university first you know you're used to an all out male atmosphere so okay girls it's kind of wo= what's that creature over there is that a girl...

Very frequently in our data, we find that when speakers talk about themselves, they try to mitigate directness by using *would* as an epistemic downtoner, even where the propositional content is undisputed.

Extract 19 (RPI)

Caller: I told him he could have piercing I mean no problem any organ of the body he wanted anything you could undo but tattoos they frighten me and as regards that lady yeah **I would be really in sympathy** with **her I would be saying** "do you know what you're doing? Do you know who you are identifying yourself with?"

Extract 20 (RPI)

Here the caller was convicted of murdering her colleague in Saudi Arabia. After an extended period, she was released and cleared of the charge.

Presenter: You figure you were stitched up?

Caller: Oh yes very definitely.

Presenter: Why?
Caller: Am again ah **I would have many theories on this**.

We see that the caller expresses certainty in her agreement with the presenter's formulation, but in her next turn when it comes to asserting the reasons why, we find *would* is used to downtone the assertion. In Extract 24 below, the topic is the problem of female facial hair and we find *would* used systematically by the caller to downtone facts about the past and present colour of her facial hair.

Extract 21 (RPI)
Caller: …two years ago I discovered waxing+
Presenter: Yeah.
Caller: +and I thought it was brilliant. The best thing ever. Now I get it done every about every two weeks and it takes longer to grow back and it's am brighter than it was. **I would have had black hair** you know **my hair would be brownish now** but it was+
Presenter: Right.
Caller: +**black** in the teenage years.

We find similar downtoning of fact in the POTTI data.

Extract 22 POTTI
Trainer: I live in ah I never know whether I live in west Clare or north Clare no I suppose I **would be** north Clare I live in Ennistymon.
Trainee: Oh you're north.

7. Conclusion

Comparative corpus evidence showed us that the occurrences of *would* are higher in Irish English. We found that it was used substantially as a hedge in the Irish institutional data and the quantitative colligational and collocational patterns were consistent with this. Closer scrutiny revealed that much of its use was context specific, where a need to redress the asymmetry of the dyadic power semantic gave rise to downtoning, especially on the part of the power role holder. However qualitative examination of the data suggested that not all examples of *would* could be attributed to softening in the normal sense of mitigating or downtoning the force of an utterance. Over and above this category, we identified the use of hedges to downtone facts where the propositional content was not in dispute, which led us to conclude that hedges had a broader pragmatic function for speakers of Irish English in our data. That is to say that by framing a fact in a hedged way a speaker can attend to face needs in a given context at a sociocultural level. This conclusion gives rise to a three-tiered model for the analysis of hedging in spoken interaction (see Table 9).

Table 9.

Level 1
– Mode
– Interactive online production
– Shared immediate situation
– Main communicative purpose/content
– Audience
– Dialect domain
– Spoken genre range

Level 2
– Institutional context
– Institutional role of speaker
– Institutional power semantic

Level 3
– Sociocultural norms

These levels can be considered in a hierarchical manner where *level 1* is confined by *level 2* and this in turn is restricted by *level 3*. At a schematic level, this illustrates the way in which sociocultural norms guide our interactions, and like institutional norms they have a defining influence at the level of register (level 1). To fully understand why we hedge in any given interaction, it is necessary to take all three levels into consideration. Together, register, setting and society weave a complex and intricate web which determines language choice and use in any particular variety.

Notes

1. The Limerick Corpus of Irish English is broadly based on the framework outlined in McCarthy (1998: 8–12).

2. Results from CANCODE and CIC are based on an oral presentation by Prof. Michael McCarthy, University of Limerick 1999, and reproduced here with his kind permission.

References

Aijmer, K. 1987. "Discourse Variation and Hedging". *Costerus* 57: 1–18.

Asián, A. and McCullough, J. 1998. "Hiberno-English and the teaching of modern contemporary Irish Literature in an EFL context". *Letters and Links* 5: 37–60.

Bakhtin, M.M. 1986. "The Problem of Speech Genres" In *Speech Genres and Other Late Essays*, C. Emerson and M. Holquist (eds), 60–102. Austin: University of Texas Press.

Berry, M. 1981. "Systematic linguistics and discourse analysis: a multi-layered approach to exchange structure" In *Studies in Discourse Analysis*, M. Coulthard and M.M. Montgomery (eds), 120–145. London: Routledge.

Biber, D. 1988. *Variation across Speech and Writing.* Cambridge: Cambridge University Press.

Biber, D. 1990. "Methodical Issues Regarding Corpus-based Analyses of Linguistic Variation". *Literary and Linguistic Computing* 5(4): 257–269.

Biber, D. 1995. *Dimensions of Register Variation.* Cambridge: Cambridge University Press.

Biber, D., Johansson, S., Leech, G., Conrad, S. and Finegan, E. 1999. *Grammar of Spoken and Written English.* London: Longman.

Bradac, J., Mulac, A. and Thompson, S. 1995. "Men's and Women's Use of Intensifiers and Hedges in Problem-Solving Interaction: Molar and Molecular Analysis". *Research on Language and Social Interaction* 28(2): 93–116.

Brown, P. and Levinson, S. 1978. "Universals in Language Usage: Politeness Phenomena". In *Questions and Politeness: Strategies in Social Interaction,* E.N. Goody, (ed), 56–310. Cambridge: Cambridge University Press.

Channell, J. 1990. "Precise and Vague Quantities in Writing on Economics". In *The Writing Scholar,* W. Nash (ed), 95–117. Newbury Park: Sage.

Clark, H. and Carlson, T. 1982. "Hearers and Speech Acts". *Language* 58: 332–373.

Clemen, G. 1997. "The Concept of Hedging: Origin, Approaches and Definitions". In *Hedging and Discourse: Approaches to the Analysis of a Pragmatic Phenomenon in Academic Texts,* R. Markkanen and H. Schröder (eds), 235–248. Berlin: Walter de Gruyter.

Crismore, A. et al. 1993. "Metadiscourse in Persuasive Writing: A Study of Texts written by American and Finnish University Students". *Written Communication* 10(1): 39–71.

Dixon, J.A. and Foster, D.H. 1997. "Gender and Hedging: From Sex Differences to Situated Practice". *Journal of Psycholinguistic Research* 26(1): 89–107.

Fahnestock, J. 1986. "Accommodating Science: The Rhetorical Life of Scientific Facts". *Written Communication* 3(3): 275–96.

Fraser, B. 1975. "Hedged Performatives". In *Syntax and Semantics (vol. 3),* P. Cole and J.L. Morgan (eds), 187–210. New York: Academic Press.

Fraser, B. 1980. "Conversational Mitigation". *Journal of Pragmatics* 4: 341–350.

Givón, T. 1984. "The Speech Continuum" In *Interrogativity: a colloquium on the grammar, typology and pragmatics of questions in seven diverse languages,* W.S. Chisholm (ed), 245–254. Amsterdam: Benjamins.

Halliday, M.A.K. 1978. *Language as Social Semiotic.* London: Edward Arnold.

Halliday, M.A.K. and Hasan, R. 1976. *Cohesion in English.* London: Longman.

Harris, S. 1995. "Pragmatics and Power". *Journal of Pragmatics* 23: 117–135.

Hinkel, E. 1995. "The Use of Modal Verbs as a Reflection of Cultural Values". *TESOL Quarterly* 29(2): 325–343.

Holmes, J. 1984. "Hedging Your Bets and Sitting on the Fence: Some Evidence for Hedges as Support Structures". *Te Reo* 27: 47–62.

Holmes, J. 1986. "Functions of *you know* in Women's and Men's Speech". *Language in Society* 15(1): 1–21.

Holmes, J. 1988. "Doubt and Certainty in ESL Textbooks". *Applied Linguistics* 9(1): 21–44.

Holmes, J. 1990. "Hedges and Boosters in Women's and Men's Speech". *Language and Communication* 10(3): 185–205.

Holmes, J. 1993. "New Zealand women are good to talk: An Analysis of politeness strategies in interaction". *Journal of Pragmatics* 20: 91–116.

Hosman, L.A. 1989. "The Evaluative Consequences of Hedges, Hesitations, and Intensifiers. Powerful and Powerless Speech Styles". *Human Communication Research* 15(3): 383–406.

Hübler, A. 1983. "Understatement and Hedges in English". *Pragmatics and Beyond* IV(6). Amsterdam: John Benjamins.

Hyland, K. 1994. "Hedging in Academic Writing and EAP Textbooks". *English for Specific Purposes* 13(3): 239–256.

Hyland, K. 1996. "Writing without Conviction? Hedging in Science Research Articles". *Applied Linguistics* 17(4): 433–454.

Lakoff, G. 1972. "Hedges: A Study in Meaning Criteria and the Logic of Fuzzy Concepts". *Papers from the eight regional meeting Chicago Linguistic Society,* 183–228.

Lakoff, G. 1973. "Hedges: A Study in Meaning Criteria and the Logic of Fuzzy Concepts". *Journal of Philosophical Logic* 2(4): 458–508.

Lakoff, R. 1975. *Language and Women's Place.* New York: Harper and Row.

Loewenberg, I. 1982. "Labels and Hedges: The Metalinguistic Turn". *Language and Style* XV(3): 193–207.

Luukka, M.R. and Markkanen, R. 1997. "Impersonalisation as a Form of Hedging". In *Hedging and Discourse: Approaches to the Analysis of a Pragmatic Phenomenon in Academic Texts,* R. Markkanen and H. Schröder (eds), 168–187. Berlin: Walter de Gruyter.

Lysvag, P. 1975 "Verbs of Hedging". In *Syntax and Semantics (vol. 4),* J. Kimball (ed), 125–154. New York: Academic Press.

Markkanen, R. and Schröder, H. 1997. "Hedging: A Challenge for Pragmatics and Discourse Analysis". In *Hedging and Discourse: Approaches to the Analysis of a Pragmatic Phenomenon in Academic Texts,* R. Markkanen and H. Schröder (eds), 3–18. Berlin: Walter de Gruyter.

McCarthy, M.J. 1994. "It, This and That" In *Advances in Written Text Analysis,* M. Coulthard (ed), 197–208. London: Routledge.

McCarthy, M.J. 1998. *Spoken Language and Applied Linguistics* Cambridge: Cambridge University Press.

Myers, G. 1989. "The Pragmatics of Politeness in Scientific Articles". *Applied Linguistics* 10(1): 1–35.

Myers, G. 1992. "Textbooks and the Sociology of Scientific Knowledge". *English for Specific Purposes* 11: 3–17.

Nikula, T. 1997. "Interlanguage View on Hedging". In *Hedging and Discourse: Approaches to the Analysis of a Pragmatic Phenomenon in Academic Texts,* R. Markkanen, R. and H. Schröder (eds), 188–207. Berlin: Walter de Gruyter.

O' Keeffe, A. 1999. "Questions of Endearment — asking questions based on expectation in radio phone-in". Paper read at The North-West Centre for Linguistics Second Conference on Questions, University of Liverpool, November 12–14, 1999.

Preisler, B. 1986. *Linguistic Sex Roles in Conversation: Social Variation in the Expression of Tentativeness in English.* Berlin: Mouton de Gruyter.

Prince, E. F., Bosh, C. and Frader, J. 1982. "On Hedging in Physician-Physician Discourse". In *Linguistics and the Professions,* J. di Pietro (ed), 83–97. Norwood/New Jersey: Ablex.

Rosch, E. 1978. "Principles of Categorization". In *Cognition and Categorization,* E. Rosch and B. Llyod (eds), 27–48. New Jersey: Erlbaum Ass.

Rounds, P. 1982. *Hedging in Academic Discourse: Precision and Flexibility.* Ann Arbor: The University of Michigan.

Salager-Meyer, F. 1994. "Hedges and Textual Communicative Function in Medical Written English Discourse". *English for Specific Purposes* 13(2): 149–170.

Schröder, H. and Zimmer, D. 1997. "Hedging Research in Pragmatics: A Bibliographical Research Guide to Hedging". In *Hedging and Discourse: Approaches to the Analysis of a Pragmatic Phenomenon in Academic Texts,* R. Markkanen and H. Schröder (eds), 249–271. Berlin: Walter de Gruyter.

Sinclair, J McH. 1991. *Corpus Concordance Collocation* Oxford: Oxford University Press.

Sinclair, J. McH. 1996. "The Search for Units of Meaning". *Textus* IX: 75–106.

Skelton, J. 1988. "The Care and Maintenance of Hedges". *ELT Journal* 42(1): 37–43.

Thomas, J. 1983. "Cross-Cultural Pragmatic Failure". *Applied Linguistics* 4(2): 91–112.

Winter, S. and Gärdenfors, P. 1995. "Linguistic Modality as expressions of Social Power". *Nordic Journal of Linguistics* 18: 137–166.

Chapter 3

Good listenership made plain

British and American non-minimal response tokens in everyday conversation

Michael McCarthy
University of Nottingham

1. Introduction

In this chapter I propose to examine a set of English adjectives and adverbs which typically occur at points of speaker change in everyday talk, and which either account for the whole of the listener response or are the first item in the listener response. The items are all taken from the 2000 most frequent items in two contemporary spoken English corpora, one British-based, one American (see 3, below). The items share the characteristic that they occur with high frequency as single-word response-tokens by listeners to incoming talk. Most of their occurrences are in situations where, on the purely transactional level (i.e. on the level of 'getting the conversational business done'), *yes* or *no* would have sufficed just as well. They are, therefore, in a sense, *yes-plus* words; they do more than just acknowledge or confirm, and show engagement and interactional bonding with interlocutors. The set of words that routinely perform these interactional/relational responsive functions also assists in our understanding of what might constitute the concept of 'good listenership', which is an under-researched area of spoken discourse analysis and one which linguists have, with few exceptions (see 2 below), ignored in favour of a concentration on the main speaker as primary input.

2.   Research into responding

2.1 Exchange structure

Founding what was to become a British tradition of discourse analysis, Sinclair and Coulthard (1975) established a useful labelling system for spoken exchanges that was based on *initiating* moves (i.e. an utterance not structurally dependent on a previous turn), and *answering* or *responding* moves by recipients of initiating moves (1975:26–7; see also Sinclair and Brazil 1982:49). In the teacher-fronted classroom discourse which Sinclair and Coulthard initially focussed on, there was also a third move, the *follow-up*, whereby teachers acknowledged and evaluated the responding moves of their pupils as they answered the teacher's questions. A typical three-part speech exchange is seen in the following corpus extract (⟨$1⟩, ⟨$2⟩, etc. indicate different speakers):

⟨$1⟩ What time are you open?   Initiating move
⟨$2⟩ Erm until about half past five.   Responding move
⟨$1⟩ Okay.   Follow-up move

Responding moves may be expanded after the initial acknowledgement/ answer/feedback, with some additional comment, as in the following example. Such turns may be referred to as extended responses.

⟨$2⟩ That's it. It's done.   Initiation
⟨$1⟩ **Great. // Well done. Congratulations.** Response (acknowledge// comment)
⟨$2⟩ Thanks.   Follow-up

Sinclair and Coulthard's labelling system also allows for a single speaking turn to include a new initiating move by the respondent, as in the following extract. The new initiation, which transfers the status of ⟨$2⟩ from listener to speaker, is, in its turn, responded to by the initial speaker.

⟨$2⟩ And his mum paid for them as well so. Initiation 1
⟨$1⟩ **Good. Great. Good good good. //**
     Did he buy them both?   Response 1 // Initiation 2
⟨$2⟩ Yep.   Response 2

The kinds of response items this chapter deals with also occur in the follow-up (third) slot of the three-part exchange:

[Customer ⟨$1⟩ and waiter ⟨$2⟩ in restaurant]
⟨$1⟩ Is that with rice as well?   Initiation
⟨$2⟩ It comes with rice.   Response
⟨$1⟩ **Yeah. Great.Okay.**   Follow-up

In the present chapter I shall treat both the responding move and the follow-up as types of responses, and refer to *response moves* to cover both cases.

Sinclair and Coulthard's tripartite classification is highly relevant to the study of spoken corpora, where the sequential positioning of words within the *initiation* → *response* → *follow-up* framework says a great deal about their typical environments of occurrence and their associated conversational functions. Thus the interpretation of a word may be affected not only by its syntactic function or by its basic lexical meaning, but by where it most typically occurs in the conversational exchange structure. In this chapter, I wish to examine a set of words which display a proclivity to occur as single-word responding or follow-up moves or as the first word in extended responding or follow-up moves, or to be a lexical element in those moves alongside functional particles such as *yes, no, oh* and *okay*. The words under scrutiny, I shall argue, play a key role in how effective listeners act verbally.

2.2 Listener behaviour in conversation analysis

The discourse- and conversation-analysis literature contains a number of useful studies of listener behaviour, but focuses mainly on how listeners retain their status without taking over the floor or the role of 'main speaker'. Fries (1952), investigated listener responses in telephone calls, and, since then, numerous items have been described and identified that occur as short responses by which listeners keep the communication channel open, acknowledge and show understanding of incoming talk. Fries' catalogue of items included *yes*, non-lexical vocal noises such as *unh* and *hunh*, and fully lexical items such as *good* and *I see* (Fries, 1952:49). Following Yngve's paper on 'getting a word in edgewise' (Yngve, 1970), many studies have concentrated on the non-lexical vocalisations that have become widely known as 'backchannel noises'. Yngve looked at minimal responses such as *uh-huh, yes, okay*, and short comments such as *Oh, I can believe it.* Yngve called such activity by listeners 'behavior in the back channel' (p.574). Numerous investigations into listener activity have succeeded Yngve's, but what is included within back channel behaviour (as opposed to turns which assume the speaker-role) varies from study to study.

Duncan and Niederehe (1974) reassert the basic notion that the back-channel encodes an understanding between speaker and listener that the turn has not been given up, but they point to uncertainties over the boundary between brief utterances and proper turns. Drummond and Hopper (1993a) and Zimmerman (1993) take up just this issue in debating the range of roles of acknowledgement tokens vis-à-vis retention of listenership or claim to speaker-ship. And indeed it is probably the inherently scalar nature of the options that listeners exercise, ranging from non-vocal acknowledgement (e.g. through body language), through minimal responses (including non-lexical vocalizations), tokens such as *yes* and *okay*, single lexical tokens, brief clauses and more extended responses, that has resulted in the more stable and clearly circum-scribed territory of non-lexical vocalisations being the nexus of more research than in the other areas.

Duncan (1974) expands the typology of backchannel responses from non-lexical vocalisations and *yeah*, and includes items such as *right* and *I see*, sentence completions, clarification requests, brief restatements and head nodding and shaking. Duncan's range of items is indicative both of the potential range of behaviour that may be considered relevant to the study of listenership and, once again, of the difficulty in establishing the boundary between backchannelling, turn-taking and floor-grabbing (e.g. whether a brief clarification request is a case of the listener assuming the floor, albeit only momentarily).

A key paper in the interpretation of listener responses is Schegloff (1982). Schegloff asserts that the turn-taking system is fundamentally designed to 'minimize turn size' (p. 73), that is to say there is an economy immanent in communication: speakers say no more than is barely essential (although this condition may be overridden by any speaker). Indeed, brief responsive turns of various kinds which occur in everyday talk would seem to confirm the concept of communicative economy. But central to my argument in this chapter is that the 'additional' content which regularly occurs in response moves indicates that listeners direct their attention as much towards the interactional/relational aspects of the talk as to the transactional content and the need to keep the back channel open, to mark boundaries and to acknowledge the incoming talk. 'Economy', therefore, takes both transactional and relational needs into account. Schegloff recognises the role of vocalisations such as *mm hmm, yeah* and *uh huh* and the importance of research paying attention to listeners in general. To neglect the listener, and to focus only on the main speaker, Schegloff states, leads to the unfortunate tendency to regard discourse as 'a single speaker's, and a single mind's, product' (p. 74). And it is true that discourse analysts have, by and large, undervalued the contribution of listeners in general (notable exceptions are the papers in McGregor, 1986, Bublitz, 1988 and McGregor and White, 1990). I believe it is important to continue to redress that balance. Schegloff also draws attention to the multi-functioning of short response tokens such as *yeah*: they not only mark acknowledgement and confirm understanding, but may also express agreement, and in this way, social action is co-ordinated and fine-tuned on several levels simultaneously. He also suggests that repetition of the same response token by the same listener over a given stretch of talk could be interpreted as indicative of inattention or boredom, and so, to guard against this, in general, listeners vary their responses. However, as we shall see below, repeated tokens in immediate sequence may also indicate an enthusiastic or encouraging response, and it is only the local context which is a reliable guide to the exegesis of affective meanings. Other possible affective functions may also be realised by response tokens, such as incredulity, sarcasm, etc., any of which may be realised in particular contexts where repetition occurs. Nonetheless, the data presented in the present chapter certainly suggest that listeners have a range of options available for response, and do vary their use of the potential tokens.

Gardner (1997 and 1998) refers to backchannels as 'the vocalisation of understandings' and locates them as existing 'between speaking and listening' (both quotations from the title of the 1998 paper). Gardner (1997) looks at what he terms 'minimal responses', such as *mm hm* (which he labels as a 'continuer', encouraging the main speaker to go on speaking), *mm* (which operates as a 'weak acknowledging' token), and the 'stronger, more aligning/agreeing' *yeah* (p. 23). The same tokens are also examined with different intonation contours, along with *oh* as a signal of new information, and *okay* marking a change of activity. Gardner (1998) divides types of listener behaviour into backchannel items such as acknowledgements and brief agreements and continuers (e.g. *yeah, Mm hm*), newsmarking items (e.g. *oh, really*), evaluative items (e.g. *wow, How terrible*), and clarification requests.

Closer again to the preoccupations of the present chapter as regards variation is work by Stubbe and Holmes. Stubbe (1998) refers to 'supportive verbal feedback' in her title. She compares two groups of indigenous New Zealanders' listener behaviour in English conversation. She examines clusters of minimal responses, distinguishing between neutral response tokens (e.g. *mm, uhuh*, typically with level intonation patterns) and supportive tokens (e.g. *oh gosh*, typically with wider pitch spans). Stubbe's aim is cross-cultural understanding, and the avoidance of negative evaluations and stereotyping which may arise from differences in types of listener feedback across different cultural communities. Holmes and Stubbe (1997) further introduce a gender dimension to the study of variation in listener behaviour.

2.3 Corpus-based research

Continuing the tradition of studying the backchannel, Öreström (1983), basing his research on a 50,000-word sample of the London-Lund spoken corpus, examined paralinguistic features of backchannels such as loudness and degree of overlap with the main speaker's turn. He too extended the range of items under scrutiny beyond typical non-lexical vocalisations such as *m* and *aha* to lexical items such as *quite* and *good*.

Tottie (1991), like the present chapter, uses British and American English corpus data to look at backchannel behaviour, and includes items such as *m*, *mhm* and *uh-(h)uh*, along with 'bona fide words and phrases' (p. 255). Her data are taken from the London-Lund corpus and the University of California, Santa Barbara, corpus. Tottie also focuses on the difficulty of establishing the boundaries of backchannels. She notes that there are cases where an utterance is very brief and looks like a backchannel but is itself responded to by the recipient, such that there is a strong case for re-classifying these items as full turns. Tottie and others rightly perceive the cline that runs from general body language and head movements, through non-lexical vocalisations, through single words, through phrasal utterances, through short clauses (such as *that's fine*), through longer utterances (e.g. clarification requests) to the other extreme where the listener's utterance assumes full speaker status. Another dimension of the problem of this boundary is to see it in Sinclair and Coulthard's (1975) terms, that is to say the point where the responding move ends and a new initiating move begins, itself not always a straightforward matter in the operation of their labelling system. Tottie also makes a useful distinction between *backchannel items* (i.e. the individual words or vocalisations, the 'types' of backchannel language) and *backchannels*, which may consist of more than one token, as when a listener says *yeah, sure, right* in quick sequence (p. 261).

With regard to relevance to the present chapter, Tottie concludes that there are vocalisations and variations of items which differ between British and American English. American English favours *yeah, mhm, hm, right* and *sure* with greater frequency than does British English. British English, in its turn, favours *yes, m, no,* and *really* with greater frequency than does American. As to whether American English speakers use more backchannels generally than

British English speakers, and why this and the variation in items may be so, Tottie is more hesitant, rightly concluding that her two relatively small samples simply cannot provide reliable answers.

In the studies reported above, much important insight is offered, but problems also emerge. One difficulty is the problem of terminology, which can vary considerably (see Fellegy, 1995, for a brief discussion). In the present chapter I will use the term *non-minimal response* to refer to the single-word response moves exemplified, in order to reinforce the argument that speakers regularly use tokens that more than satisfy the minimal requirements of keeping the backchannel open, acknowledging and showing understanding of the incoming talk, and marking discourse boundaries. In most cases, *yes/yeah, no, okay*, or a conventionalised vocalisation would be sufficient to maintain the economy and efficiency of the talk, to show agreement and/or acquiescence, and to function as an appropriate response move. Nonetheless, listeners regularly choose to do more, to orientate affectively towards their interlocutors, and to create and consolidate interactional/relational bonds.

3. Corpus data

The present chapter is a corpus-based investigation, as are some of the studies reviewed above, but with considerably more data than previous studies and looking at a wider range of single-word items across two varieties, British and American English. For the sake of economy and so as not to duplicate extensive work already done (e.g. Drummond and Hopper, 1993b; Beach, 1993; Condon, 2001), I exclude non-lexical vocalisations and the words *yes/yeah, no, oh* and *okay* from the present study, and focus on the most frequent lexical words that occur as single-word responses. However, I include *wow* and *gosh*, even though they are on the fuzzy border between vocalisations and lexical words, since they do have accepted spellings and display other word-like characteristics.

This study uses two corpora: a 3.5 million-word sample of the CANCODE spoken corpus and a similar-sized sample of the Cambridge North American Spoken Corpus. Both corpora are the copyright of Cambridge University Press, from whom permission to use or reproduce any of the corpus material must be sought. CANCODE stands for 'Cambridge and Nottingham Corpus of Discourse in English'; the corpus was established at the Department of English Studies, University of Nottingham, UK, and is funded by Cambridge University Press. The total corpus consists of five million words of transcribed conversations.

The corpus audiotape recordings were made in a variety of settings including private homes, shops, offices and other public places, and educational institutions in non-formal settings across the islands of Britain and Ireland, with a wide demographic spread. The CANCODE corpus forms part of the much larger Cambridge International Corpus. For further details of the CANCODE corpus and its construction, see McCarthy (1998). For the sake of convenience, these data will be referred to as 'British'. The Cambridge North American Spoken Corpus is, similarly, a collection of a wide range of different types of conversation collected in the USA and funded by Cambridge University Press. The corpus includes casual talk among friends, telephone calls, and a variety of other everyday types of talk. The corpus currently stands at eight million-plus words, and the present sample was chosen with a view to an optimum balance with the CANCODE corpus conversations (i.e. across the genres, ranging from transactional contexts to collaborative exchanges of ideas, to collaborative tasks, etc, see McCarthy 1998: Chapter 1). The balance is not perfect; the American corpus data contains far fewer public service encounters than does the British corpus. However, it is clear that the general distribution of the high-frequency response tokens in both corpora as regards casual conversational contexts is robust and reliable for the broad comparative purposes of the present chapter. Nonetheless, results for service encounters alone might produce bigger differences for the two varieties. For the sake of convenience, the North American data will be referred to as 'American'.

4.   Frequency of response tokens

For the purposes of this chapter, the top-2000 word frequency lists for both the British and American corpora were examined and most likely candidates (based on the previous studies reviewed above, and on observation and intuition) for occurrence as single-word responses were listed. As a limiting criterion, at least 100 occurrences in each corpus was set as the level below which items would be excluded from consideration, and after the initial count, a maximum of 1000 entries from each corpus was analysed for each item (via random sampling options in the analytical software). This initial investigation produced the following items (Tables 1 and 2), in descending order of frequency, for the British and American data, respectively.

These are simply gross frequencies, and tell us little about actual occurrences as responses. However, it is notable that there are differences in overall

Table 1. Total frequency of items occurring more than 100 times in the British corpus

Item	Occurrences
Right	20823
Really	11731
Good	6351
Quite	4816
Sure	1690
Great	1292
Lovely	1039
Fine	956
Exactly	831
Absolutely	726
True	592
Definitely	549
Certainly	532
Brilliant	363
Wonderful	387
Excellent	187
Cool	192
Gosh	188
Wow	175
Perfect	122
Marvellous	104

frequency which exclude some items from the American list which occur in the British list (*viz. brilliant* and *marvellous*), both of which fall below the 100 lower limit in the American data. The 100 lower limit is not an otiose choice; in both corpora, an occurrence of 100 or more places a word within the core vocabulary which occurs within the 'hump' of high frequency words before the marked fall-off in frequency occurring round about the 1700–1800th word in the rank order frequency lists for the corpora (see McCarthy 1999 for further details). All of these items occur as single-word responses. As a next step to gross frequency, it is necessary to measure what percentage of the total occurrences for each item realise the response-token function. If a very high percentage of the occurrences of any word occur in that function, then this feature will be an important component of the lexical profile of that word, and any description of that word not taking its response-prone behaviour into account will be inadequate.

Let us consider, then, how many occurrences of each word are in fact single-word responses, and calculate what percentage this represents. As stated above, the maximum number of occurrences analysed for any individual token is 1000 from each corpus, generated by random sampling of the total number

Table 2. Total frequency of items occurring more than 100 times in the American corpus

item	occurrences
Really	17738
Right	15445
Good	10091
Great	2437
True	2392
Quite	1872
Exactly	1459
Wow	1265
Wonderful	844
Certainly	773
Gosh	746
Fine	742
Cool	574
Absolutely	642
Sure	638
Definitely	563
Excellent	231
Perfect	164
Lovely	106

of occurrences. Tables 3 and 4 show the occurrences and the respective percentages, in descending order of percentage frequency, for both corpora.

There are some interesting differences between the two corpora, some of which can be explained by the make-up of the data. Figure 1 brings together items where there is a marked difference in distribution between the American and British data.

Right, fine and *good* all occur more frequently in the British data, and this could be explained by the fact that the British corpus contains more service encounters than does the American corpus, and these three tokens serve characteristically as transactional boundary markers in such encounters, or it could relate to a broader difference in preferences. Such a claim could only be borne out, however, by further research into corpora more carefully balanced in terms of genre. *Lovely* is a different matter, and on the basis of firm anecdotal support and public reaction whenever British corpus extracts are presented to American audiences, is perceived as a very British, and non-American, response token. *Absolutely* has no obvious explanation for its uneven distribution and may be a case of genuine dialect variation. The figures certainly confirm my

Table 3. Occurrences of relevant tokens as single-word responses: British data

item	occurrences as response	% of total occurrences analysed (max. 1000)
Right	771	77
Exactly	275	33
Fine	267	28
True	266	70
Great	233	23
Defenitely	203	37
Good	198	20
Lovely	189	17
Absolutely	161	22
Gosh	144	76
Wow	121	69
Really	118	12
Sure	91	9
Cool	85	44
Brilliant	85	23
Excellent	78	42
Wonderful	57	15
Certainly	49	9
Marvellous	16	15
Perfect	14	11
Quite	8	0.8

own subjective impression that American speakers use *absolutely* more frequently than British speakers in the response slot. Similarly, the absence of *brilliant* and *marvellous* from the American data is almost certainly indicative of a feature of dialect variation. *Wow* and *sure* would be felt by many British speakers to be very typically American, and their greater frequency in the American data would seem to confirm this. *Cool* might equally be thought of as classically American, and indeed, most older generation British speakers would consider it a relatively recent American import into British English via pop culture. And yet its distribution is unexpectedly higher in the British data. This is probably explained by the demographic spread of the two corpora; the CANCODE British corpus contains a good deal of data collected by and involving university students aged 18–25, while the American data has a much broader age spread. Other items in Tables 3 and 4 are more closely matched: *true, great, definitely, gosh, really, excellent, wonderful, certainly, perfect* and *quite* all display consistency across the two varieties of English in terms of frequency as response tokens.

Table 4. Occurrences of relevant tokens as single-word responses: American data

Item	Occurence as response	% of total occurences analysed (max. 1000)
Wow	978	98
True	614	61
Gosh	602	81
Exactly	597	60
Absolutely	433	67
Right	379	38
Sure	258	40
Great	260	26
Definitely	162	28
Cool	144	25
Wonderful	138	16
Excellent	122	53
Good	115	11
Really	96	10
Fine	81	11
Certainly	52	7
Perfect	19	11
Lovely	7	7
Quite	0	0

Tables 3 and 4 show more than just the frequency with which the listed items operate as response tokens; the percentage figures show to what extent each item is what might be called 'response-prone'. For example, *gosh* and *wow* are overwhelmingly used as reactive responses, with only a very small number of their occurrences accounted for by other contexts (mostly in speech reports). *Quite* is the opposite: it is a frequent word in both corpora (in its role as an modifying adverb), but its occurrence as a response token is minimal in the British corpus and non-occurring in the American. Intuition and subjective impressions suggest that *quite* as a single word response token is at the very least rather formal in contemporary British speech, and may be on the verge of being perceived as an archaism.

In the British list, 13 words have over 20% of their occurrences as single-word response tokens, and for eight of the words over 30% of all occurrences are single-word responses. In the American list, 11 words have over 20% of their occurrences as single-word response tokens, and, as in the British list, for eight of the words over 30% of all occurrences are single-word responses. The two lists for occurrences in the response slot in excess of 30% of all occurrences are as in Table 5.

Expressing percentage figures as in Table 5 also enables at least a glimpse to be obtained of possible degrees of pragmatic specialization which the words may have undergone or are undergoing. There are interesting differences displayed in the table, which may relate to different degrees of pragmatic specialisation in each variety; for instance, *absolutely* and *sure* would seem to be more exclusively pragmatically specialized as responses in American English than in British, with *right* and *definitely* representing the opposite case, though again caution must be expressed as regards possible imbalances in generic contexts.

5.   Contexts and functions

In this section I consider the environments in which the response tokens occur and illustrate the kinds of functions they typically fulfil. Each extract is labelled according to its variety, British (Br.) or American (Am.), and items for comment are in bold.

American & British response tokens

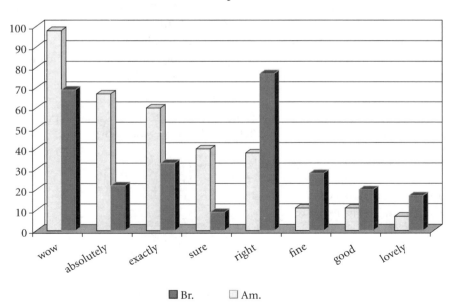

Figure 1. Items showing a marked difference in distribution between the two corpora

Table 5. Occurrences in the response slot in excess of 30% of all occurrences: British and American data

British	%	American	%
right	77	wow	98
gosh	76	gosh	81
true	70	absolutely	67
wow	69	true	61
cool	44	exactly	60
excellent	42	excellent	53
definitely	37	sure	40
exactly	33	right	38

5.1 Non-minimal single-word responses without further turn content

The first set of examples show the response tokens occupying the whole response move, or only minimally accompanied by *yes/yeah/no/okay/oh*, after which the turn reverts to the speaker of the previous move. Extracts 1 and 2 show a characteristic use of items such as *lovely, fine* and *right* as signals of transactional or topical boundaries, where speakers jointly coordinate phases of business such as making arrangements, agreeing on proposed courses of action, and marking the satisfactory exchange of information, goods or services. But, as stated several times already, the response tokens do more than just mark boundaries; they contribute to affective and social well-being between interlocutors, and both varieties display the same functions (for transcription conventions, see the end of this chapter).

Extract 1 (Br.)
[Assistant ⟨$2⟩ and customer ⟨$1⟩ in a post office concluding a transaction]
⟨$1⟩   Thanks very much. That's all. Then I owe you for the stamp.
⟨$2⟩   Thirty six yeah.
⟨$1⟩   I've got the six actually. There we go.
⟨$2⟩   There we are.
⟨$1⟩   **Lovely.**
⟨$2⟩   Thank you.
⟨$1⟩   Thanks very much. Bye bye.
⟨$2⟩   Thank you. Bye bye.

Extract 2 (Am.)
[Colleagues talking]
⟨$4⟩   You and I, you wanted to discuss things with me later in the afternoon but we can also do that over dinner can't we?

⟨$1⟩   Yeah. In fact I don't have any any plans.
⟨$4⟩   **Right.**
⟨$1⟩   Like we can even go out early before dinner.
⟨$4⟩   **Right. Okay. Fine.**

Extract 3 illustrates sociable agreement asserted with *right* and reinforced with *definitely*. Duplicated and clustered tokens will be returned to in Sections 5.5 and 5.6.

> **Extract 3** (Am.)
> ⟨$2⟩   Everybody has some idiosyncrasy.
> ⟨$1⟩   Right.
> ⟨$3⟩   ⟨$E⟩ laughs ⟨$\E⟩
> ⟨$1⟩   **Right.** Yeah **definitely. Definitely.**
> ⟨$3⟩   ⟨$E⟩ laughs ⟨$\E⟩ Oh I can vouch for that. I can vouch for that.

The tokens may often be used for ironic effect. In Extract 4, the response token functions as acknowledgement but also (it may be inferred) with an intended irony. The irony is inferable from the lack of a response indicating surprise or horror (e.g. *wow*, or *gosh* or *really!*), which might have been predicted had the main speaker's initiating move been taken seriously, and the use instead of a response token normally associated with assent/acquiescence:

> **Extract 4** (Am.)
> [Casual conversation]
> ⟨$1⟩   I made that myself. It's for signing your name to get sick soon cards and and hate mail and poison pen letters.
> ⟨$2⟩   **Sure.**

Wow and *gosh*, in both varieties, represent strong affective reactions of surprise, incredulity, delight, shock, horror, etc., by the listener:

> **Extract 5** (Am.)
> ⟨$2⟩   This would not be the tournament. But she says we can get it. Would be six hundred and four dollars. And so it's almost a hundred dollars more.
> ⟨$1⟩   **Wow.**
> ⟨$2⟩   To, not do the tournament but if just the two of us go.

> **Extract 6** (Br.)
> ⟨$1⟩   Well we left about seven in the morning. Went home at seven at night then seven at morning. Then had to go home and then start and milk the cows by hand.
> ⟨$2⟩   ⟨$E⟩ laughs ⟨\$E⟩ **Gosh.**

⟨$1⟩   There were no milking machines.
⟨$2⟩   **Right.**

Extract 6 also contains a typical use of *right*, to acknowledge reception progressively, as complex messages unfold.

Really as a response token is special in that it invites continuation by the
previous speaker, or at the very least some expression of confirmation before
the talk can continue, and before the complete listener reaction is given (in the
British Extract 7 *right*, and *wow* in the American Extract 8). For this reason,
really may be termed a 'continuer' in both varieties:

Extract 7 (Br.)
[Casual conversation]
⟨$5⟩   Have you got your friends in the car Claire?
⟨$8⟩   No. They're+
⟨$5⟩   Oh.
⟨$8⟩   +not here yet. Er they're, someone else hired them back or, believe it or
        not.
⟨$5⟩   Oh **really**.
⟨$8⟩   Yeah.
⟨$5⟩   Oh **right**.

Extract 8 (Am.)
⟨$2⟩   There you go. The forecasts of sales came back all fine.
⟨$1⟩   Oh **really**?
⟨$2⟩   Yeah.
⟨$1⟩   **Wow.**

5.2 Tokens preceding expanded responses

The examples in Section 5.1 show the response tokens occupying the whole of
the response move. Response tokens also frequently occur at the beginning of
expanded response moves, where they feed back on initiating turns (or on
responding moves as follow-ups) and preface longer moves. Typical examples are:

Extract 9 (Am.)
⟨$4⟩   But Marsha and Rob are gonna come out hopefully.
⟨$3⟩   **Great. That would be so much fun.**

Extract 10 (Br.)
⟨$2⟩   Three colour sets yeah. And then just one O H P hopefully just with the
        front cover.
⟨$3⟩   Oh right. Cos you've already got the other ones.

⟨$2⟩   Yeah.
⟨$3⟩   Yeah. **Fine. Okay Laura. That sounds fine.**

5.3 Premodified response tokens

A subset of the response tokens (principally *fine, true, good, definitely, brilliant, perfect*) may be premodified by intensifying adverbs, which serve to focus their interactive/affective meanings. Some examples follow from both varieties:

Extract 11 (Br.)
[Business meeting]
⟨$2⟩   Mark and Kevin are looking into that at the moment.
⟨$1⟩   Right. Okay. But it's all under control.
⟨$2⟩   It's actioned.
⟨$1⟩   **Jolly good.**

Extract 12 (Am.)
⟨$1⟩   But to be the actual one of the ones that decide, that would be tougher
          for me.
⟨$2⟩   Yes, **very true.** I, uh, I agree with you there.

Extract 13 (Br.)
[Discussing tenancy problems]
⟨$1⟩   Doesn't, isn't there something in your tenancy agreement about it? You
          have a written agreement don't you?
⟨$2⟩   **Most definitely.**
⟨$3⟩   Oh of course. Yeah. Yeah.

Intensifying the tokens in this way is reminiscent of what Antaki (2000, 2002) calls 'high-grade assessments', which in his data (phone calls and interview data) relate to either institutional power or speakers claiming 'ownership' of the stages of the interaction, in other words an assertion of power or (in our case here) at the very least of confident equality of participation. Extracts 11 and 12 hardly manifest powerless or diffident speakers.

5.4 Negated tokens

Absolutely, certainly and *definitely* may be negated as response tokens by adding *not*. This is not very frequent, accounting for only nine, six and four occurrences in the American data of the three items, respectively, and two, eight and 19 in the British, respectively. *Definitely not* is notable as a British feature, occurring almost five times more frequently than in the American corpus.

Examples include:

> **Extract 14** (Br.)
> [Colleagues talking]
> ⟨$2⟩   We're not environmentally sound in the Union.
> ⟨$1⟩   Oh **definitely not.**
> ⟨$2⟩   Even though we've got an environmental officer.
> ⟨$1⟩   No I know.
>
> **Extract 15** (Am.)
> ⟨$1⟩   It was like twelve hundred calories or something.
> ⟨$2⟩   Yeah and um
> ⟨$1⟩   Don't go to a hospital if you want to get well.
> ⟨$3⟩   Yeah.
> ⟨$2⟩   **Absolutely not.**

5.5   Double and triple tokens, and tokens in short clauses

Single-word responses often occur in doublets, uttered by the same listener, as illustrated in Extracts 16 and 17. This is particularly evident in (pre-)closing phases at topic-boundaries, where the doublet may function both to signal a boundary (whether transactional or topical) and to add a relational element (of satisfaction, agreement, social bonding). Doublets also occur at points of strong conversational convergence or concurrence between speakers. They occur in both varieties.

> **Extract 16** (Br.)
> [Assistant ⟨$2⟩ and customer ⟨$1⟩ in a post office. Assistant advises customer about a customs declaration label]
> ⟨$2⟩   Well if you don't put it on the customs will open it.
> ⟨$1⟩   **Right. Fine.**
> ⟨$2⟩   Mm.
> ⟨$1⟩   Thank you.
> ⟨$2⟩   Right.
>
> **Extract 17** (Am.)
> [Colleagues talking about another colleague doing sales forecasts]
> ⟨$2⟩   Because she keeps telling me+
> ⟨$1⟩   Cause she hasn't been doing these for awhile.
> ⟨$2⟩   +oh she says I haven't done them in a long time.
> ⟨$1⟩   **Right. Exactly.**

The doublet may also be a repetition of the same token:

Extract 18 (Br.)

⟨$1⟩   And how is Elaine?

⟨$2⟩   Erm now she was very well about a month ago.

⟨$1⟩   **Right. Right.**

⟨$2⟩   And then she had a really bad couple of days.

⟨$1⟩   Yeah.

⟨$2⟩   And now she's sort of picking up again slowly.

⟨$1⟩   **Right. Right.**

Occasionally, triplets occur, which clearly serve greatly to intensify the response:

Extract 19 (Br.)

⟨$1⟩   So I'll I'll just phone you when you know and ask er where you want it sent or whatever and erm we'll sort it out from there.

⟨$2⟩   **Right. Fine. Fine. That's great.**

Triplets are most frequently repetitions:

Extract 20 (Br.)

[Colleagues at work]

⟨$3⟩   But what he's saying now is that that the big one would affect would not just affect that but a wind shift it'd affect it'd affect the whole the whole area wouldn't it.

⟨$1⟩   **Right. Right. Right.** Yep.

Extract 21 (Br.)

⟨$1⟩   It sort of it intrigues me really because consultants and registrars tend to be male you know and you trust them so I mean what's the problem.

⟨$2⟩   **Exactly. Exactly. Exactly.**

Extract 22 (Am.)

[Giving street directions]

⟨$1⟩   Now when you come out of this building and you make a left to get over the corner.

⟨$3⟩   **Right. Right. Right.**

⟨$1⟩   Walk straight up two or three blocks. And in on twenty-second street right off sixth you'll see Flora Rhodes.

Many of the items that occur as single words also occur frequently in short clauses with *that's*.

Extract 23 (Am.)

[Giving street directions]

⟨$4⟩   You'll come to a stop sign take a right and just follow it all the way out.

⟨$2⟩   Oh. Perfect.

⟨$1⟩   Great.

⟨$2⟩   **That's excellent.** Thank you very much.
⟨$1⟩   Thank you so much. Thanks.

The minimal clause is particularly evident with *true*, which seems to show a preference for the clausal environment over the single-word option:

Extract 24 (Am.)
⟨$1⟩   I know there's a lot of salt in bread.
⟨$1⟩   **That's true.**
⟨$1⟩   This doesn't have much salt though.

Other words with a high occurrence of *that's* clauses are *good*, *great* and *fine*, for example:

Extract 25 (Br.)
[Assistant and customer in car spare parts department]
⟨$2⟩   Yeah. Bob's up in erm Manchester tomorrow so he can't come tomorrow.
⟨$1⟩   **That's fine.**
⟨$2⟩   Er but I'll get one of the lads in to come and do it for you.
⟨$1⟩   Lovely.

5.6 Sequences and clusters

The response tokens may also cluster in consecutive series across speakers, where coordinated joint actions realise multiple signals of (pre-)closure and simultaneous relational consolidation. Often they cluster with other markers of closure such as thanks, checks, confirmations and salutations.

Extract 26 (Am.)
⟨1⟩   How are you doing in there? Let's see eleven thirty.
⟨3⟩   I'm tired actually. ⟨$E⟩ laughing ⟨$\E⟩ Oh. **Yeah. Yeah.** Looks good. **Okay.**
⟨2⟩   **Okay great. Thanks Irene.**

Extract 27 (Br.)
[Telephone call concerning a printing order]
⟨$2⟩   Do you think it needs editing?
⟨$1⟩   Erm I shouldn't think so.
⟨$2⟩   **Good. Brilliant. Okay well** I'll be round to pop it up.
⟨$1⟩   **Okay.**
⟨$2⟩   Pick it up today.
⟨$1⟩   **Okay** [male name].

⟨$2⟩   Have you got the compliment slips?
⟨$1⟩   Yes.
⟨$2⟩   On all er
⟨$1⟩   They they look very good.
⟨$2⟩   **Great.**
⟨$1⟩   Yes.
⟨$2⟩   **Fabulous.**
⟨$1⟩   **All right. ⟨$E⟩ laughs ⟨\$E⟩**
⟨$2⟩   **Okay. Thanks for that.**
⟨$1⟩   **Okay [male name].**
⟨$2⟩   **Cheers.**
⟨$1⟩   **Bye.**

Extract 28 (Br.)
[Waiter ⟨$3⟩ and customer ⟨$2⟩ in restaurant]
⟨$3⟩   If you need some more just order some more. **All right.**
⟨$2⟩   **Right. Fine.**
⟨$3⟩   **Okay. Thank you.**
⟨$2⟩   **Thank you.**
⟨$3⟩   **You're welcome. Thank you.**

6. Conclusion

The analysis of non-minimal response tokens shows a set of items in British and American English which occur within the core, first 2000 frequency lists for each variety. Although there are differences between the two varieties (see Figure 1 above), they have more in common than that which separates them. Their commonality is seen in the examination of local contexts and functions, and both varieties show a strong orientation by listeners towards relational aspects of the discourse. In both varieties, 'good listenership' seems to demand more than just acknowledgement and transactional efficiency, and listeners orientate towards the creation and maintenance of sociability and affective well-being in their responses.

Cross-corpora comparisons of this inter-varietal type and comparisons across languages are useful in two major respects. In the first place they may confirm or may refute functional interpretations made from one variety or language as not being idiosyncratic to one culture or speech community. Spoken corpora as a locus for research into human communication always run the risk that features of talk may be culture-bound, and it is only in intervarietal and interlingual studies that one can find safer ground for generalisations.

Secondly, in this case, the inter-varietal study offers the possibility of amalgamating the two lists of tokens (and similar lists from other varieties of English) to point towards some sort of 'average' list for English as an international language which could have powerful resonance in current English as a second language pedagogy, where the debate over models of spoken English and the status of individual native-speaker varieties is growing in tandem with the expansion of spoken English corpora (see McCarthy, 2001, Chapter 6). Either way, the study of corpora of different varieties of the same language offers a powerful tool for an overall understanding of the common ground that typically exists alongside differences between one variety and another. Problems remain: not least that of the comparability of corpora, and efforts to build parallel spoken corpora are to be applauded, albeit they are fraught with difficulties in achieving consistency of data collection. The ICE corpus of English is a notable attempt to achieve some sort of comparability across varieties of English (see Nelson, 1996). Whatever our resources, inter-varietal corpus-based comparisons of spoken English can only add to our overall understanding of a major, global language in its widely differing contexts of use.

Transcription conventions

⟨$1⟩, ⟨$2⟩, etc.   used to label each speaker consecutively in each conversation.
⟨$E⟩ and ⟨\$E⟩   beginning and end of non-verbal language event (e.g. laughter)
+   'latched' turn, where a speaker continues a turn as if uninterrupted after an interruption or overlap.

References

Antaki, C. 2000. 'Brilliant. Next question…': High-grade assessment sequences in the completion of interactional units. *Research on Language and Social Interaction*, 33 (3): 235–262.

Antaki, C. 2002. 'Lovely': turn-initial high-grade assessments in telephone closings. *Discourse Studies*, 4 (91): 5–24.

Beach, W. 1993. Transitional regularities for 'casual' "okay" usages. *Journal of Pragmatics*, 19: 325–352.

Bublitz, W. 1988. *Supportive Fellow-Speakers and Cooperative Conversations*. Amsterdam: John Benjamins.

Condon, S. 2001. Discourse *ok* revisited: default organization in verbal interaction. *Journal of Pragmatics*, 33: 491–513.

Drummond, K. and Hopper, R. 1993a. Backchannels revisited: acknowledgement tokens and speakership incipiency. *Research on Language and Social Interaction*, 26 (2): 157–177.

Drummond, K. and Hopper, R. 1993b. Some uses of *yeah*. *Research on Language and Social Interaction*, 26 (2): 203–212.

Duncan, S. 1974. On the structure of speaker-auditor interaction during speaker turns. *Language in Society* 2: 161–180.

Duncan, S. & Niederehe, G. 1974. 'On signalling that it's your turn to speak', *Journal of Experimental Social Psychology*, 10, 3, 234–47.

Fellegy, A. 1995. Patterns and functions of minimal responses. *American Speech*, 70 (2): 186–199.

Fries, C.C. 1952. *The Structure of English*. New York: Harcourt, Brace.

Gardner, R. 1997. The listener and minimal responses in conversational interaction. *Prospect*, 12 (2): 12–32.

Gardner, R. 1998. Between speaking and listening: the vocalisation of understandings. *Applied Linguistics* 19 (2): 204–224.

Holmes, J. & Stubbe, M. 1997 Good listeners: gender differences in New Zealand conversation. *Women and Language*. 20 (2): 7–14.

McCarthy, M.J. 1998. *Spoken Language and Applied Linguistics*. Cambridge: Cambridge University Press.

McCarthy, M.J. 1999. What constitutes a basic vocabulary for spoken communication? *SELL*, 1: 233–249.

McCarthy, M.J. (2001). *Issues in Applied Linguistics*. Cambridge: Cambridge University Press.

McGregor, G. (ed) 1986. *Language for Hearers*. Oxford: Pergamon Press.

McGregor, G. and White, R. 1990. *Reception and Response: Hearer Creativity and the Analysis of Spoken and Written texts*. London: Routledge.

Nelson, G. 1996. The design of the corpus. In S. Greenbaum (ed.) *Comparing English Worldwide: the International Corpus of English*. Oxford: Oxford University Press, 27–35.

Öreström, B. 1983. *Turn-taking in English Conversation*. Lund: Gleerup.

Schegloff, E. 1982. Discourse as interactional achievement: some uses of 'uh huh' and other things that come between sentences. In D. Tannen (ed.) *Analysing Discourse. Text and Talk*. Washington: Georgetown University Press, 71–93.

Sinclair J. McH. 1991. *Corpus, Concordance, Collocation*. Oxford: Oxford University Press.

Sinclair J. McH. and Brazil, D. 1982. *Teacher Talk*. Oxford: Oxford University Press.

Sinclair J. McH. and Coulthard, R.M. 1975. *Towards an Analysis of Discourse*. Oxford: Oxford University Press.

Stubbe, M. 1998. Are you listening? Cultural influences on the use of supportive verbal feedback in conversation. *Journal of Pragmatics* 29: 257–89.

Tottie, G. 1991. Conversational style in British and American English: The case of backchannels. In K. Aijmer and B. Altenberg (eds.) *English Corpus Linguistics*. London: Longman, 254–71.

Yngve, V. 1970. On getting a word in edgewise. *Papers from the 6th Regional Meeting, Chicago Linguistic Society*. Chicago: Chicago Linguistic Society.

Zimmerman, D. 1993. Acknowledgement tokens and speakership incipiency revisited. *Research on Language and Social Interaction*, 26 (2): 179–194.

CHAPTER 4

Variation in the distribution of modal verbs in the British National Corpus

Graeme Kennedy
Victoria University of Wellington

In his major study of English modal verbs, F. R. Palmer (1979:1) made the claim that "there is, perhaps, no area of English grammar that is both more important and more difficult than the system of the modals". It is not entirely clear what led Palmer to accord such status and difficulty to modals verbs, nor the extent to which he had in mind either linguistic description or language learning. However, like most other studies of modals since the 1970's, it was the semantics of modal use which was the central focus of his rich and detailed analysis. Palmer's study made use of the Survey of English Usage Corpus, the last major pre-electronic corpus. Modern electronic corpora now make it possible to explore the nature and use of linguistic phenomena in a much wider variety of texts. Such descriptions go beyond exploring what is grammatically and semantically possible, and add a distributional dimension which characterizes linguistic features in terms of probability of occurrence. Corpus-based distributional analysis also makes it possible to extend our understanding of linguistic variation across different genres in different domains of use. This will be illustrated in the present paper by exploring the distribution of modal verbs and the complex verb phrase structures in which they occur in the British National Corpus.

Verbs constitute about 20 per cent of all the word tokens used in English, and in written texts, modal verbs typically constitute about 8 per cent of all verb forms. Modals form a small, semi-closed set of nine auxiliary verbs, most of which express both core 'deontic' meanings such as 'obligation', 'intention' or 'permission' (e.g. '*You must be home by 10 pm*') or 'epistemic' meanings associated with truth conditions and assessment of degrees of certainty (e.g. '*You must be our new neighbours*'). The 'central' English modals are usually considered to be *will, would, can, could, may, might, shall, should, must*. In addition to these nine central modals there is a small group of 'marginal modals', *ought to, need to, used to* and *dare* (Quirk et al 1985: 135) which can behave in some ways like modals and in other ways like main verbs. Although they are not the focus of the present paper, there is also a small group of expressions known as 'semi-modals', which function like modals — *(had) better, (have) got to, be about to, be going to, be supposed to.* Biber et al (1999: 487) have noted increasing use of semi-modals and have suggested that in the LSWE Corpus, the historically-older semi-modals such as *have to* and *be going to* tend to be used more in US English than in British English, whereas the more recently developed semi-modals *(had)better,* and *(have) got to* are more common in British English conversation.

Part of the difficulty of English modal verbs for linguists and language learners is that although they are few, most modals are polysemous, and several have similar core meanings (e.g. *can* is used for marking ability, possibility and permission; *must, should* and *ought to* can each express obligation). Furthermore, modal meanings can be expressed in a number of different ways involving other grammatical and lexical means apart from modal verbs. For example, *You can go outside* and *You have permission to go outside* provide alternative ways of giving permission, but only the former makes use of a modal verb.

In addition to Palmer's study of English modals there have been a number of other important corpus-based studies over the last two decades. While some have explored the distribution of modals others have focused on aspects of the semantics of modals. From a distributional perspective Quirk et al (1985: 136) observed that the frequency of individual modals varies greatly in the Brown, LOB and SEU corpora, that the modals as a whole are much more frequent in spoken than in written English, and that the four modals, *will, would, can* and *could* are notably more frequent than the other modals. Coates (1983) undertook an innovative study of the relative distribution of core and epistemic uses of modals in British English and demonstrated the extent of these distributional differences. Her analysis of modals in spoken texts was based on the half-million-word London-Lund Corpus, while the analysis in written texts was based on the one-million-word LOB corpus. The distribution of the nine major modals in Coates' study is summarized in Table 1.

Regional and historical variation in the use of modals has been studied by other researchers. Collins (1991), for example, compared the distribution of the modals of obligation and necessity in Australian, British and American English. Biber et al (1998: 205–210) described how the distribution of the modals *must* and *should*, which mark obligation and necessity, has changed from the 17th

Table 1. Estimate of relative frequency of modals: Coates, 1983. (%)

	Spoken UK English LLC	Written UK English LOB	Spoken and Written
Will	24.2	19.3	22.0
Would	19.9	20.6	20.2
Can	19.9	14.7	17.6
Could	11.3	12.0	11.6
Should	6.3	8.8	7.5
Must	6.5	7.8	7.1
May	5.0	9.1	6.8
Might	4.1	5.3	4.6
Shall	2.8	2.4	2.6
Total	100	100	100

century to the present in different genres, with increasing use of "semi-modals" such as *have to* and *have got to*, which are now more frequent than *need to* and *ought to*.

A comprehensive distributional account of modals, based mainly on an analysis of some 30,000 verb phrases mainly from British fiction, was undertaken by Mindt (1995). This study covers many aspects of modal use but focuses especially on the relative frequency of modals used for expressing some 17 types of modal meaning. Like his predecessors, Mindt (1995: 37–38) observed that "modal verbs are not distributed evenly". According to his analysis "their distribution varies according to text type....In fictional texts the most frequent...modals are *would* and *could*....In spoken conversation the most frequent...modals are *would* and *can*....In expository prose the most frequent...modals are *will* and *would*". However, text type does not only affect the choice of which modals get to be used most. Mindt also noted that the use of the verb phrase structures in which modals occur is also influenced by text type, and varies from modal to modal with considerable implications for studies of variation and for language teaching. Most recently, Biber et al (1999: 483–502) undertook a major description of the distribution of modals in the 40-million-word LSWE Corpus. This study included a description of the relative frequency of different uses of each of the modals in conversation, fiction, news and academic prose.

When it became available in 1995 the British National Corpus (BNC) was the largest structured corpus ever compiled. This huge 100-million-word representative sample of spoken and written texts of British English, mainly from the last two decades of the 20th century makes it possible to explore variation in a wide range of domains and genre types and to extend our understanding of how modals are used. The BNC consists of 10 million words of spoken English sampled from many domains of use by participants from four socio-economic groupings in some 38 geographical locations in Great Britain. There are also 90 million words of written English prose in the BNC, selected from nine genres. Eighty percent of the written texts are 'informative' and twenty percent 'imaginative'. The written texts from informative genres were selected from Natural and Pure Science, Applied Science, Social Science, World Affairs, Commerce and Finance, Arts, Leisure, Belief and Thought. The project has been sponsored by major British universities and publishers and the British government.

This paper is based on an analysis of all 1.45 million words which are grammatically tagged as modals in the BNC, with the exception of a very small number of forms such as *shalt, wilt* and *mayst*. In such a large corpus there is inevitably a margin of error in word counts because of incorrect tagging. For example, word breaks with forms such as *toucan*, or *can-can* sometimes lead to tagging errors. Occasional tagging of the month of May as a modal appears to be one of the most persistent errors. Analysis of a carefully checked two-million-word sample from the corpus shows that because of tagging errors, the number of tokens of the modals *may* and *will* may be slightly exaggerated, whereas the numbers of *can, could, must* and *should* may be slightly under-estimated. However, mistagging is not considered to have had an undue influence on the present analysis and this is supported in that the overall rank ordering of the central modals in the BNC as shown in this study is identical to that in the 40-million-word LSWE Corpus (Biber et al 1999: 486).[1]

1.   Distribution of modal verbs in the BNC

The relative frequency of occurrence of modal verbs in the BNC is summarized in Table 2. Column 1 of that table lists the modal forms which are analyzed. Column 2 shows that 1,457,721 of the word tokens in the BNC (1.45%) are tagged as modals. Column 3 shows the percentage contribution of each of the modals. *Will, would, can,* and *could* account for 72.7% of all the modal verb tokens, with the most frequent model (*will*) accounting for almost 23% of all modal tokens in the corpus.

Table 2. Distribution of Modal Verbs in the British National Corpus

1	2	3	4	5	6	7	8	9
	No. of tokens in BNC	All BNC texts (100 m words) %	All BNC spoken texts (10 m words) %	All BNC written texts (90 m words) %	All BNC affirmative modals %	All BNC negative modals %	All BNC spoken negative modals %	All BNC written negative modals %
will	244,822	16.8	9.0	18.1	18.2	6.6	1.6	7.8
'll	72,591	5.0	14.8	3.3	5.6	0.3	0.4	0.3
won't	16,164	1.1	2.7	0.8	—	9.4	16.6	7.5
		22.9	26.5	22.2	23.8	16.3	18.6	15.6
would	255,192	17.5	15.8	17.8	17.5	17.4	18.7	17.1
'd	34,314	2.4	5.7	1.8	2.6	0.2	0.2	0.2
		19.9	21.5	19.6	20.1	17.6	18.9	17.3
can	234,386	16.1	17.1	15.9	16.5	12.9	2.7	15.4
can't	31,730	2.2	6.0	1.5	—	18.4	37.6	13.6
		18.3	23.1	17.4	16.5	31.3	40.3	29.0
could	168,397	11.6	9.4	11.9	10.7	18.3	12.2	19.8
may	113,025	7.8	2.3	8.7	8.3	4.0	1.5	4.7
might	61,446	4.2	3.9	4.3	4.6	1.7	1.4	1.7
shall	20,235	1.4	1.3	1.4	1.5	0.7	0.1	0.9
shan't	527	0.04	0.01	0.03	—	0.3	0.4	0.3
		1.4	1.3	1.4	1.5	1.0	0.5	1.2
should	111,237	7.6	5.7	8.0	7.8	6.6	4.9	7.0
must	72,085	4.9	2.8	5.3	5.4	1.7	0.9	1.9
ought to	5,979	0.4	0.6	0.4	0.4	0.2	0.1	0.2
need to	3,356	0.2	0.1	0.3	0.1	1.3	0.4	1.6
dare	722	0.1	0.1	0.1	—	0.2	0.2	0.2
used to	11,513	0.8	2.8	0.4	0.9	0.01	0.0	0.01
Total %		100.0	100.0	100.0	100.0	100.0	100.0	100.0
Total tokens	1,457,721	1,457,721	215,485	1,242,236	1,284,839	172,882	34,446	138,436
Modals per 1,000 words		14.6	21.5	13.8	12.9	1.7	3.4	1.5

Columns 4 and 5 show that modals occur with much greater frequency in spoken texts than in written. In the spoken texts in the corpus there are 215,485 modals in 10 million words. Whereas column 3 shows that overall in the BNC modals occur at the rate of 14.6 per thousand words, they occur in spoken texts at a rate of 21.5 modals per thousand words. *Will, would* and *can* are all more frequent proportionately in spoken than in written texts. In the written texts of the BNC there are 1,242,236 modals in 90 million words, occurring at the rate of 13.8 modals per thousand words. In Coates' 1983 study of modals in LOB and the LLC, with texts from the 1960's, she estimated that spoken British English had 17.7 modals per thousand words, and written British English had 14.6 per thousand words. The difference between spoken and written texts in the frequency with which modals are used is thus shown in the BNC to be even greater than Coates estimated.

Column 3 in Table 2 shows that overall in the BNC, 10.7% of all the modals occur in elided or contracted forms (not counting the contraction of *not*). However, there is clearly a much higher proportion in spoken English. In the spoken texts in the corpus (column 4), 29.2% of the modals occur in contracted forms. In the written texts (column 5), the proportion of modals occurring in contracted forms is 7.4%.

Column 7 shows that 172,882 of the modal tokens in the BNC (11.9%) occur in negative contexts. Overall, columns 6 and 7 show that there are about eight times as many modals in affirmative contexts as compared with negative contexts, with 12.9 affirmative modals per thousand words, and 1.7 negative modals per thousand words. But here too, there is obviously substantial variation. If columns 6 and 7 are compared, the four most frequent modals account for 71% of the tokens in column 6 for affirmative contexts, whereas these same four account for 83.5% of the negative tokens. Further, in negative contexts (column 7), almost half of the modal tokens come from just two modals, *can(not)/can't* and *could (not)*.

Columns 8 and 9 show the distribution of modals in negative contexts in the spoken and written texts. The 34,445 tokens in column 8 are almost 16% of the total spoken modals and represent 3.4 negative modals per thousand words. This should be compared with the 138,436 negative modals in the written texts (column 9). Only 11.1% of the modals in written texts are in negative contexts, occurring at 1.5 negative modals per thousand words. Thus negative modals are over twice as frequent in spoken British English as in written in the 1990s — especially *can't, won't, wouldn't*. In the spoken texts of column 8, *can't/cannot* is more frequent than *won't/will not* and *wouldn't* combined.

The rank ordering of individual modals in the BNC clearly varies consider-ably according to whether the medium is spoken or written and whether or not negation is involved. In spoken texts, the rank order of the modals is somewhat different from the order in the written corpus. In spoken texts, *can* rises in the ranking in negative contexts. The importance of examining the occurrence of modals in negative contexts is well-illustrated with *can*. Columns 7 and 8 show that where there is negation users of British English clearly prefer to say *can't*, or *couldn't*, rather than *won't*, *mustn't* or *shouldn't*, whereas in affirmative contexts there is proportionally lower use of *can* and *could*. The high incidence of *can* in negative contexts suggests that perhaps in speech, which is typically face-to-face, external constraints prevail, or are preferred, rather than expressions of volition or obligation (*I can't help you* rather than *I won't help you*). Unpleasant things like refusals and prohibitions are perhaps best left to a faceless written medium or are more appropriately expressed through the use of the passive voice, (e.g. *Something must be done* rather than *You must do it*), where external constraints beyond the control of the speaker can also be implied.

2.   Modal verbs in different genres of the BNC

The variation in the distribution of individual modal verbs shown in Table 2 can be further exemplified across the range of genres in the BNC. Table 3 shows the distribution of modals in nine written genres. (The distributions in the whole BNC and in all spoken and written texts are also repeated in rows 1,2 and 3 of Table 3 for ease of reference.)

As noted earlier the most frequent modals, *will*, *would*, *can*, and *could* account for almost 73% of all modal tokens in the BNC, and over 71% in the written texts (row 3 of Table 3). These four modals typically have a high incidence of epistemic uses (certainty, possibility, probability) as well as the core meanings of intention, ability, hypothesis. However, rows 4 through 12 show that different written genres have substantially different distributions for each modal. *Will* gets greater use proportionately in Applied Science, Com-merce and Finance, and Leisure than it does in other genres. *Would* and *could* get much higher use in Imaginative Prose and World Affairs (journalism) probably because of narrative and reporting functions. On the other hand *would* and *could* have relatively much lower incidence of use in Natural, Pure, Applied and Social Sciences (rows 5 through 7). *Can* and *may* feature strongly in Natural and Pure Science, and to a lesser extent in other academic and

Table 3. Distribution of Modal Verbs in Genres of the BNC (%)

	1 will	2 would	3 can	4 could	5 may	6 might	7 shall	8 should	9 must	10 ought to	11 need to	12 dare	13 used to	14 Total %
1 All BNC	22.9	19.9	18.3	11.6	7.8	4.2	1.4	7.6	4.9	0.4	0.2	0.1	0.8	100
2 All BNC spoken	26.5	21.5	23.1	9.4	2.3	3.9	1.3	5.7	2.8	0.6	0.1	0.1	2.8	100
3 All BNC written	22.2	19.6	17.4	11.9	8.7	4.3	1.4	8.0	5.3	0.4	0.3	0.1	0.4	100
4 Imaginative prose	19.1	26.8	12.7	19.0	2.5	5.3	1.8	5.4	5.9	0.6	0.2	0.1	0.6	100
5 Natural and pure science	17.6	11.8	27.3	7.5	17.4	4.0	1.2	7.3	5.4	0.2	0.3	0.0	0.1	100
6 Applied science	27.5	12.2	22.6	8.0	12.2	3.2	0.4	8.3	5.0	0.2	0.2	0.0	0.2	100
7 Social science	19.8	14.5	19.5	7.7	14.8	4.4	1.8	10.5	5.8	0.4	0.4	0.0	0.5	100
8 World affairs	18.9	27.0	11.7	13.7	7.3	4.6	1.8	8.8	5.1	0.4	0.2	0.1	0.3	100
9 Commerce and finance	26.3	14.3	18.0	6.6	13.6	3.7	1.7	10.2	5.0	0.3	0.3	0.0	0.2	100
10 Arts	22.1	18.6	21.0	11.2	7.8	4.7	1.1	7.2	4.9	0.3	0.2	0.1	0.9	100
11 Belief and thought	16.6	16.9	22.6	9.7	11.6	5.2	2.0	7.2	6.7	0.6	0.4	0.1	0.4	100
12 Leisure	28.1	15.0	23.0	9.7	7.2	2.9	0.5	8.4	4.3	0.2	0.2	0.0	0.6	100

commercial genres to express the epistemic meanings of 'logical possibility' and perhaps a suitably cautious degree of certainty. The high incidence of *can* may also reflect its use in some genres for expressing the non-epistemic meaning of 'ability'. For the remaining modals there are much less striking differences in their use in different genres. *Should* has a slightly higher use in Social Science and Commerce and Finance genres, perhaps reflecting 'predicting' and 'advising' functions.

Overall, in different written genres, the evidence of the BNC is thus that some modals get used more than others presumably because the semantic functions associated with particular modals get used more than others, (e.g. those associated with future orientation, logical possibility, speculation).

3.   Modal verb phrase structures in the BNC

At a formal level of analysis, the modal verbs might seem to be used in quite a simple canonical paradigm followed by the bare infinitive (including *be* and *have*) of a lexical verb. (e.g. *Fred and Sue will/ would/ can/ etc go to the movies.*) Greenbaum (1996: 246–7) noted however, that modals are followed not only by the infinitive of a lexical verb. He wrote, "the auxiliaries appear in a set sequence: modal – perfect have – progressive be – passive be – main verb....It is not usual for all to be present in one verb phrase though it is certainly possible".

Table 4 shows the nine verb phrase structures in which modal verbs can occur, at least two of which can have a noun or adjective instead of a past participle (# 6, 9), and one of which (# 2) has about 25% of its tokens with *be* or *have* as the infinitive. Mindt (1995) has explored the distribution of modal verb phrase structures in a corpus of fiction texts. These modal verb-phrase structures are sometimes given names such as 'modal perfect passive ' (e.g. *He could have been told*). All structures except 1 and 5 have *be* either as part of the passive or progressive, or as a lexical verb in its own right. The multifunctional *be* is probably responsible for many learners' difficulties with modal verbs. Without a distributional analysis a learner might conclude that all nine structures are used equally since most grammars do not provide an analysis of their relative frequencies. For language learners who are trying to learn to sequence the items correctly, such an assumption would be a serious misconception, as Biber et al 1999: 498–501 has demonstrated. "While the majority of modals do not co-occur with marked voice or aspect, particular modals show differing preferences for these combinations". They note, for example, that while *can, could, should,*

Table 4. Modal verb phrase structures

1	Modal alone	(Who will go?) *I will.*
2	Modal + infinitive	Sam *can swim.* She *must be* hungry. You *should have* a rest.
3	Modal + *be* + past participle (Modal with Passive)	It *should be replaced.*
4	Modal + *be* + present participle (Modal with Progressive Aspect)	They *will be arriving* soon.
5	Modal + *have* + past participle (Modal with Perfect Aspect)	He *might have done* it. You *must have been* hungry.
6	Modal + *be* + *being* + past participle (or adjective) (Modal with Perfect and Progressive Aspect)	It *might be being done* tomorrow. He *could be being* awkward.
7	Modal + *have* + *been* + past participle (Modal with Passive and Perfect Aspect)	It *should have been fixed.*
8	Modal + *have* + *been* + present participle (Modal with Perfect and Progressive Aspect)	He *must have been lying.*
9	Modal + *have* + *been* + *being* + past participle (or adjective) (Modal with Passive and Perfect and Progressive Aspect)	He *might have been being blackmailed.* They *must have been being* careless.

and *must* are fairly common in passive constructions, *may, might, should* and *must* are the most frequently used modals with perfect aspect. Data from the BNC strongly support the general picture of variation in the use of verb phrase structures painted by Mindt and Biber et al.

Table 5 contains an analysis of the distribution of the nine modal verb phrase structures in different genres of the BNC. For the corpus as a whole, column 1 shows that there are huge differences in the relative distributions of use of the nine structures. The modal + infinitive structure (structure 2) accounts for 76% of all modal tokens in the corpus. Column 2 shows an even higher proportion of use of structure 2 in spoken texts (84.9%) and imaginative prose (81.3%). Structure 3 contains the passive voice, and together with structure 2 accounts for over 90% of all modal tokens in the BNC as a whole, as well as in most genres. Structure 1 (modal alone) occurs proportionately more

Table 5. Modal verb phrase structures in genres of the BNC (%)

Modal structure	1 All BNC	2 All BNC spoken	3 All BNC written	4 Imaginative prose	5 Natural and pure science	6 Applied science	7 Social science	8 World affairs	9 Commerce and finance	10 Arts	11 Belief and thought	12 Leisure
1 Modal alone	1.9	6.0	1.3	3.1	0.4	0.5	0.5	0.6	0.6	1.1	0.7	0.9
2 Modal + infinitive	76.0	84.9	74.5	81.3	67.4	71.0	69.4	71.0	72.0	75.3	75.0	76.7
3 Modal + be + past ptc	14.7	3.4	16.6	4.8	27.1	24.3	25.2	19.2	23.1	15.0	17.3	14.9
4 Modal + be + pres ptc	1.5	1.8	1.5	1.7	0.7	1.2	1.0	1.1	1.1	1.8	1.3	2.0
5 Modal + have + past ptc	5.1	3.6	5.4	8.4	3.7	2.5	3.1	6.8	2.6	5.9	5.0	4.8
6 Modal + be + being + past ptc	0.0	0.0	0.0	0.0	0.0	0.0	0.0	0.0	0.0	0.0	0.0	0.0
7 Modal + have + been + past ptc	0.7	0.2	0.7	0.5	0.7	0.6	0.7	1.2	0.6	0.8	0.7	0.6
8 Modal + have + been + pres ptc	0.1	0.1	0.1	0.2	0.0	0.0	0.1	0.1	0.0	0.1	0.1	0.1
9 Modal + have been being + past ptc	0.0	0.0	0.0	0.0	0.0	0.0	0.0	0.0	0.0	0.0	0.0	0.0
Total	100	100	100	100	100	100	100	100	100	100	100	100

in speech and imaginative prose, and reflects the use of ellipsis in conversational discourse. (e.g. *Can any of you come back tomorrow? — Yes, I can.*) In the spoken texts 6% of the modal tokens occur in structure 1. Conversely, structure 3 (modal with passive) is used much less in spoken English and imaginative prose than in other genres, but proportionately more in the various 'Sciences', 'World Affairs' and 'Commerce and Finance' (columns 5–9). In the 'Social Science' texts in the BNC 25% of the modal verb tokens occur in structure 3. Structures 4, 5, 7 and 8 do not have high use in any genre, and structures 6 and 9 are extremely rare. In the BNC most tokens of structures 4,5,7 and 8 express epistemic modality (e.g. '*She must have known about it*').

Whereas Table 5 shows the distribution of the nine modal verb phrase structures in different genres of the BNC, Table 6 shows the extent to which different modals make use of the nine verb phrase structures.

As noted above, overall for all modals in the BNC, structure 2 (modal + infinitive) is predominant with 76% of modal tokens occurring in this structure. There is considerable variation, however. Whereas *dare* and *used to* have over 94% of their tokens occurring in structure 2, *should* and *must* have about 63% and 65% respectively, perhaps because both *should* and *must* have a lower proportion of deontic uses, and a correspondingly higher proportion of epistemic uses than other modals in the active voiced structure 2.

In structure 3, on the other hand, where the mean for all tokens is 14.7%, *should* (26.3%), *must* (19.5%) and *can* (21.9%) have a much higher proportion of their tokens than any of the other modals. This structure contains the passive voice which, by means of agent deletion, can be used to imply possibly externally-imposed obligation. Things *should be done, must be done* or *can be done* but not necessarily by the speaker or listener. *Would*, which seems to have many of its tokens in reported speech, has a notably lower use of structure 3, with only 7% of its tokens in that structure. *Would, could, may, might,* and *must* also have a notably higher proportion of their uses in structure 5, typically in epistemic uses (*Mary must have known*) than is the case for the other modals. *Will, can* and *shall* are rarely used in structure 5. Table 6 also shows clearly that none of the modals have a significant proportion of their uses in the BNC in structures 6–9.

Table 7 shows the extent to which each individual modal contributes to the total number of tokens of modal use for each of the nine modal verb phrase structures. For structure 1 (the modal alone), 83% of the modal tokens come from *will, would, can* and *could,* with *can* contributing over a quarter of all tokens. In structure 2, it is *will* which contributes the highest proportion (24.9%)

Table 6. Distribution of modal verbs in verb phrase structures of the BNC

Modal structures	1 Mean for all modals in BNC %	2 Will %	3 Would %	4 Can %	5 Could %	6 May %	7 Might %	8 Shall %	9 Should %	10 Must %	11 Ought to %	12 Need to %	13 Dare %	14 Used to %
1 Modal alone	1.9	2.0	2.0	2.8	2.4	0.5	1.5	3.1	1.6	1.0	2.5	1.9	5.0	1.2
2 Modal + infin.	76.0	82.6	78.8	74.6	75.7	72.4	70.9	83.4	63.2	65.3	72.8	76.7	94.2	94.5
3 Modal + *be* + past ptc.	14.7	11.6	7.1	21.9	13.6	17.3	11.3	9.5	26.3	19.5	13.5	14.7	0.1	3.9
4 Modal + *be* + pres. ptc.	1.5	2.8	1.5	0.3	0.6	1.5	1.8	3.4	1.7	1.4	4.0	0.3	0.0	0.3
5 Modal + *have* + past ptc.	5.1	0.9	9.7	0.3	6.6	7.0	12.4	0.5	6.1	11.3	5.9	5.9	0.7	0.1
6 Modal + *be* + *being* + past ptc.	0.0	0.0	0.0	0.0	0.0	0.0	0.0	0.0	0.0	0.0	0.0	0.0	0.0	0.0
7 Modal + *have* + *been* + past ptc.	0.7	0.2	0.9	0.1	1.1	1.3	1.8	0.1	0.9	1.0	1.2	0.5	0.0	0.0
8 Modal + *have* + *been* + pres. Ptc.	0.1	0.0	0.1	0.0	0.1	0.1	0.3	0.0	0.2	0.5	0.1	0.1	0.0	0.0
9 Modal + *have been being* + past ptc.	0.0	0.0	0.0	0.0	0.0	0.0	0.0	0.0	0.0	0.0	0.0	0.0	0.0	0.0
Total	100	100	100	100	100	100	100	100	100	100	100	100	100	100

of the modal tokens, while in structure 3, on the other hand, *can* is again the most frequently-occurring modal (27.2%).

As noted above, structure 5 is commonly used epistemically. It is particularly noteworthy how *will* (4%) and *would* (37.7%) differ in the contribution they make to the overall total for structure 5, and how this is the reverse of the relationship between *will* (41.3%) and *would* (20%) in structure 4. Structures 6 and 9 are highly infrequent. Structure 6 has only 48 tokens in the whole of the BNC, of which 25% of the tokens occur with *may* as the modal verb. Structure 9 has only two tokens in the whole BNC. Both of these occur with the modal *may*. Structure 8, which is also relatively infrequent, has almost half of the modal tokens contributed by *must* and *would*, typically with epistemic uses. The marginal modals, *ought to, need to, dare* and *used to* are very infrequent.

4. Conclusions

Analysis of the BNC thus confirms the findings of earlier studies, often in smaller and less representative corpora that there is substantial and multidimensional variation in the use of modal verbs and the structures they occur in. First, there are differences in the relative use made of individual modals. The BNC generally supports the estimate of the relative frequency of the modal verbs made by Coates (1985) based on the LLC and LOB texts from the 1960s. The BNC suggests that in the 1990's the use of *must* and *shall* may be proportionately less than found in Coates' study, but the frequency of *can* and to a lesser extent, *will* may have increased. In the BNC *will* accounts for almost 23% of all modal tokens, followed by *would, can,* and *could,* with *can* being especially frequent in spoken texts. Semantically, those modals associated with the deontic meanings of 'willingness/intention', 'ability', 'habit' and 'hypothesis', and the epistemic uses of 'prediction', 'certainty' and 'possibility/probability' account for 73% of the modal tokens in the BNC. The use of modals to express the deontic meanings of 'obligation/necessity' and 'permission' is relatively infrequent in the BNC.

Tables 2–7 suggest that there is also systematic variation associated with whether the texts are of spoken or written origin, whether the verb phrase is affirmative or negative, what genre a particular modal occurs in, and which complex verb phrase structure a particular modal token is used in.

There are over 56% more modals per 1000 words in speech than in writing. This is possibly because of the role of modality, especially in face-to-face spoken

Table 7. Distribution of modal verb phrase structures in the BNC

Modal structures	1 Tokens in all BNC	2 Will %	3 Would %	4 Can %	5 Could %	6 May %	7 Might %	8 Shall %	9 Should %	10 Must %	11 Ought to %	12 Need to %	13 Dare %	14 Used to %	15 Total %
1 Modal alone	28,643	23.0	19.8	26.0	14.1	1.8	3.2	2.2	6.1	2.4	0.5	0.2	0.1	0.5	100
2 Modal + infin	1,108,046	24.9	20.6	17.9	11.5	7.4	3.9	1.6	6.4	4.3	0.4	0.2	0.1	1.0	100
3 Modal + be + past ptc	213,906	18.1	9.6	27.2	10.7	19.1	3.2	0.9	13.7	6.6	0.4	0.2	0.0	0.2	100
4 Modal + be + pres ptc	22,190	41.3	20.0	3.8	4.7	7.6	5.0	3.2	8.5	4.7	1.1	0.1	0.0	0.2	100
5 Modal + have + past ptc	74,082	4.0	37.7	1.2	14.9	10.7	10.3	0.1	9.2	11.0	0.5	0.3	0.1	0.0	100
6 Modal + be + being + past ptc	48	10.4	14.6	2.1	8.3	25.0	10.4	0.0	12.5	12.5	4.2	0.0	0.0	0.0	100
7 Modal + have + been + past ptc	9,433	6.1	27.2	1.0	19.0	15.0	11.7	0.3	11.0	7.9	0.7	0.2	0.0	0.0	100
8 Modal + have + been + pres ptc	1,371	2.8	22.6	1.3	10.1	11.7	14.3	0.2	11.3	25.1	0.6	0.2	0.0	0.0	100
9 Modal + have been being + past ptc	2	0.0	0.0	0.0	0.0	100.0	0.0	0.0	0.0	0.0	0.0	0.0	0.0	0.0	100
Total	1,457,721														

interaction, to hedge and soften utterances and express subtle differences in degrees of certainty, attitudes, value judgements and the truth conditions of propositional content. These differences are described in terms of 'stance' by Biber et al (1999: 966). In the BNC, speakers (rather than writers) seem to like to invoke external constraints through the use of particular modal verbs or modal structures. As noted above, this is seen for example, with the use of passive structures when obligation is being expressed (Things *must be done* or *should be done*), or when negation is used, BNC speakers *can't* or *couldn't* do things, rather than *won't* or *wouldn't*. The BNC confirms the frequent use of contracted forms especially in the spoken occurrences of just three modals, *will, can, would*, where about a third of the tokens are contracted.

Negation has a particularly profound effect on the distribution of modals. In spoken texts where modals occur in negative grammatical contexts (Table 2, column 8) they do so with twice the frequency of written. (3.4 per 1000 as against 1.5 per 1000). This effect is particularly shown in the high use of *can't, won't, wouldn't* and *couldn't*. In general, negation appears to have a bigger effect on modal use than genre, or whether the medium is spoken or written.

The BNC shows that while there can be considerable differences between genres in modal use, the distinction between 'imaginative' and 'informative' texts which has often been noted in corpus-based analyses, can be less strong than that between other genres in the BNC. Tables 3 and 5, for example, suggest that on some dimensions the use of modals in the journalistic texts of 'World Affairs' have more in common with 'Imaginative Prose' than with other 'Informative' texts.

There are very great differences in the relative frequency of use of the nine verb phrase structures in which modals can occur. Structure 2 in Tables 4–7 (modal followed by the bare infinitive) is overwhelmingly dominant for all modals. Structures 2 and 3 account for over 90% of all the modal tokens in the BNC. Although structure 1 accounts for only 1.9% of modal tokens in the BNC as a whole, this averaging masks considerable variation. In spoken negative contexts 14% of the modal tokens occur in structure 1.

Table 5 shows that modals occurring in passive voice structures (structure 3) are particularly important in certain 'informative' genres. For example, about 25% of all modals in 'Natural and Pure Science,' 'Applied Science', 'Social Science' and 'Commerce and Finance' occur in this structure, compared with only 15% overall. On the other hand, structure 3 is comparatively infrequent in imaginative prose and spoken texts. When modals are used with perfect aspect in structure 5 there is a comparatively higher use of this structure in 'Imaginative

Prose' and 'World Affairs' than in other genres. The use of modals with progressive aspect in the BNC is extremely rare as is shown in Table 5 for structures 4, 6, 8, and 9. Tables 6 and 7, suggest that the variation in the use of individual modals in the extent to which they each use the nine modal structures is even more striking than variation among genres.

It can be argued that corpus-based descriptions of aspects of language are of interest in their own right because they can improve descriptive adequacy by adding a distributional dimension to linguistic description (Kennedy, 1998). Corpus-based descriptions of English are already being reflected in innovative new grammars. The most comprehensive of these, by Biber et al 1999, is a major work of scholarship. Although the uses which are made of grammatical descriptions are not entirely predictable, their use in language education to develop curricula and new teaching materials is well-established. For teaching and learning the use of modal verbs this analysis of their occurrence in the BNC suggests that among the individual modals, the nine 'central' modals and their elided and negative forms continue to be especially important, (although *shall* is considerably less frequent than the other eight), and some should be the focus of particular pedagogical attention so that learners can develop proficiency handling the semantic functions of 'willingness/intention', 'certainty', 'possibility/probability', 'prediction', 'ability', and 'hypothesis' in both affirmative and negative contexts.

This analysis also suggests that while there is pervasive variation in the distribution of modal verbs in different genres and media, there is substantial stability in their use in complex verb phrase structures. The 100 million words in the spoken and written texts of the BNC represent the equivalent of about 10,000 hours of continuous spoken discourse, equivalent to the exposure which an individual might receive if exposed to English for 8 hours per day for 3.5 years. Over this period of time, Table 7 shows that we could expect to meet structure 9 twice, structure 6   48 times, and structure 8   1371 times. On the basis of this evidence, structures 1,2,3 and 5 clearly have a high priority in language pedagogy. As part of the consciousness-raising of teachers, we might expect that such insights from corpus-based analysis will help associate use with usefulness, so that linguistic items become part of language education not just because they exist, but because they are used often enough to justify inclusion in instruction.

The analysis of the use of modal verbs in a large corpus also demonstrates that linguistic variation is characteristically a probabilistic phenomenon rather than an absolute one. In the present study this has been illustrated at the level of genre. It can be anticipated nevertheless that sociolinguistic or regional varieties of the language are similarly likely to show not the presence or absence of particular linguistic phenomena, but a tendency for them to be used more or less than in other varieties.

Note

1. I am particularly grateful to Gunnel Tottie, Sebastian Hoffmann, Hans Martin Lehmann, and Peter Schneider whose support when I was teaching at the Englisches Seminar of the Universitat Zurich enabled me to carry out this analysis.

References

Aijmer, K. and Altenberg, B. (eds) 1991. *English Corpus Linguistics: Studies in Honour of Jan Svartvik*. London: Longman.
Biber, D., Conrad, S., and Reppen, R. 1998. *Corpus Linguistics*. Cambridge: Cambridge University Press.
Biber, D., Johansson, S., Leech, G., Conrad, S. and Finegan, E. 1999. *Longman Grammar of Spoken and Written English*. Harlow: Pearson Education.
Coates, J. 1983. *The Semantics of the Modal Auxiliaries*. London: Croom Helm.
Collins, P. 1991 "The Modals of Obligation and Necessity in Australian English". In Aijmer and Altenberg (eds) 145–165.
Greenbaum, S. 1996. *The Oxford English Grammar*. Oxford: Oxford University Press.
Kennedy, G. 1998. *An Introduction to Corpus Linguistics*. London: Longman.
Mindt, D. 1995. *An Empirical Grammar of the English Verb: Modal Verbs*. Berlin: Cornelsen.
Palmer, F. 1979. *Modality and the English Modals*. London: Longman.
Quirk, R., Greenbaum, S., Leech, G. and Svartvik, J. 1985. *A Comprehensive Grammar of the English Language*. London: Longman.

CHAPTER 5

Strong modality and negation in Russian

Ferdinand de Haan
University of New Mexico

1. Introduction

One of the purposes of corpus-based research is the testing of theoretical claims made in the literature. When the claims concern a highly complex and heterogeneous area like modality, it becomes all the more important to test claims against a corpus of naturally occurring data in order to provide a distinction between what is claimed by theory and what is actually is occurs in natural language.

This paper examines the interaction of strong modality in Russian with a particular emphasis on the relation between strong modality and negation. Strong modality refers to the modality of necessity and obligation, as opposed to weak modality, which is concerned with possibility and permission (cf. Palmer 1986).

While much work has been done on modality in English, including some very fine corpus-based studies (e.g., Tottie 1985 on negation and epistemic modality; Collins 1991 on strong modality in Australian English and various papers by Merja Kytö 1987, 1991), corpus investigations of modality in other languages is lagging behind. This is not doubt due to of the higher degree of availability of English corpora as opposed to corpora of other languages. This situation, however, is now changing as many more corpora of different languages have become available, either on CD-ROM or on-line. For this study I have made use of the Uppsala corpus of contemporary Russian texts. This corpus was developed at the University of Uppsala and is available free of charge on-line through the University of Tübingen.[1] The corpus contains one million words and consists of a collection of journalistic prose from various sources (both political and scientific) from the period 1985–1988 and of literary works from the 1960s-1980s. The recentness of the material ensures that any study deriving from the corpus is based on a current description of the language. All too often people make use of 19th and early 20th century texts in Russian studies.

The study of modality and negation in Russian is important because there are a number of areas in which Russian potentially differs from English. First, the modal system of Russian is not as grammaticalized as the English system (see Section 2), and this may lead to duplications and ambiguities. Second, the Russian sentence structure differs from the English one. In English, scope of negation and modal is expressed by means of different modal verbs, while in Russian it can depend on the position of the negation which scope interpretation is meant (see De Haan 1997 for a typological discussion of the interaction of modality and negation). A better understanding of the relationship between syntactic and semantic scope is needed. This paper is a start in that direction.

One note on terminology. In this paper I will use the traditional terms *epistemic* and *deontic* modality, for ease of reference. The two meanings are shown in (1) below, using the English strong modal verb *must* as example:

(1) a. John must go to New York tomorrow.
     b. John must be at home: the light is on.

Sentence (1a) shows the deontic use: there is an obligation for John to perform an action. Deontic modality deals with obligation and permission. Sentence (1b) is epistemic: the speaker assigns a likelihood to the statement that John is home. The relative degree of likelihood, or confidence on the part of the speaker in what he or she is saying is the domain of epistemic modality (see Palmer 1986 for an introduction to these terms). These terms are the traditional terms, but in recent years other terms have been coined. Instead of deontic modality, quite often the term *root* modality is used (e.g., in Coates 1983) and terms like *agent-oriented* modality (Bybee, Perkins and Pagliuca 1994) or *participant-oriented* modality (Van der Auwera and Plungian 1998) have been used. While all these terms are supposed to have slight differences in meaning, in practice these terms tend to be used interchangeably. There is no consensus on terminology and the traditional terms are used in this paper, if only for the reason that these terms are the most familiar.

The rest of this paper is structured as follows: Section 2 discusses the basic modal elements in Russian and its relation with negation. Section 3 is an introduction to indeterminacy as defined in Coates 1983. Sections 4 through 7 discuss the modals most commonly used in the literature when discussing strong modality and negation. Section 8 summarizes the implications of NEG-raising while Section 9 draws some conclusions.

2. Modality in Russian

Unlike the English system of modal verbs, modality in Russian is not as grammaticalized. Russian modals do not form a separate syntactic category as the English modals do for the most part. In Russian, modality is very much a semantic category rather than a syntactic one. It is the meaning rather than the syntactic characteristics that define a modal in Russian. Unlike in English, Russian modals form a diverse morphological and syntactic lot. Some modals are adverbs, some are verbs, some modals are personal, some are impersonal. Some can be used across the board, some can only be used in restricted environments. What they have in common is that they can all be combined with a main verb, the verb serving as the object of modality. In (2) below, a partial list of Russian modals is shown with a rough English gloss:

(2) *Partial list of Russian modals*

Modal verbs:	*moč'*	'may, can'
Impersonal verbs:	*sledovat'*	'have to'[2]
	prixodit'sja	'have to'
Modal adverbs:	*dolžen*	'must'
Impersonal adverbs:	*nado*	'have to'
	nužno	'have to'
	dólžno	'must'
	možno	'possible'
Negative modals:	*nel'zja*	'impossible'

Some of these modals (namely the verb *moč'* and the adverb *dolžen*) require a subject in the Nominative (if there is one), while the impersonal modals require that the subject is in the Dative (*nado, nužno, nel'zja*, for instance). Some modals have an inherent past and future tense (e.g., the verbs *moč'*, past tense *mog; prixodit'sja*, past tense *prišlos'*), others (the adverbs) need the auxiliary verb *byt'* 'to be' to form past and future tenses (e.g., *dolžen*, past tense *dolžen byl*).[3]

Simple negation in Russian is expressed with the particle *ne*, placed before the verb. In case of a modal word in the sentence, *ne* can be placed before the modal (as in sentence (3a) below), before the main verb (3b), or before both (3c). all examples come from the scholarly literature.

(3) a. Ne **nado** <u>vyzvat'</u>[1] ego, on priedet sam.[4]
          'There is no **need** to <u>summon</u> him, he'll come himself.'
     b. **Nado** ne tol'ko vsestoronne <u>podgotovit'sja</u>[P] k igre, nado tak že osno-
          vatel'no gotovit'sja k každoj trenirovke.

'It is **necesssary** not only to <u>prepare</u> fully for a game, it is necessary
to prepare just as thouroughly for each practise.'
(Rappaport 1985:210)

c.   Govorja o jazyke žestov, **nel'zja** ne <u>videt'</u>[I] tex izmenenij.
'In speaking of sign language, it is **impossible** not to <u>see</u> those changes.'
(Grenoble 1992:740)

The placement of *ne* in principle determines the relative scope of the negation
and the modal. If the negation precedes the modal, the modal is in the scope of
the negation. If the negation immediately precedes the main verb, it is in the
scope of the modal. When the modal is in the scope of the negation we speak of
wide scope of the negation, when the negation is in the scope of the modal, it is
called *narrow scope*.

However, when the negation immediately precedes the modal, the modal
can still have scope over the negation. This is a process related to the well-
known phenomenon of NEG-raising, also known as negative transport or
transferred negation (see e.g., Horn 1989 for a discussion). This leads to
sentences in which the negation precedes the modal in linear order to have a
narrow scope interpretation. An example is shown in (4):

(4)   On očen' punktual'nyj čelovek, *on* ne **dolžen** <u>opazdat'</u>[P].
'He is a very punctual person, *he* **should**n't <u>be late</u>.'
(Rappaport 1985:212)

Even though the linear order would lead us to expect a wide scope interpretation (i.e, a translation with *need not* or its equivalent), we have instead a narrow
scope interpretation, translated by *should not*.

This is the theory, but as the examples from the corpus will illustrate, in
practise the situation is more complicated. It is not quite clear, for instance, why
sentence (4) above is not translated with *need not* (and the interpretation of the
sentence then becomes *He is a very punctual person so there is no need for him to
be late*). In other words, can we always distinguish between both scope interpretations? This leads us to the problem of *indeterminacy* which is addressed in the
next section

It has been claimed in the literature (e.g., Forsyth 1970, Rappaport 1985)
that there is a relation in Russian between modality, negation, and the choice of
aspect of the main verb.[5] An example will illustrate this (example and discussion from Rappaport 1985:206). The modal *nel'zja* (see Section 6 for details) is
ambiguous between a negated possibility and a negated obligation. When the
interpretation of *nel'zja* is 'impossible' the main verb must be in the perfective

aspect form (as illustrated in sentence (5a)), but if the sense is 'must not', the main verb has to be in the imperfective aspect form (sentence (5b)).

(5)   a.   Zdes' net telefona, otsjuda **nel'zja** <u>pozvonit'</u>^{P}.
            'There is no telephone here; it **is impossible** to <u>call</u> from here.'
       b.   Otsjuda **nel'zja** <u>zvonit'</u>^{I}, my pomešaem ljudjam rabotat'.
            'One **mustn't** <u>call</u> from here; we will disturb people working.'

In other words, the choice of aspect is completely determined by the interpretation of the modal. The negated epistemic interpretation of *nel'zja* requires the perfective aspect, but negated deontic modality requires the imperfective aspect. The aspectual choice of the main verb is *opaque* in Rappaport's terminology. The aspect of the main verb is not determined by the normal rules that govern aspectual choice in Russian but is wholly determined by the interpretation of *nel'zja*. The modal "blocks" the normal rules of aspectual choice. Not all modals are opaque, most do allow the normal rules of aspectual choice and these modals are said to be *transparent*.

3.   Indeterminacy

In her corpus study of modality in English, Coates (1983) showed that it is often difficult to determine the precise status of a given modal. This problem is known as indeterminacy. Coates (1983:14–7) distinguishes three types of indeterminacy:

–   *Gradience*, or the continuum of meaning of a given modal.
–   *Ambiguity*, when it is not possible to determine which meaning is intended and when the interpretation makes a difference.
–   *Merger*, similar to ambiguity but with the difference that the two meanings are not mutually exclusive.

Especially the last two types of indeterminacy are of importance in this study. In (6), an example of *ambiguity* is shown (Coates 1983:16):

(6)   He must understand that we mean business.

This sentence can be interpreted either epistemically (*Surely he understands that we mean business*) or deontically (*It is essential that he understand that we mean business*). In order to disambiguate the sentence we need context but if the correct interpretation cannot be determined from the context, then either one must be chosen. Given that the two meanings are distinct, this proves, according to Coates, the existence of the epistemic-deontic distinction.[6]

Sometimes, in the case of *merger*, the two meanings are not mutually exclusive. In such a case, given the context, both interpretations can make sense and it is not necessary to determine the correct interpretation. The classic example is the exchange of (7), from Coates (1983:17):

(7) A: Newcastle Brown is a jolly good beer.
     B: Is it?
     A: Well it ought to be at that price.

In this exchange, the modal *ought* in the third sentence can be interpreted as either a deontic modal (the brewers of Newcastle Brown have an obligation to put out a good beer given the high price) or an epistemic modal ("It costs a lot, therefore it is good"). In English, merger occurs often with the modals *should* and *ought*. Indeterminacy occurs in Russian as well as will be demonstrated in the next sections.

4. The modal dolžen

We now turn to a discussion of the Russian modals that exemplify strong modality, starting with the prototypical modal *dolžen*.[7] The modal form *dolžen* combines a number of different meanings (cf. Chvany 1974:78–9). It can have both epistemic and deontic interpretations.

In the corpus the most common use of *dolžen* is deontic, and examples are shown in (8):

(8) a.   Konečno, *komandirovannyj čelovek* **dolžen** <u>polučat'</u>[I] kakuju-to
           kompensaciju za dorožnye neudobstva.
           'Of course, *the person in charge* **must** <u>receive</u> some form of compen-
           sation for travel expenses.'   (Izvestija, 1988)
     b.   Po každomu ugolovnomu delu *sud* **dolžen** liš' <u>otvetit'</u>[P] na vopros,
           ..., soveršil li ego podsudimyj.
           'For every criminal case *the court* **must** only <u>decide</u> ... whether the
           accused committed the crime.'   (Literaturnaja Gazeta, 1987)

The modal *dolžen* is the prototypical modal to express strong deontic modality, or obligation in Russian. In sentence (8a) above, the obligation is an opinion expressed by the writer of the article and is more subjective in nature. Typically, the obligation stems from an unspecified source rather than from the discourse participants. For this reason, subjects with *dolžen* are quite often inanimate. In the examples under (9) below, the obligation is more objective in nature. Sentence (9a), from an article on new equipment for ambulances, shows an obligation in the form of a rule or law, while sentence (9b), from a text on equipment for a new rocket ship, shows an obligation imposed by the laws of physics (the discussion revolves around weight in space).

(9) a. V každoj takoj mašine **dolžen** byt'[I] i defibrilljator .
'In every such car must also be a defibrilator.'
(Izvestija, 1987)

   b. Sama *radioantenna* **dolžna** vesit'[I] 700 kilogrammov.
'The *radio antenna* alone **must** weigh 700 kilograms.'
(Izvestija, 1988)

The aspect of the main verb following *dolžen* is *transparent*. The presence of the modal has no effect on the choice of aspect of the main verb. As can be seen from the examples in (8) above, both aspects are possible, because the normal rules for determining the aspectual choice of the main verb apply.[8]

Tense of the modal is expressed by means of adding the auxiliary verb *byt'* 'to be' as is shown in (10) below. The function of the auxiliary is to show that the obligation existed in the past (but not in the present) as in sentence (10a), or will exist in the future, as in (10b). In sentence (10a) the obligation existed in the past but is no longer relevant for the present, hence the use of the past tense *byla*. Sentence (10b) shows that there will exist an obligation in the future, but this obligation does not yet exist in the present.

(10) a. A dal'še *reč'* ... **dolžna byla** pojti[P] o preémnike.
'And further *the speech* (FEM) ... **had to** be (lit. go) about the successor.'
(Izvestija, 1987)

   b. Esli že narodnye zasedateli ... budut ob"edineny v samostojatel'nuju organizaciju , *oni* **dolžny budut** prinjat'[I] rešenie sami, bez učastija sud'i-professionala.
'If then the people's assessors ... will be united in an independent organization, *they* will **have to** take decisions by themselves, without participation of a professional judge.'
(Izvestija, 1987)

Most of the time the obligation is a present obligation (in the corpus this occurs in 86.5% of all cases, as opposed to 12.8% of cases with a past tense and only 0.7% of *dolžen* with a future tense), or includes the present in its obligation.

While *dolžen* does occur with an epistemic interpretation, this is much rarer. In only about 7.5% of the time, *dolžen* is epistemic. Most of the time, moreover, epistemic *dolžen* occurs as the fixed comination *dolžno byt'* 'must be', usually as an interjection:

(11) Pet'ka očen' ljubil čitat'; **dolžno byt'**, poètomu on i byl takoj umnyj. On povadilsja čitat', kogda drugie rebjata ešče spali.
'Pet'ka really loved to read; that **must** have been, because he was so smart. He had the habit of reading, while the other children were still asleep.'   (Kaverin, V., *Pesočnye časy*, 1971)

We now turn to the combination of *dolžen* and negation. As mentioned in Section 2 above, the negation *ne* can both preced and follow the modal. Ideally, the relative position of modal and negation determines its scope, as in (12) below. Sentence (12a) shows a wide scope negation (*ne dolžen*) and the inter-pretation is also one of wide scope, translated in English by *need not* (i.e., *there is no obligation to*). In sentence (12b) the negation has wide scope as well. Sentence (12c) shows a narrow scope negation and the interpretation is that there is an obligation not to, translated in English with *must not*.

(12) a.   On ne **dolžen** opravdyvat'sja[I] pered vami.
'He does not **have to** justify himself to you.
(Rappaport 1985:210)
     b.   Zatmenie ne **dolžno** proizojti[P] v pjat' časov.
'The eclipse **need** not take place at five o' clock.
(Chvany 1974:97)
     c.   My gluboko ubeždeny, čto *novyj komitet* **dolžen** ne kontrolirovat'[I] prirodoispol'zovanie , a upravljat' im.
'We are strongly of the opinion that *the new committee* **must** not control the use of nature, but guide it.'   (Ogonek, 1988)

However, it is quite often the case that the linear order does not reflect the relative scope of the modal. The linear order is that of a wide scope negation (i.e, *ne dolžen*), but the interpretation is narrow scope (i.e., *dolžen ne*, translated as *must not*), and examples are shown in (13) below.

(13) a.   Zapomni ešče raz : *nikto* pro menja ne **dolžen** daže dogadyvat'sja[I].
'Remember once again: *nobody* **must** even guess about my exist-ence.'   (Rasputin, V., Zhivi i pomni)
     b.   Samo po sebe èto položenie edva li možet vyzvat' vozraženija. No pri opredelenii statusa èstonskogo jazyka ne **dolžny** uščemljat'sja[I]

prava graždan drugix nacional'nostej, kotoryx v respublike
dovol'no mnogo.
'By itself this situation can hardly be objectionable. But in the deter-
mination of the status of the Estonian language one **must** not <u>curtail</u>
the *rights* of citizens from other nationalities, of which there are
quite a few in the republic.   (Izvestija, 1989)

In fact, raising of the negation in contexts of strong modality is very common
and the order *dolžen ne* is very rare (less than 10% of all occurrences of *dolžen*
and a negation and less than 1% of all occurrences of *dolžen* in total). All
occurrences of *dolžen ne* were in contrastive contexts, such as the one shown in
(12c) above; in effect, sentences with *dolžen* and a narrow scope negation are
positive sentences, because there is an obligation to do something.[9] What is
negated is not the obligation but rather the action to be performed, which is
contrasted with the action that is under obligation. For instance, in sentence
(12c) the verb *kontrolirovat'* 'control' is negated, and the verb *upravljat'* 'guide'
is contrasted with it to show what is under obligation.

   Sentence (12a) and (b) are not from the corpus, but from the literature on
scope of modality. In the corpus, no clear examples of a wide scope interpretation of *ne dolžen* (i.e., translated as *need not*) are found. Sometimes it was
unclear from the context whether a wide scope or a narrow scope interpretation
of *ne dolžen* was meant (the *ambiguity* problem, see Section 3), but in those
instances where the interpretation was clear, the combination *ne dolžen* had to
be interpreted as narrow scope.

5.   The impersonal verb prixodit'sja and negation

Unlike *dolžen*, the impersonal verb *prixodit'sja* 'have to' is a relatively straightforward modal.[10] It is in the corpus often used to denote multiple events, as in
sentence (14) below whereas *dolžen* rarely is used for multiple events.

   (14)   *Mne* **prixodilos'** ne raz <u>slyšat'</u>[1] slova kolleg.
          '*I* (DAT) **had to** <u>listen</u> more than once to the words of my colleagues.'
                                                          (Nauka i Zhizn', 1988)

This confirms Nichols' (1985:99) observation that *prixodit'sja* often occurs with
explicit expressions of multiplicity, such as *ne raz* 'more than once', *často* 'often'
whereas *dolžen* occurs rarely in such contexts. There is no 100% correlation
between *prixodit'sja* and its use to denote strong modality in multiple events,

however (see, e.g., sentence (15) below). Because of this occurrence with multiple events, the main verb accompanying *prixodit'sja* is almost always in the imperfective. In the corpus, only one occurrence had a main verb in the perfective. Sentence (15) uses the main verb *priznat'* 'admit' in the perfective due to the fact that we are dealing with a singular event with an inherent end.

(15)   No teper' **prixoditsja** priznat'[P], čto èto uže ne čisto biologičeskaja nauka, a kompleksnaja, v kotoruju vovlečeny praktičeski vsestorony žizni i dejatel'nosti čeloveka.
'But now one **must** admit that this is no longer a pure biological science, but a complex one, which involves practically every aspect of life and human endeavor.'   (Nauka i Zhizn', 1987)

The verb *prixodit'sja* is a deontic modal. No examples of epistemic modality were attested in the corpus.

As far as the interaction of negation and *prixodit'sja* is concerned, in almost all examples the negation precedes the modal. Examples are shown in (16) below:

(16)   a.   ...ne **prixodilos'** li *nam* polučat'[I] vot takie netrudovye doxody?
'**Should**n't *we* (DAT) receive such non-work related income?'
(Socialističeskaja Industrija, 1988)

        b.   Nemcy byli uže tret'ju nedelju okruženy v Stalingrade, kazalos', blizok konec, i xotelos' dovoevat' do nego, komanduja svoim batal'onom. Xotelos', no ne **prišlos'**.
'The Germans were already in the third week of the siege of Stalingrad and it appeared the end was near. And (I) wanted to fight on till the end, commanding the battalion. I wanted to, but **couldn't**.'
(Simonov, K., *Soldatami ne roždajutsja*,1965)

        c.   *Mne* nikogda v žizni ne **prixodilos'** byvat'[I] v bjuro poxoronnogo obsluživanija. Pri vide magazina s vyveskoj "Poxoronnye prinadležnosti" ja perexožu na druguju storonu ulicy.
'Never in my life did *I* **have to** go (lit. be) to a funeral parlor. Whenever I see a store with a sign "services for the dead" I cross to the other side of the street.'
(Solouxin, V., *Poxorony Stepanidy Ivanovny*, 1987)

The modal *prišlos'* in (16b) occurs without explicit main verb, but the intended verb is *dovoevat'* ('to fight on').

As is the case with *dolžen*, NEG-raising also occurs with *prixodit'sja*. In sentence (16c) the interpretation is one of wide scope (there is clearly a negative obligation), while sentence (16a) conveys an obligation not to do something. Again, as is the case with *dolžen*, the negation most often comes before the modal, regardless of the scope interpretation. In only one instance of modal *prixodit'sja* and negation, the negation occurs before the main verb and after the modal:

(17) Esli by *mne* kogda-nibud' **prišlos'** ne <u>trenirovat'sja</u>[I], ne znaju, čto slučilos' by.
'If *I* **had to** not <u>train</u> at some point, I don't know what would happen.'
(Fizkul'tura i Sport, 1987)

Sentence (17) is clearly an instance of a narrow scope negation: the reference is to an obligation not to do something. When the negation follows the modal, the interpretation is therefore unambiguously narrow scope, as expected.

6. The modal nel'zja

The modal *nel'zja* is an inherently negative form with a fairly broad set of meanings. In textbooks, it is usually stated that *nel'zja* can denote negated ability (*impossible*), negated possibility (*cannot*), and negated permission (*must not*). It is frequently seen as the negative counterpart to the adverb *možno* 'possible, allowed' which cannot be combined with a negation.[11]

In addition, it is usually mentioned that *nel'zja* quite often occurs without overt subject. In the corpus, *nel'zja* most often occurs without overt subject. Of the 301 occurrences of *nel'zja* in the corpus, 280 were without overt subject (93.0%), 15 occurrences were with a third person subject (5.0%), 4 with a first person subject (1.3%), and two occurrences were with a second person subject (0.7%). While most modals can not occur with an overt subject, none has such a high correlation with the absence of the subject.

There is also an idiomatic expression with *nel'zja*, namely *kak nel'zja lučše* 'better than ever' (or a variation of this idiom) of which there are ten occurrences in the corpus. This use of *nel'zja* has been disregarded in this study.

In the corpus, the range of *nel'zja* is restricted. The epistemic interpretation of *nel'zja* is by far the most common interpretation (170 out of 301 examples). This epistemic reading is in all cases the *cannot*, or, *impossible* one. Typical examples are:

(18) a. Odnako mnogie iz nix naxodjatsja sejčas kak by na pereput'e-ponimajut, čto <u>dejstvovat'</u>[I] po-staromu **nel'zja**, a po-novomu ne

mogut, ne umejut.
'However, many of them find themselves at a crossroads as it were. They understand that they **can't** <u>act</u> as in the old days, but they cannot, are not capable, of doing thing the new way.'   (Pravda, 1988)
b.   Slovami ètot zapax opisat' nevozmožno. <u>Pripomnit'</u>[P] ego usiliem mysli tože **nel'zja**. Kakoj on byl?
'This smell could not be described in words. It was also **impossible** to <u>remember</u> it with all (my) might. What was it?
(Grekova, I., *Kafedra*, 1980)

In sentence (18a), the modal *nel'zja* describes an epistemic impossibility, the impossibility to continue as before. This is an external impossibility. Note the juxtaposition of *nel'zja* with the modals *ne mogut* 'cannot' and *ne umejut* 'physically cannot' in the continuation of the sentence; the latter two modals show the internal impossibility. Sentence (18b) juxtaposes *nel'zja* with *nevozmožno* 'impossible'.

In the corpus, 19 occurrences have a double negation construction; *nel'zja* is comined with a negation occurring before the main verb. This construction is interpreted in the same way as the English double negation construction *can't not V = must V*. An example is (19):

(19)   V ètoj svjazi **nel'zja** ne <u>zametit'</u>[P], čto "vojna nervov", kotoruju SŠA zatejali   protiv Livii, vstrečena v Tel'-Avive kak podarok sud'by.
'In this respect we **can't** not (= must) mention that the "war of nerves" that the USA is engaged in with Libya is treated in Tel-Aviv as a gift from heaven.'
(Izvestija, 1989)

In 17 cases, the interpretation is one of denied permission (*may not*):

(20)   Medsestra podošla k Margo i skazala, čto <u>plakat'</u>[I] **nel'zja** ni v koem slučae, potomu čto ej vredno rasstraivat'sja.
'The nurse went up to Margo and said that she wasn't **allowed** to <u>cry</u> under any circumstance, because it was bad for her concentration.'
(Tokareva, V., *Ničego osobennogo*, 1987)

We now turn to the role of the aspect of the main verb. It has been often observed in the literature (e.g., Forsyth 1970, Rappaport 1985) that the choice of aspect has an influence on the interpretation of *nel'zja*. Example sentences were shown in (5) above. These sentences were all unambiguous because of context. The claim that is frequently made is that the choice of aspect without context points to the interpretation of the modal, as evidenced by the following example from Rappaport (1985:206):

(21) Ètu vstreču **nel'zja** <u>otložit'</u>[P] / <u>otkladyvat'</u>[I].
      'This meeting **cannot** [P] / **must not** [I] <u>be postponed</u>.

If the main verb is perfective, the interpretation is negated ability, if it is imperfective, it denotes negated permission. Of course, the difference in modal interpretation is not all that great. The difference between the impossible (*cannot*) and the prohibitive (*must not*) interpretation. There is an area of indeterminacy and sometimes aspect is not the predictor of modality, as in the case of (22), also from Rappaport (1985:207):

(22) a. V ètom kinoteatre **nel'zja** <u>pokazyvat'</u>[I] širokoèkrannye fil'my.
          'In this movie theater it is **not possible** to <u>show</u> widescreen films.'
      b. **Nel'zja** <u>razrušit'</u>[P] Pariž, èto sdelaet nevozmožnym soglašenie.
          'Paris **must not** be <u>destroyed</u>, it will make an agreement impossible.'

Even though the inability reading is present in sentence (22a), and therefore the main verb should be in the perfective aspect, the imperfective form is used to show that the action described (the showing of movies) is an ongoing activity, which is expressed by the imperfective aspect in Russian. Conversely, because the act of destroying a city is an action with an inherent endpoint, the perfective aspect is appropriate in sentence (22b). In both cases, the normal rules that govern aspectual choice override the alleged opacity of the modal.

This is certainly also the case in the corpus. In many cases there was no clear relationship between the choice of aspect and the choice of modal interpretation. In many cases the precise modality was not clear (as in sentence (23a) below), and in other cases a different aspect than predicted was obtained.

(23) a. Slovno by zabyvaetsja i o tom, čto est' vozrast, fiziologičeski naibolee blagoprijatnyj dlja obučenija, kotoryj **nel'zja** <u>upustit'</u>[P].
          'It is as though one forgets as well that it is the age which is physically best suited for education, and which we **can't** (**mustn't**) <u>let go to waste</u>.'   (Izvestija, 1987)
      b. <u>Upravljat'</u>[I], kak prežde, uže **nel'zja**.
          '<u>Govern</u>, like before, is now **impossible**.'   (Izvestija, 1988)

Since the main verb is perfective in sentence (23a) we would expect the negated ability (*impossible*) interpretation. While this is certainly possible, the *must not* interpretation is also possible, and we are dealing with indeterminacy. Since both interpretations are possible, we are dealing with a case of *merger*. Sentence (23b), on the other hand, is clearly a case of negated ability and the perfective would have been appropriate. The imperfective is used, however, because the action expressed (*upravljat'* 'to govern') is durative in nature, and durative verbs in Russian require the imperfective aspect.

7.   Nado and negation

The adverb *nado* 'necessary' in its modal sense can only be used as a strong deontic modal.[12] Thus, a sentence such as (24) below can only be interpreted as an obligation, not as an epistemic necessity (Forsyth 1970:264).

(24)   Knigi **nado** <u>sdavat'</u>^I v biblioteky vsegda vovremja.
        'Books **must** always <u>be returned</u> to the library on time.'

The aspect of the main verb in positive sentences is not influenced by *nado*, but rather by the general rules that govern aspectual choice. Thus, the main verb is in the imperfective in sentence (24) because we are dealing with a general truth. When a negation is present, the situation changes.

The modal *nado* can be combined with *ne* 'not' by placing it either before *nado* or before the main verb (it is also in principle possible to have two negations, but this was not attested in the corpus). Examples from the corpus are:

(25)   a.   Ne **nado** <u>zabyvat'</u>^I , čto reč' idet ne tol'ko o rybe.
              'One **must** not <u>forget</u> that we are not just talking about fish.'
                                                              (Nauka i žizn', 1989)
        b.   …, mnogie trudnosti, odolevajušč ie naše narodnoe xozjajstvo, kak, estestvenno, i puti ix preodolenija, <u>iskat'</u>^I **nado** ne v samoj èkonomike.
              '(the cause of the) many problems that plague our economy, and of course the way to their solution **must** not be <u>found</u> just in economics.'
                                                              (Izvestija, 1988)

It has been noted in the literature (e.g., Forsyth 1970:246; Rappaport 1985:212–3) that the aspect of the main verb after *ne nado* is always imperfective. This is also true in the corpus. Of the 68 (out of 78) examples of the corpus with *ne nado* and a main verb, all main verbs were in the imperfective aspect. Sentence (25a) above is an example of the imperfective aspect of the main verb. The aspectual choice of the main verb combined with *ne nado* is therefore opaque: it always has to be in the imperfective and this is due to the presence of *ne nado*.

Similarly, the statement that *ne nado* (and *nado ne*) are always deontic in nature is also borne out by the corpus. Examples with *nado* and a negation always refer to either a lack of obligation (which can be translated with *need not*) or to an obligation not to do something (in which case it can be translated with *must not*).

The problems surrounding *nado* and negation are similar to those that occur with *dolžen* and negation. Scope relations are not always straightforward. In principle the linear order should determine the scope of the negation. In sentence (25b) the negation follows the modal, so that the *must not* translation is appropriate, while in (26) below the negation precedes the modal and the *need not* translation is appropriate.

(26) Ne **nado** dolgo naprjagat'[1] pamjat', čtoby vspomnit' lučšie kinoroli Eleny
      Proklovoj.
      'One **need** not think long and hard in order to remember the best
      movieroles of Elena Proklovaja.'   (Socialističeskaja industrija, 1988)

However, in many cases the linear order is not indicative of the scope relation between the modal and the negation. In sentence (25a) above, the surface order suggest a wide scope interpretation, yet it is clear that the intended interpretation is narrow scope. This occurs quite often in the corpus. Of the 72 cases of *ne nado*, 34 have a wide scope interpretation, 24 a narrow scope interpretation, and a further 14 cases in which the intended scope interpretation is ambiguous. The narrow scope linear order is unambiguous: the interpretation always follows the linear order and *nado ne* is always interpreted as narrow scope.

The interesting fact about the narrow scope interpretation is not that it can occur with a wide scope linear order (i.e., *ne nado*), but that it rarely occurs with a narrow scope order (i.e., with the order *nado ne*). This order only occurs 6 times in the corpus. Of those 6 times, only 2 times a true narrow scope situation occurred and sentence (25b) is an example. In 4 instances, *nado ne* occurred in a contrastive situation (*one must not do X, but Y*), and an example is shown in (27) below.

(27) Oni ponjali, čto iskat'[1] **nado** ne točnye kopii izučaemogo gena, a vsex ego
      rodstvennikov, to est' geny, blizkie emu po strukture .
      'They understood, that they **had to** find not exact copies of the gene
      under investigation, but of all of its relatives, that is to say, genes that
      resembled it in structure.'   (Sputnik, 1986)

Examples such as (27) show that *nado ne* in these cases is actually a positive sentence. The negation is not sentential but only refers to the constituent (see De Haan 1997 for a discussion and tests of sentence versus constituent negation), since the action expressed is not denied but the object of the verb. In the concrete case of sentence (27) the negation has only the object of the verb *to find* in its scope (*the exact copies of the gene under investigation*), not the verb itself or the modal so that the sentence expresses a positive obligation to perform a certain action.

A wide scope linear structure with a narrow scope interpretation, i.e., situations in which the form *ne nado* has the interpretation *must not*, is very common. As mentioned above, this occurred 24 times in the corpus. Thus, the form *ne nado* is potentially ambiguous between a wide and a narrow scope interpretation of the negation. This difference in interpretation has no impact on the choice of the aspect of the main verb (it is still imperfective), showing that the scope interpretation of *nado* and the negation is not a factor but that *ne nado* inherently requires its main verb to be in the imperfective.[13]

In a number of cases it is not possible to decide without a doubt from the context whether we are dealing with narrow or wide scope negation. An example is shown in (28).

(28)   Ne **nado** <u>vygonjat'</u>[I] iz školy Sašu Stameskina ... Pered licom svoix
        tovariščej po Leninskomu komsomolu ja toržestvenno obeščaju, čto
        Stameskin stanet xorošim učenikom, graždaninom i daže
        komsomol'cem.
        ' (We) **mustn't/need**n't <u>expel</u> Sasha Stameskin from school. Before the
        faces of his comrades of the Lenin Komsomol I swear that Stameskin will
        become a good student, citizen, and even a (good) Komsomol member.'
                                    (Vasil'ev, B., *Zavtra byla vojna*, 1984)

From the context it is not possible to determine whether we are dealing with a wide or a narrow scope. Either interpretation is possible in this situation. However, since both interpretations are mutually compatible, we are dealing here with a case of *merger*. With *merger*, it is not necessary to decide which of the two meanings is intended, and this is clearly going on in example (28). Since 14 out of 72 cases, or 19.4%, are indeterminate in this way, the correct scope interpretation cannot be determined in a sizeable portion of all occurrences of *ne nado*. But given that the two scope interpretations are not far apart in meaning, this rarely creates any problem. Compare the findings of *ne nado* with the analogous German combination *nicht müssen* "must / need not" which is similarly ambiguous. Scope ambiguity also occurs when there is no main verb that accompanies *ne nado*, as in (29)

(29) A prinimat' snotvornoe ne privykla . — I ne **nado**, — podderžal ee Gil'e.
'But I didn't get used to taking something to help me sleep. — "And you **must**n't / **need**n't," insisted Gil'e.'   (Lidin, V., *Fedra*, 1962)

Sentence (29) shows indeterminacy in the form of *ambiguity*. It can be interpreted as either a warning to not get addicted, or as a statement that there is no need to take painkillers. This is an either/or indeterminacy, hence the ambiguity. It is necessary to disambiguate the discourse fragment in order for it to be understood.

8. The implications of NEG-Raising

The main function of NEG-raising in examples such as (13) and (16) is to show that we are dealing with a negative sentence. The best way of ensuring that the listener is aware that we are dealing with a negative sentence is to place the negative element as early as possible, i.e., right before the modal. This view is well attested in many languages (see De Haan 1997 and the references there for discussion). Compare this with the English situation: the constructions *must not* and *need not* have syntactically identical structures; in both cases, the negation is sentential.[14] Not so with the constructions *modal + ne* and *ne + modal* in Russian. Only in the second case is the negation sentential. In the case of *modal + ne*, we are actually dealing with a positive sentence, but with a negated constituent (the VP). Apparently it is felt that in the construction *modal + ne* the negation in its narrow scope interpretation is still somehow sentential in nature (as it is in English) and since the negation in the *modal + ne* construction is not syntactically sentential, the modal is shifted to the beginning, creating the construction *ne + modal*. This frees up the construction *modal + ne* and it can be used for contrastive situations which is one of the natural functions of constituent negations crosslinguistically. This situation is found almost without exception in the corpus. Cases in which the combination *modal + ne* is not contrastive may involve an implicit contrast.

The process of NEG-raising does entail that the construction *ne + modal* is now ambiguous between a wide and a narrow scope interpretation. This creation of ambiguity is clearly not considered to be a big problem. However, there is some indication that the modal *dolžen* combined with *ne* is now mainly used to denote the narrow scope, i.e., it must be translated by *must not* rather than *need not*. Most of the clear-cut cases in the corpus (those not involving indeterminacy) have the narrow scope interpretation. This could mean that *dolžen* is moving in the direction of a verb with only one possible scope interpretation when it is combined with a negation. If this is the case, it will have the same status as English *must* and *need*, namely verbs which have only one scope interpretation when they are combined with a negation.

9.   Conclusions

As far as the interaction of negation and strong modality is concerned, Russian paints a complex picture. Several different processes (indeterminacy, aspectual choice of main verb, NEG-raising) go on simultaneously. These processes create problems of interpretation and speakers of Russian must find ways to get around ambiguity problems. One such strategy, reserving a certain verb for just one scope representation (as demonstrated by the verb *dolžen*), could be an important clue to the direction of change languages take when they decide on how to encode ambiguities of scope. Based on the Russian data presented here, it would appear that languages go from a syntactic approach (where the placement of the negation in the sentence determines its scope) to a semantic approach (where the scope of the negation is determined by the modal verb). Possibly the process of NEG-raising is a determining factor in the change from one state to the other.

Finally it must be mentioned that there was little difference between the behavior of modality and negation in the two registers used here. I take this to mean that the processes described in the previous sections hold for most, if not all, registers of the language and that we are therefore dealing with a phenomenon which represents a true shift in Russian as a whole. This in turn may mean that we are dealing with a universal mechanism of scope disambiguation.

Notes

1. The corpus can be consulted at http://www.sfb441.uni-tuebingen.de/b1/korpora.html.
2. This verb comes from a full verb with the meaning 'to follow.'
3. The present tense of *byt'* 'to be' is zero.

4. In citing the Russian examples, I make use of the following conventions. First, the modal is printed in bold and the main verb is underlined. If a subject is present, it is italicized. Finally, according to standard practise, the aspect of the main verb (if present) is indicated by means of either a superscript I (for imperfective aspect) or P (for perfective aspect).

5. In Russian, most verbs have two morphological forms, depending on the choice of aspect. For instance, the Russian translation of the verb 'to write' is either *pisat'* for situations requiring the imperfective aspect (broadly speaking, actions in progress), or *napisat'* when a perfective interpretation is required (when an action is viewed in its totality). Both *pisat'* and *napisat'* are infinitives and can be inflected for tense and person. The relationship between imperfective and perfective verb forms is for the most part idiosyncratic and for almost every verb, both forms must be memorized.

6. Coates uses the term root modality instead of deontic modality.

7. The form of the modal *dolžen* depends on the gender of the subject. The forms are *dolžen* (for masculine singular nouns), *dolžna* (feminine singular), *dolžno* (neuter singular) and *dolžny* (plural). The subject is in the nominative.

8. In the corpus, *dolžen* is very often accompanied by a main verb. Only in 1.7% of all cases was there no main verb present. With other modals it is more common to omit a main verb when it can be recovered from the context.

9. Syntactically, *dolžen ne* does not behave like *ne dolžen*, as explained in De Haan 1997. Narrow scope negation fails the tests for sentence negation and must be considered instances of constituent negation. The combination *dolžen ne* is not the only combination with this behavior, see Section 7 below on *nado ne*.

10. The impersonal verb *prixodit'sja* is the imperfective member of an aspectual pair, of which the verb *prijtis'* is the perfective member. It is one of a very few aspectual modal pairs in Russian and the existence of the two verbs is due to the fact that their origin lies in motion verbs. In fact, the pair *prixodit'sja/prijtis'* can still be used as full verbs, with the meaning of 'end up'. The distribution of *prixodit'sja* and *prijtis'* is unclear and no attempt is made in this paper to explain the reasons underlying the choice of *prixodit'sja* and *prijtis'*.

11. In the corpus, the combination *ne možno* does not occur, although *možno ne* does sporadically.

12. In addition, *nado* can also serve as an adverb meaning 'need', as in the following sentence:
(i)   Odna iz našix ženščin zajavila , čto ne **nado** nam nikakix plat'ev iz-za granicy.
'One of our females explained that we don't **need** any dresses from abroad.'
(Literaturnaja gazeta, 1989)
This use of *ne nado* occurred 21 times in the corpus. Because this is not a modal usage, these 21 cases are disregarded in the rest of the paper.

13. Rappaport (1985:212–3) explains this by stating that *ne nado* in its narrow scope interpretation can be looked at as a negated deontic possibility by applying the elementary modal logic conversion rule *necessary not == not possible*, or *must not == can't*. In contexts of negated possibility in Russian, the imperfective is also required. This explanation entails that the modal *nado* can be viewed as either a strong modal (*need*) and a weak modal (*can*) but the latter only in negative contexts. This seems strained.

14. This can be demonstrated with syntactic tests, such as the addition of tag questions or tags with *not even* (or its equivalent in the language under discussion). See De Haan (1997) for discussion.

References

Bybee, J., Perkins, R. and Pagliuca, B. 1994. *The Evolution of Grammar: Tense, Aspect, and Modality in the Languages of the World.* Chicago: University of Chicago Press.

Chvany, C. V. 1974. The grammar of Dolžen: Lexical entries as a function of theory. In *Slavic Transformational Syntax. Michigan Slavic materials 10,* D. Richard D. Brecht and C. V. Chvany (eds) , 78–122. Ann Arbor: University of Michigan.

Coates, J. 1983. *The Semantics of the Modal Auxiliaries.* London: Croom Helm.

Collins, P. 1991. The modals of obligation and necessity in Australian English. In *English Corpus Linguistics,* Karin Aijmer and Bengt Altenberg (eds), 145–65. London and New York: Longman.

De Haan, F. 1997. *The Interaction of Modality and Negation: A Typological Study.* New York: Garland.

Flier, M. S. and A. Timberlake (eds). 1985. *The Scope of Slavic Aspect.* Columbus, OH: Slavica Publishers, Inc.

Forsyth, J. 1970. *A Grammar of Aspect: Usage and Meaning in the Russian Verb.* Cambridge: Cambridge University Press.

Grenoble, L. A. 1992. Double negation in Russian. *Linguistics* 30, 731–52.

Horn, L. R. 1989. *A Natural History of Negation.* Chicago: University of Chicago Press.

Kytö, Merja. 1987. On the use of the modal auxiliaries indicating "possibility" in Early American English. In Martin Harris and Paolo Ramat (eds.). *Historical development of auxiliaries.* Berlin: Mouton de Gruyter, 145–70.

Kytö, Merja. 1991. *Variation and diachrony, with Early American English in focus: studies on can/may and shall/will.* Frankfurt a.M.: Peter Lang Verlag.

Nichols, J. 1985. Aspect and Inversion in Russian. In Flier and Timberlake (eds) 94–117.

Palmer, F. R. 1986. *Mood and Modality.* Cambridge: Cambridge University Press.

Rappaport, G. C. 1985. Aspect and Modality in Contexts of Negation. In Flier and Timberlake (eds) 194–223.

Tottie, G. 1985. The negation of epistemic necessity in Present-day British and American English. *English World-Wide* 6, 87–116.

Van der Auwera, J. and Plungian, V. A. 1998. Modality's semantic map. *Linguistic Typology* 2, 79–123.

CHAPTER 6

Formulaic language in English academic writing

A corpus-based study of the formal and functional variation of a lexical phrase in different academic disciplines[*]

David Oakey
University of Birmingham

1. Introduction

Evidence pointing to the existence of formulaic language has been found in a variety of research fields. Approaches to language teaching have in the last decade recognised the need to take such formulaic language linguistic phenomena into account, the most comprehensive presentation to date being the taxonomy of "lexical phrases" by Nattinger and DeCarrico (1992). They suggested the lexical phrase as a pedagogically applicable formulaic sequence, and they specified lexical phrases to be used in the teaching of academic writing to learners of English as a foreign language. However, some of these lexical phrases did not intuitively seem typical of those used in academic writing in English, possibly due to the limitations of the linguistic data on which they were based. It was felt that corpus research may provide a clearer, less intuitive insight into these units, and illuminate how their form and use differs in different academic contexts. This paper thus investigates the formal and functional variation of one of these lexical phrases as it is used in academic writing in social science, medical, and technical disciplines. It will highlight the relationship between the syntagmatic and paradigmatic variation of this lexical phrase and its discourse signalling and organising functions across different academic disciplines.

2.   Research into formulaic language

There has long been evidence from cognitive psychology, from studies of first and second language acquisition, and from textual description, which suggests that speakers may possess a non-homogeneous store of language knowledge consisting of a system of generative grammatical rules and a store of pre-assembled patterns, and that a speaker at times 'bypasses' the rules and retrieves a pre-fabricated pattern instead. From a cognitive perspective Pawley and Syder argued that the majority of a speaker's output is in some part memorised, and only "a minority of spoken clauses are entirely novel creations in the sense that the combination of lexical items is new to the speaker." (Pawley and Syder 1983:205). Bolinger drew on the work of Van Lancker and suggested that lateralisation of functions in the cortex "points to a side which files things and a side which puts them together," (Bolinger 1976:13), and that formulaic language is "part of the automatic or semi-automatic store which continues to be more or less automatic, even when passed through the analytical sieve that separates them." (ibid.: 13). From a psycholinguistic perspective, Peters (1983 cited in Weinert 1995:181) found evidence of formulaic language in first language acquisition, and Hakuta (1974) saw it in data from child second language learning.

Evidence for formulaic language is also apparent from the study of written texts, particularly in corpus-driven research into collocation and patterns. Sinclair's 'idiom principle' resulted from the observation that speakers and writers can use "a large number of semi-preconstructed phrases that constitute single choices, even though they might appear to be analyzable into segments." (Sinclair 1991:110). Hunston and Francis (2000) developed their previous work on grammar patterns to propose a corpus-driven grammar of English described in terms of patterns. Partington (1998) and Wray (1999) have presented thorough surveys of formulaic language across these different fields of reference.

3.   Formulaic sequences for English language teaching: lexical phrases

The above evidence suggests that formulaic language of some kind features widely in language learning and language use and thus may be important for learners and users of second languages, as well as their teachers. This was pointed out by Cowie, for example, who held that "the sheer density of ready-made units in various types of written text is a fact that any approach to the teaching of writing to foreign students has to come to terms with." (Cowie 1992: 10). Lewis, a influential force in raising awareness of formulaic language in English language teaching during the 1990s, similarly contends that

> chunking of written text principally involves words, word partnerships and, for those learning to write in a particular genre such as academic English, developing an awareness of the sentence heads and frames typical of the genre.
> (Lewis 1996: 15)

As already mentioned, the focus of the present study is the lexical phrase, a term which has been used frequently in the English language teaching literature over the past decade, not least due to the contribution made by Lewis. The term dates back at least to an Artificial Intelligence paper by Becker (1975), although it is also used to refer to types of compound nouns in the field of Information Retrieval (c.f. Krovetz 1997).

Nattinger and DeCarrico (1992) used the term to describe a pedagogically applicable unit of formulaic language; one which had a categorical form and pragmatic discourse function. They specified lexical phrases for, among other uses, helping students with the organisation and form of their essays, based on the observation that:

the typical essay a student writes in North American universities…adheres to the following structure:

(1) Opening
  a. Topic priming: sets the scene and prepares the reader for what is to follow.
  b. Topic nomination:
    (a) statement of purpose: explains what the writer intends;
    (b) statement of topic: explains what the writer will talk about;
  c. Statement of organisation: explains how the writer will talk about the topic
(2) Body: sets forth the argument, conveys the information.
(3) Closing: brings the argument to a close.
    (Nattinger and DeCarrico 1992: 164)

They then provide lists of "representative lexical phrases for the above categories." (Nattinger & DeCarrico, 1992: 165). However, this model of academic discourse organisation, with three complex stages for 'opening', yet only one each for 'body' and 'closing,' appears rather superficial when compared with the texts which more advanced university students are expected to produce and publish. While Nattinger and DeCarrico specified these lexical phrases for wider application in the teaching of English academic writing, it is not clear to what degree these phrases are "representative" of other genres such as theses, journal articles and so on. One reason for this lack of clarity is the data used by Nattinger and DeCarrico in formulating these lexical phrases. This data is rather briefly described as "written discourse collected from a variety of textbooks for ESL, textbooks for academic courses, letters to the editor of various news publications, and personal correspondence." (Nattinger and DeCarrico 1992: xvi). There is little information about the quantity and attestedness of this data which obviously crosses a number of genres. Since Nattinger and DeCarrico's work, genre analysis has revealed much about the complex ways in which texts in different genres are produced, leading to an interest in the patterning and construction of writing in individual disciplines. It would seem that lexical phrases may need to be more genre-specific than currently specified.

There arise, therefore, two questions which this study attempts to answer: Are lexical phrases replicable *as specified* in authentic corpus data? — i.e. do word strings with the same form as these lexical phrases occur in published academic prose? The second question relates to the functional discourse model: If such phrases do occur, what is their function in different disciplines? The answer to this question has relevance for teachers: if lexical phrases are seen to vary across disciplines, then a one-size-fits-all pedagogical approach will not be sufficient. There now follows a brief description of the lexical phrase used in this study.

4. Form and function of *it is/has been (often) asserted/believed/noted that X*

The object of the present study is the lexical phrase *it is/has been (often) asserted/believed/noted that X*. Nattinger and DeCarrico term this a "sentence builder" lexical phrase which provides the framework for whole sentences (ibid.: 42). This "sentence builder" category is discontinuous and highly variable, and this particular lexical phrase has the potential to frame a long and complex sentence. A writer whose first language was not English would need a sound grasp of what variation is and is not permissible in order to do this successfully. It would seem that more paradigmatic variation is possible than specified, for example verbs such as *argue* or *claim* could be used here. Similarly, syntagmatic variation would also seem possible: there is no reason why *often* need stay in the specified position after *been*. The function of this lexical phrase is intended to be "topic priming", something defined by Nattinger and DeCarrico for academic writing as the way the writer "sets the scene and prepares the reader for what is to follow." (ibid.: 164).

5.   Methodology

5.1 The corpus subset

The corpus data used in this study was chosen to allow replicability. Applying functional labels to linguistic units is a highly subjective activity, and researchers in the field often compile their own subcorpora which are not available to other researchers. This means that previous studies can not easily be replicated, and thus the consistency of subjectivity can be hard to gauge. With this in mind, a subset of the British National Corpus (Oxford University Press 1995) was chosen, based on categorisations by Lee (2001), and so the study may be replicated by anyone with access to the BNC.

At the time of this study, the BNC classification relied on a broad categorisation of texts by "domains" such as leisure, business, imaginative, informative, and so on, which made it difficult to isolate texts from different academic subject disciplines from the corpus. Lee's categorisations provide a different way of dividing the BNC fields. He opts for a prototypical approach where some texts fit better into categories than others; boundaries are fuzzy, and roughly match those of the ICE-GB and LOB categories. He proposes a "super genre" of academic prose, comprised of 6 sub-genres: humanities/arts, medicine, natural science, politics/law/education, social science, and technical/engineering.

For the purpose of this study, three of Lee's sub-genres were chosen, and the resulting subset searched comprised all texts in social science, medicine, and technical/engineering sub-genres (see Table 1 below). The texts were a mixture of published journal articles and book extracts, and a full list of the files used is available from this author on request.

The study can still be replicated by users of the current BNC World edition (2000) which allows selection of texts according to Lee's criteria. It should be pointed out here that the BNC was not built with studies of this type in mind (Aston 2001). The sampling methods used in its construction meant that partial texts were included, and thus some areas of discourse may not be represented

Table 1. The subset of the BNC

Subject area	Social Science	Medicine	Technical/Engineering
Texts	91	23	18
Total words	2,607,749	1,413,493	620,424
Average words per text	28,657	61,456	34,468

equally. Nonetheless, it is fair to say that a subset of this size yields sufficient occurrences for meaningful comparisons to be made between sub-genres.

5.2 Searches

The subset was searched using WordSmith Tools Version 3.0 (Scott 1999) and strings identified which had the same form as Nattinger and DeCarrico's lexical phrase. These occurrences were not immediately classed as lexical phrases. By definition a lexical phrase is a discontinuous formulaic sequence which has been assigned a pragmatic function, and thus each occurrence of a pattern needs to be examined in context in order to identify the function it appears to have in the text. Thus, two conditions need to be satisfied in order to identify a lexical phrase: its form must approximate to the specified string, and then the pragmatic function of the phrase must be the one specified.

Corpus analysis can speed the identification of word strings in a large corpus, but traditional intuitive judgement must still play a large part in deciding whether a particular string performs a particular function. For example, if a researcher is looking for examples of *it is the case that X* , the concordancing software could be instructed to search the corpus for all occurrences of *case* where *that* occurs within nine words to the right. However, it is still the researcher's task to identify and remove those examples which refer to legal or medical cases and so on. In proposing a pragmatic function for *it is the case that,* such as "topic priming", it is still the researcher's intuition which makes the judgement based on the context in which the string occurs.

As mentioned above, sentence builder lexical phrases are highly variable and discontinuous. This possibility of variation means that a search using a fixed search string, e.g. *it has been shown that,* would yield only occurrences of that string and miss any syntagmatic and paradigmatic variation. Similarly, searching this corpus subset using the wild card search string *it has been * that* would only highlight paradigmatic variation, and miss syntagmatic variation such as the insertion of adverbs or conjunctions.

Allowance must also be made for scanning infelicities in the corpus subset. There were many instances where two spaces occur between words, (e.g., it is assumed that ...).

This would not be picked up by a search string with a single space. Cumulative wildcard search strings were therefore (Table 2 below) used in order to ensure that all possible patterns, not just a particular string, were found.

Table 2. Search strings

search strings for occurrences of *it has been (often) asserted/believed/noted that X,*	search strings for occurrences of *it is (often) asserted/believed/noted that X,*
it * is	has been
it is * that	has * been
it is * * that	has * * been
it is * * * that	has * * * been
it is * * * * that	has * * * * been
it is * * * * * that	has * * * * * been

WordSmith sorted the occurrences alphabetically by verb, then the context of each occurrence was examined and a function, if any, was identified. Occurrences which had the same form as a lexical phrase but did not have a discourse signalling function were discarded (see Appendix 4).

6.   Results: Form

The first question relating to the form of lexical phrases is easily answered. It seems that in general strings of the form *it is/has been (often)_____ that X* containing a passive verb form are not very frequent in the corpus subset. There are a total of 362 simple present occurrences per million words, and 261 present perfect occurrences (see Table 3 below). Biber *et al.* (1999:674) find around 2000 *that*-clause types per million words of academic prose. Looking for the exact forms specified by Nattinger and DeCarrico, the simple present form with *believed* is the only form to occur across all three sub-genres, and the present perfect form only occurs with *noted*.

In general, occurrences of word strings of the form *it is/has been ____ that X* containing a passive verb form vary across sub-genres (see Appendix 1). Writers of medical texts use most over all, a total of 269 per million words, and

Table 3. Occurrences of word strings of the form *it is/has* ____ *that X* per million words

	Social Science	%	Medicine	%	Technical/ Engineering	%	Total
it is ____ *that X*	104	29	110	30	148	41	362
it is asserted that X	1.2	100	0	0	0	0	1.2
it is believed that X	1.8	28	3	47	1.6	25	6.4
it is noted that X	0.8	100	0	0	0	0	0.8
it has been ____ *that X*	65	25	159	61	37	14	261
it has been asserted that X	0	0	0	0	0	0	0
it has been believed that X	0	0	0	0	0	0	0
it has been noted that X	1.9	66	1	34	0	0	2.9

social science use the fewest. Medical writers are also alone in using more of these strings in the present perfect than in the simple present. Technical writing, by contrast, uses nearly four times as many strings in the present simple than in the present perfect.

Turning to other verbs used in the simple present form of this string, i.e. *it is* ____ *that X*, no verb occurs more than 17 times per million words (see Appendix 2). Biber *et al.* (1999:663), when discussing verbs which control *that*-clauses, deem features which occur this infrequently "less common". The strings *it is known that* and *it is concluded that* occur most frequently, both of them in medical texts. The verb which occurs most across all three sub-genres is *assumed,* which occurs between 10 and 12 times.

For strings in the present perfect, i.e. with the form *it has been* ____ *that X,* the most striking feature of the results is that *show* and *suggest* are the most common verbs for all three disciplines. In medical texts these verbs occur more than 40 times per million words, which makes them "relatively common" by the Biber criteria (see Appendix 3).

7.   Results: Function

The second question relates to the function of these strings: whether or not they can be termed lexical phrases in Nattinger and DeCarrico's sense, and whether variation across sub-genres is important for teachers of writing to students in different academic disciplines. One example will serve to illustrate the importance of context in judging the function of a string of the form *it is/has been* ____ *that X*. In example 1 below, it is the writer who is doing the recognising,

Appendix 1 Results: occurrences of strings of the form
it is/it has been _____ *that X*   (per million words)

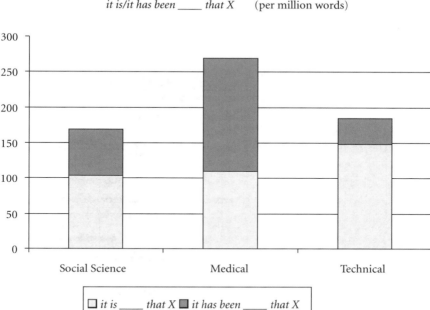

i.e. recognising that more research is needed. In example 2, the recognition is of a fact recognised by the writer and the wider discourse community, and which the writer intends the reader also to recognise. Example 1 seems to be using the verb in its performative sense, with no metadiscoursal function of signalling or organising, whereas example 2 does have a pragmatic function of bringing in outside support to a proposition. Example 1 can not therefore be classed as a lexical phrase, and is discarded, whereas example 2 is considered as a lexical phrase and put into a category "support cited" (see 7.2 below). In the present simple tense at least, the insertion of the adverb *widely* changes the verb sense and thus alters the function of the string.

(1)   The empirical research carried out here is intended to test the feasibility of this approach, as well as providing some general indications of what the effects might be and of one way by which they can be represented on the final output map. In so doing **it is recognized that** many of the questions raised are left open for subsequent investigation and that the results are initial and tentative.

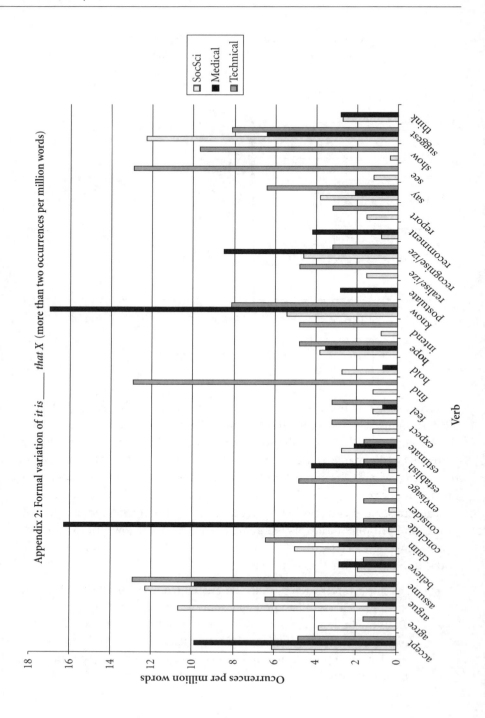

Appendix 2: Formal variation of *it is* _____ *that X* (more than two occurrences per million words)

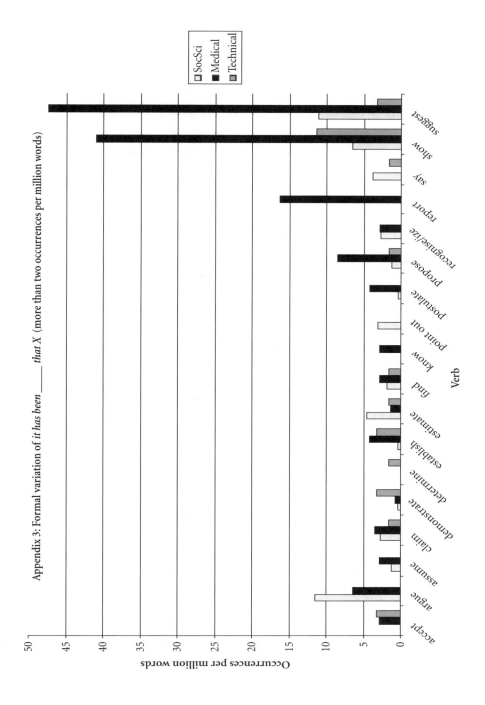

Appendix 3: Formal variation of *it has been* ___ *that X* (more than two occurrences per million words)

(2)   **It is widely recognized that** the proportion of women who suffer mental disorders — particularly depression — exceeds that of men (Cochrane, 1983).

A related phenomenon in strings of this type has been noted by Johns (1991) who observed that tense choice also affects function. He suggests that:

> in English science and engineering academic abstracts, the present perfect is specifically used to refer to the work of other scientists. For example *It is proposed that* ... suggests that the writer of the abstract is doing the proposing, but *It has been proposed that* ... suggests that the proposing is done by someone other than the writer.
> (Johns 1991 quoted in Baker 1992: 101)

This would appear to relate tense choice to function. *It is proposed that* ... contains a performative verb so the string does not qualify as a lexical phrase, while *It has been proposed that* ... performs a support function and thus can be judged a lexical phrase.

The first finding of this study is that in all three sub-genres between 40% and 60% of occurrences of *it is* _____ *that X* were rejected, i.e. judged not to be lexical phrases, while fewer than 10% of occurrences *of it has been* _____ *that X* were discarded. Next, in addition to Nattinger and DeCarrico's "topic priming", four other discourse functions were identified for the remaining occurrences which qualifies them as lexical phrases. These other functions are described below.

7.1 Topic priming

In all three sub-genres strings of the form *it is/has been* _____ *that X* occur which have some kind of topic priming function, although it is not surprising that in published academic journal articles and book extracts this seems to be a more complex function than that proposed by Nattinger and DeCarrico for student essays. It can occur at higher or lower levels to introduce or "prime" a topic or idea which controls a greater or lesser amount of text such as a chapter, section, or paragraph. The phrases are much more likely to be varied by the insertion of an adverb such as *often* or *generally* when they are in the present simple (see example 3 and 4 below). As mentioned above, the occurrences of word strings with a topic priming function will have been influenced by the incomplete nature of many of the texts in the corpus, but the occurrences do suggest that lexical phrases are used for a function of this type, although with far more paradigmatic variation allowed than simply *asserted, believed,* or *noted.*

(3) 7.2.1. Lexical Stress
     An alternative means of increasing the number of units in the input utterance, and thereby decreasing the number of word paths found, would be to include stress in the lexicon and input utterance. **It is** generally **recognised that** there is a great deal of information in the speech wave — particularly prosodic information — which we are not yet able to isolate and use.

(4) Abstract
     It has been thought that aircraft maintenance problems i.e. planning/-scheduling activities, aircraft system/equipment failure diagnosis, etc., are too large and complex to be tackled successfully with computers.

7.2 Support

The most common function of these strings in all sub-genres is to bring in support from outside sources. Writers bring in non-conflicting factual information or arguments from outside sources in order to lend authority to their position or stance. The fact that there is a clearly-identifiable and thus teachable function performed by this string means it could justifiably be termed a lexical phrase in the sense intended by Nattinger and DeCarrico.

This function was seen in two varieties, "non-cited" and "cited". "Non-cited support" is when the writer introduces outside information as support, the source of which is not attributed in any way (see examples 5 and 6 below). This is the most common function of this lexical phrase in the corpus subset (see Appendix 4), particularly in medical texts, where nearly 70% of occurrences of the phrase in the present perfect performed this function.

(5) **It is now realised that** a million words is insufficient to produce an adequate model of a language since many of the phenomena of the language are so rare that they will be absent from such a corpus.

(6) The number of strands in the tight junctions may correlate inversely with the permeability of the epithelium and **it has been shown that** the crypt tight junctions have fewer strands than the villous junctions. Therefore, the results of the current study may indicate that the tight junctions are functionally altered, thereby allowing PT-gliadin to pass into the intercellular space.

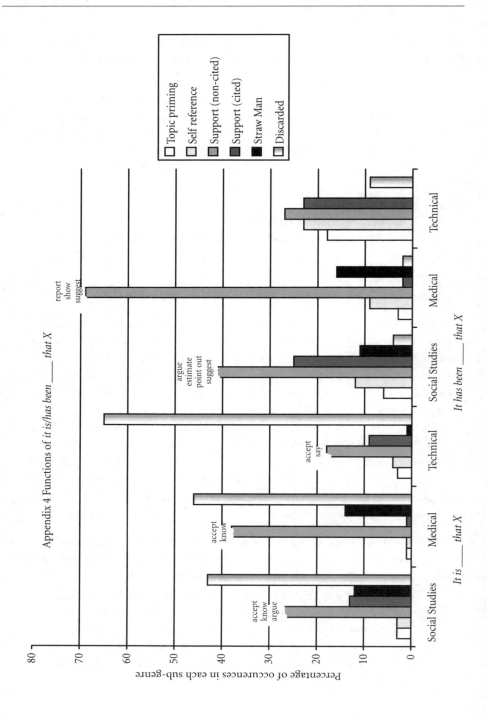

Appendix 4 Functions of *it is/has been ___ that X*

This is an interesting finding since common academic writing practice stresses the importance to students of acknowledging their intellectual debts and demonstrating their scholarship through citing other authors.

The other "support cited" function, when outside information is brought in from a source which the writer acknowledges by name (see examples 7 and 8 below), is found rather less frequently, between 10% and 25% of occurrences. The medical writers in this study are also notable in that they very seldom use this lexical phrase to attribute outside sources.

(7)   The flow of people, profits and investment between regions produces differences in living standards between them. **It is** currently widely **accepted that** regional divergence in living standards within countries is the norm (Bennett, 1980, 67). For example, there remain clear differences in unemployment levels between northern and southern Italy, or different parts of France.

(8)   **It has been suggested** by Dobbins **that** the defective T cell responses may be a secondary phenomenon, resulting perhaps from the combination of anergy triggered by infection, incomplete intestinal lymphatic obstruction, and severe malnutrition.

7.3   "Straw man"

The term "straw man" was given to the function observed when a writer wishes to introduce an argument which he or she intends to negatively evaluate, i.e. dispute (see examples 9 and 10 below). Again this is a clearly-identifiable function which can be applied pedagogically, and thus strings used in this way can be considered as lexical phrases. This use occurs mostly in medical and social science texts, between 10% and 15% of all occurrences (see Appendix 4). This function of the phrase is the first move in a debate; the writer will in the second move dispute the proposition contained in the first move. This first move thus acts as a "straw man" which the writer sets up in order to knock down in the second move. This corresponds to the attributive use of ARGUE identified by Hunston (1995) in a COBUILD corpus study of verbs of attribution which found that ARGUE + *that is* usually used in conflicts. The attributor (i.e. the writer of the principal text) uses it to state another authority's proposition (the 1ST MOVE) and afterwards gives it his or her own evaluation (the 2ND MOVE) either positively (agreeing) or negatively (disputing). Hunston finds that "an attributed statement introduced by ARGUE, irrespective of context, is likely to be negatively evaluated." (ibid.: 153). However in this subset, only twice when *it is/has been argued that* introduced a "straw man" was the writer of the proposition attributed by name.

(9) Though **it is** sometimes **said that** Hilbert's theorem killed invariant theory, this is not entirely correct. Invariant theory continued — albeit at a reduced level of intensity — and in recent years activity has begun to pick up again.

(10) **It has** recently **been suggested that** the synthesis of TNF is greatly increased in inflammatory bowel disease and that TNF could enhance the functions of natural killer cells, lymphokine activated killer cells, and polymorphonuclear neutrophils. The results in our study, however, indicate that TNF does not participate in anticolon ADCC mechanisms to kill colonic epithelial cells.

7.4 Self reference

This lexical phrase is a discourse device which links what the writer is currently dealing with in the text with a relevant area before or after (see examples 11 and 12 below). In each discipline it is used more in the present perfect than in the present simple.

(11) Indeed **it has been seen** in (212) above **that** allow can even evoke the existence of permission as a present state and leave the realization of the action permitted in the hypothetical future.

(12) **It has** previously **been shown that** there is no acetyltransferase enzyme activity in the epithelial cell membrane. The intracellular and extracellular production of Ac-ASA was therefore deemed to be the result of 5-ASA uptake and subsequent metabolism — that is, equivalent to 5-ASA uptake.

It should be pointed out here that putting linguistic items in tidy functional categories can obscure the fact that they can have multiple functions, a phenomenon described by Moon (1998:21) as "cross-functioning." So, for example, in a journal article abstract the lexical phrase *it is argued that* is at one stage "topic priming" by introducing the reader to the main idea contained in the paper, but also acting as a "straw man" since the topic is subsequently negatively evaluated.

8.   Conclusions

This study has attempted to test the notion of the lexical phrase in attested corpus data by highlighting the relationship between the form and function of one particular formulaic string. The results show that strings of this form are indeed used by academic writers, but it is also clear that, if we accept in principle the definition of a lexical phrase, the functions performed by this particular phrase are more varied than originally specified. In addition to "topic priming", instances have been found in all three sub-genres where this phrase has been used for attributed and non-attributed support, negatively evaluated statements, and reference within the text.

While the main finding of this study is clear, more work remains to be done. Since not all the texts in this BNC subset are complete, the distribution of occurrences of different functions within whole texts, e.g. at the beginnings, middles, or ends of sections or chapters, cannot be fully determined. It could be argued that these results are not useful since a corpus of *published* academic writing was searched for occurrences of something which was specified for use in *student* academic essay writing. However, if we accept the basic definition of the lexical phrase, we should also acknowledge that the functions of similar word strings are likely to vary between these forms of writing, not least because of the differences in length. For example writing *it has often been argued that X* may prime the topic of a five-paragraph student essay, but it is clear from the results of this study that it is not the only possible function of this string. Therefore it is valid for published data to be consulted in an attempt to make the lexical phrase relevant to teachers across the broader field of academic writing.

Moving on to the wider debate about whether lexical phrases and formulaic language are of use for teaching academic writing, opinions are divided. Lewis (1993: 96) argues that "*correctly identified* lexical phrases can be presented to L2 learners in identifiable contexts, mastered as learned wholes and thus become an important resource to (sic) mastering the syntax." (emphasis added). It is hoped that this study has not only "correctly identified" the various forms and uses of this particular phrase, but also has suggested pedagogically useful functions.

Notes

* The author wishes to thank the Centre for Research in Language and Linguistics, based in the Language Institute at the University of Hull for supplying the copy of the British National Corpus used in this study.

References

Arnaud, P. L. J. and Bejoint, H. (eds) 1992. *Vocabulary and Applied Linguistics.* Basingstoke: Macmillan.

Aston, G. 2001. "Text Categories and Corpus Users: A Response to David Lee." *Language Learning & Technology* 5/3: 73–76.

Baker, M. 1992. *In other words : a coursebook on translation.* London: Routledge.

Becker, J. 1975. "The Phrasal Lexicon." in Nash-Webber, B. and Schank, R. (eds) 70–77.

Biber, D., Johansson, S., Leech, G., Conrad, S., and Finegan, E. 1999. (eds) *Longman Grammar of Spoken and Written English.* London: Longman.

Bolinger, D. 1976. "Meaning and Memory." *Forum Linguisticum* 1/1: 1–14.

British National Corpus v 1.0 (1995) Oxford: Oxford University Computing Service.

British National Corpus World Edition (2000) Oxford: Oxford University Computing Service.

Cowie, A. P. 1992. "Multiword Lexical Units and Communicative Language Teaching." in P. J. L Anaud, & H. Bejoint, H. (eds). pp 1–12.

Hakuta, K. 1974. "Prefabricated Patterns and the Emergence of Structure in Second Language Acquisition." *Language Learning* 24/2: 287–297.

Hunston, S. 1995. "A corpus study of English verbs of attribution." *Functions of Language* 2/2: 133–158.

Hunston, S. and Francis, G. 2000. *Pattern Grammar.* Amsterdam: Benjamins

Krovetz, R. 1997. "Homonymy and polysemy in Information Retrieval" in *Proceedings of the 35th Annual Meeting of the Association for Computational Linguistics:* 72–29.

Lee, D. 2001. "Genres, registers, text types, domains, and styles: clarifying the concepts and navigating a path through the BNC jungle." *Language Learning Technology,* 5/3, 37–72. http://llt.msu.edu/vol5num3/lee/default.html

Lewis, M. 1993. *The Lexical Approach.* Hove: Language Teaching Publications.

Lewis, M. 1996. *"Implications of a lexical view of language".* in J. Willis, D. Willis (eds). 10–16.

Moon, R. 1998. Fixed Expressions and Idioms in English: A corpus based approach. Oxford: Clarendon Press.

Nash-Webber, B. and Schank, R.1975. (eds) *Theoretical Issues in Natural language Processing* 1. Cambridge, Mass.: Bolt, Beranek, and Newman.

Nattinger, J. R. and DeCarrico, J. 1992. *Lexical Phrases and Language Teaching.* Oxford: Oxford University Press.

Partington, A. 1998. Patterns and Meanings: Using Corpora for English Language Research and Teaching. Amsterdam: John Benjamins

Pawley, A. and Syder, F. H. 1983. "Two puzzles for linguistic theory: nativelike selection and nativelike fluency." In J. C. Richards, R. W. Schmidt. (eds). 191–227.

Richards, J.C. and Schmidt, R.W. 1983. (eds). *Language and Communication*. London: Longman.

Scott, M. 1999. *WordSmith Tools 3.0* Oxford: Oxford University Press.

Sinclair, J. McH. 1991. *Corpus, Concordance, Collocation* Oxford: Oxford University Press.

Weinert, R. 1995. "The Role of Formulaic Language in Second Language Acquisition." *Applied Linguistics* 16/2: 180–205.

Willis, J. and Willis, D. (eds). *Challenge and change in language teaching*. Oxford: Heinemann.

Wray, A. 1999. "Formulaic language in learners and native speakers." *Language Teaching* 32: 213–231.

CHAPTER 7

Lexical bundles in Freshman composition

Viviana Cortes
Iowa State University

1. Introduction

For several decades, linguists have been interested in the study of lexical association patterns, that is, the way words seem to co-occur with another word or words. Firth (1964) introduced the terms 'collocation' and 'collocability' to express the habitual occurrence of a word with another word, and he tried to explain the way in which collocations help complete the meaning of the word. While in the past the study of these frequent lexical co-occurrences was completed from a rather perceptual point of view, the growth of corpus linguistics studies and the development of computer programs specifically designed for the analyses of language corpora have introduced new research paths and tools. These research methodologies have been employed in the study of the distribution of lexical association patterns in natural contexts (Biber, 1993, 1996; Biber & Conrad, 1999; Biber, Johansson, Leech, Conrad, & Finegan, 1999; De Cock, 1998), which allowed not only the identification of collocations, which are two words that tend to frequently co-occur in real language, but also of 'lexical bundles', which are extended collocations, sequences of three, four, five, or six words that statistically co-occur in a register (Biber et al., 1999).

Biber et al. (1999) used computational analyses of a large corpus to identify the most frequent lexical bundles in academic prose and conversation, and produced a comprehensive list of examples and their grammatical categorizations. Modeled after their investigation, this study analyzes a corpus of writing from freshman composition courses to find out the most frequent 4-word lexical bundles produced by freshman university students, and to establish a comparison with those 4-word lexical bundles most frequently found in academic prose and conversation (Biber & Conrad, 1999). The study includes grammatical and functional analyses of the most frequent 4-word bundles identified in the corpus of freshman composition and an analysis of some of the functions performed by these bundles, followed by examples.

2. Review of related literature

The varied research conducted on the study of word combinations has come a long way: from the ethnographic and qualitative studies in first and second language acquisition of formulaic routines of the 70s to the quantitative corpus-based studies of natural language in the 90s. In addition, several studies tried to account for the use of word combinations and their frequency in language in an intuitive way. The purpose of this section is to present a survey of studies of word combinations that will help create a better framework of reference for the study of lexical bundles.

A wide variety of studies have concentrated on the investigation of word combinations from a pedagogical point of view (DeCarrico & Nattinger, 1988; Fillmore, 1979; Hakuta, 1974; Howarth, 1998; Pawley & Syder, 1983; Peters, 1983; Yorio, 1980). Other studies are descriptive studies of word combinations, both perceptual (Allerton, 1984; Becker, 1975; Chafe, 1994; Cowie, 1988; Fraser, 1990) and empirical studies (Altenberg, 1993, 1998; Biber et al., 1999; Butler, 1997; De Cock, 1998; Moon, 1998).

Many times studies that claim they analyze different types of word combinations use different labels to name the same type of word sequence. At other times, studies use the same label to define different types of expressions. Pawley (1985) centers his work around speech formulas, which he defines as "a conventional pairing of a particular formal construction with a particular conventional idea" (p. 88). He believes that these expressions have something in common with idioms, lexical items, and grammatical constructions, but do not fit in any of those groups. Cowie (1988) does not call these expression "speech formulas" but he uses a variety of terms like "ready-made expressions", "multi-word units", or "prefabricated routines." He divides these combinations into two groups, which are different in intended conveyed meaning and structural level. The first category contains pragmatically specialized units which have evolved meanings that reflect their function in discourse, such as *good morning*, or *how are you?*. The second category groups expressions like *kick one's heels* or *pass the buck*, which have developed referential meaning by being used as invariable units. Moon (1992) explains the importance of fixed expressions for lexicographers, as fixed expressions have significant functions in text, and the descriptions of these functions should be a part of their lexicographical exposition. She focuses on idioms and formulae, and produces a taxonomy of fixed expressions based on the contribution that they make to the structure of the text in which they occur.

The work of Altenberg in corpus-based research of word combinations deserves special mention, as he employs a different methodology for the identification of frequent fixed expressions. His earliest work with the London Lund Corpus of Spoken English (100 texts, and about 500,000 words), reports an inventory of over 68,000 different word combinations (types) representing some 200,000 examples (tokens). Altenberg and Eeg-Olofsson (1990) and Altenberg (1993) present the results of the identification and analysis of word combinations in that corpus. It is necessary to point out that these word combinations are identified by means of computer programs that yield the most frequent word sequences in the corpus. After discarding many phraseologically uninteresting examples (such as fragmented sequences), Altenberg concludes that 70% of the running words in the London-Lund Corpus form part of recurrent word combinations. The recurrent combinations in this corpus vary in length and frequency; while the majority of the combinations are fairly short (2–3 words), longer sequences (5 words or more) are comparatively rare. The list of combinations that occur over 20 times in the corpus included many discourse expressions, such as interpersonal comments (*you know, you see*), modal hedges (*I think*) , repair signal (*I mean*), responses (*thank you*), and structural links and transitions (*and he, and they*). Grammatically, these expressions are almost entirely made up of closed-class items: prepositions, determiners, conjunctions, pronouns, auxiliaries, and short adverbs. The most common functions fulfilled by these combinations were conjunctions and conjuncts, comment clauses (*you know, I mean*), complements, and adverbial adjuncts. One of Altenberg's latest studies focuses on recurrent word combinations in spoken English (Altenberg, 1998). In this study, he continues analyzing the fixed word combinations he had previously identified in the London-Lund Corpus. He argues that the most important impression that arises from these expressions is the pervasive and varied character of conventionalized language in spoken discourse.

It is important to mention the studies of other researchers who also devoted their work to the investigation of word combinations through corpus-based research. This is the case of Kjellmer (1991, 1994) who worked with the Brown Corpus of American English on the identification of recurrent collocations, that is, sequences of words that recur more often than their individual frequencies would lead us to expect. These sequences differ from fossilized or semi-fossilized phrases (such as *aurora borealis,* or *brussels sprouts*), in that even though one word may predict the others, these predictions will have to be interpreted more loosely, and the cohesion among the members of the constituents of these constructions is less compelling. Kjellmer's work was completed with the creation of the Dictionary of English Collocations (Kjellmer, 1994), also based on the Brown Corpus. This work aimed at registering all the collocations in that corpus, which were classified according to a surface structure system, together with their relative frequency.

Sinclair (1991) worked on one of the largest lexicographical analyses of the English language, the Cobuild project. Sinclair's work on collocations was later complemented by his work on collocational frameworks. Renouf and Sinclair (1991) looked at frameworks, which are "discontinuous sequences of two words, positioned at one word removed from each other" (p. 128). Frameworks are rather problematic word combinations because grammatically, they lie somewhere between word and group; lexically, they do not fit in the definitions of collocations, lexical items, or phrases; and semantics has no means of dealing with these grammatical co-occurrences, either as two independent constituents or as part of a unit with independent meaning.

In their exhaustive study of English grammar, Biber et al. (1999) identified the most frequent lexical bundles in academic prose and conversation in the Longman Corpus of Written and Spoken English. They produced an extensive list of bundles and a structural and grammatical categorization as well as a register comparison, which was further developed by Biber and Conrad (1999). They are identified empirically as word combinations that recur most commonly in a register. Following the research methodology previously used by Altenberg (1993), lexical bundles are identified by means of a computer program that counts all the times that a word combination recurs in a corpus, as well as the number of texts in which that word combination recurs. The following section defines lexical bundles and provides examples of these word combinations in different registers.

3.   Lexical bundles

Biber et al. (1999) define lexical bundles as "recurrent expressions, regardless of their idiomaticity, and regardless of their structural status" (p. 990), simple sequences of words that commonly co-occur in natural language use. They are identified empirically as word combinations that recur most commonly in a register. While three-word bundles can be considered extended collocations, four-word, five-word, and six-word bundles are more phrasal in nature and less common. Frequency is an important issue for lexical bundles. The bundles identified by Biber et al. (1999) are restricted to those word combinations that occur over 10 times in a million words, and that repeat in 5 or more texts. For the present study, a more conservative frequency cut-off point is set at 20 times per million words and 5 or more texts.

The main difference between lexical bundles and the rest of the lexical association patterns previously discussed in this paper, is the way in which bundles are identified. The search for lexical bundles needs no previous perception or intuition of which word combinations can occur frequently. Word combinations that meet the frequency criterion which are yielded by the computer program are considered lexical bundles.

For their study of lexical bundles, Biber et al. (1999) worked with the conversation and academic prose sections of the Longman Corpus. The Longman Corpus of Written and Spoken English is a collection of 40 million words of British and American English from varied registers: conversation, fiction, news, academic prose, and non-conversational speech. The conversation section of the corpus is made up of about 6.5 million words, and the academic prose section consists of over 5.3 million words.

Lexical bundles usually do not represent complete structural units. Biber and Conrad (1999) affirm that only 15% of the lexical bundles found in conversation can be considered as holding complete structural units, while less than 5% of the lexical bundles identified in academic prose can be regarded as complete grammatical units. However, lexical bundles have strong grammatical correlates, which facilitates their grouping into several basic structural types. In conversation, almost 90% of the lexical bundles are segments of declarative or interrogative clauses. Moreover, 50% of these bundles begin with a personal pronoun, which is followed by a verb phrase (as in *I don't know why*). The bundles in academic prose present completely different grammatical groupings. In fact, 60% of all lexical bundles identified in academic prose, are parts of noun phrases or prepositional phrases (*e.g., as a result of,* and *the nature of the*).

4.   Lexical bundles in freshman composition

Listening to many composition instructors comment on the struggles of their freshman writing students, it could be expected that students' use of lexical bundles would more closely match those bundles found in conversation rather than those lexical bundles in academic prose. To investigate this question, a corpus of freshman composition was compiled from the essays of students attending Northern Arizona University. The corpus consisted of 54 final portfolios, which included six different papers: two descriptions, two rhetorical analyses, a research proposal, and a research paper (see Table 1 for a description of the corpus). The topics for the research papers were selected by students; some students decided to stick to the environmental topics suggested by the curriculum of the course, while others chose to deal with topics that were related to their own interests or future majors. The freshman writing courses in which these papers were collected were four sections taught by two different instructors over two semesters. The portfolios contained 311 papers (a few portfolios were not complete). The average length of the essays in the corpus was 1,113 words (with the shortest paper being 264 words long and the longest being 6,043 words long) resulting in 360,704 total words. The corpus was carefully screened to delete any misleading headings and any signs of identification.

Table 1. Description of freshman composition corpus

54 portfolios from	6 papers:	2 descriptions
2 instructors		2 rhetorical analyses
4 sections total		1 research proposal
		1 research paper
	311 papers	
	360,704 words total	

The computer program yielded a list of 93 different sequences that occurred 20 or more times in a million words and in 5 or more texts in the corpus of freshman composition, with many bundles occurring much more frequently (60 to 90 times). All the frequency counts were normalized to a million words for comparison with the counts reported by Biber et al. (1999). The most frequent bundles present in this corpus are shown in Table 2.

Table 2. List of 4-word lexical bundles in the corpus of freshman writing

a lot of the	*at the end of*	*is one of the*	*the side of the*
a part of the	*at the top of*	*it is as if*	*to appeal to the*
a wide range of	*at the same time*	*it is difficult to*	*to be able to*
a wide variety of	*in an effort to*	*on the other hand*	*will be able to*
as a result of	*in the case of*	*the back of the*	
as well as the	*in the form of*	*the bottom of the*	
at the bottom of	*in the United States*	*the edge of the*	

Table 3 shows a comparison between the most frequent lexical bundles in freshman composition and frequent lexical bundles in academic prose and conversation as reported by Biber et al. (1999).

Contrary to any intuition which may consider freshman students' writing following a conversational style (loaded with contractions and expressions connected to narration), the highest number of bundles identified in the freshman composition corpus is nominal or phrasal rather than clausal, following the pattern in published academic prose (Biber et al., 1999). Furthermore, a closer look reveals that the types of bundles found in the freshman essays closely imitate the most frequent types of bundles occurring in academic prose, mainly noun phrase + complement (35%), and prepositional phrase + complement (32%).

The 'other category' for the freshman writing comprises 21% of the bundles, much higher than the 6% found in both conversation and academic prose by Biber et al. (1999). This is due to some topic specific bundles that reproduce the titles or fragments of the titles of books and stories that students covered in their freshmen composition classes, resulting in some fragmented bundles which have been excluded from the final analysis. For example, one of the most frequent bundles is *"a sense of place"*, which is the name of the book designed by the Composition Program at the university to cover the reading section of freshman composition courses (Northern Arizona University, Composition program, 1998). Some of the essays in the book, as in the case of an excerpt from the book "The man who walked through time" by Colin Fletcher (1967), appear as very frequent bundles on the list of lexical bundles in all its combinations (*a man who walked, man who walked through, who walked through time*), as these essays were chosen by many students to complete their rhetorical analyses.

Table 3. Distribution of four-word lexical bundles by structural patterns across conversation and academic prose

Patterns more widely used in conversation	Conv.	Acad Prose	Example	Fresh Writ.	Example
Personal pronoun + lexical verb phrase (+ complement clause)	44%		I don't know what	2%	I will use this
Pronoun/NP (+ auxiliary) + copula be (+)	8%	2%	it was in the	3%	it is as if
(auxiliary +) active verb (+)	13%		have a look at		
Yes-no and wh- question fragment	12%		can I have a		
(verb +) wh-clause fragment	4%		know what I mean		
Patterns more widely used in academic prose					
Noun phrase with post modifier fragment	4%	30%	the nature of the	35%	the side of the
Preposition + noun phrase fragment	3%	33%	as a result of	32%	as a result of
Anticipatory it + VP/-adjective phrase (+ complement clause)		9%	it is possible to	5%	it is difficult to
Passive verb + PP fragment		6%	is based on the		
(verb +) that-clause fragment	1%	5%	should be noted that		
Patterns in both registers					
(verb/adjective +) to-clause fragment	5%	9%	are likely to be	2%	to appeal to the
Other expressions	6%	6%		21%	
Total	100%	100%		100%	

4.1 Grammatical and functional analysis of freshman composition bundles

Although at first sight the bundles occurring in freshman composition seem to indicate that students are making use of the same type of bundles frequently used in academic prose, a more detailed analysis reveals some interesting distinctions in the way in which students use these bundles in their writing.

Using a concordancing program, the most frequent bundles in freshman composition are located in their contexts, and examples of their actual use could be identified. The meaning of these bundles in context are analyzed using a combination of frameworks (Wray & Perkins, 2000) and carefully observing the examples in which they were used in order to investigate the language objectives of the writers and their communicative purposes. Table 4 presents the bundles in the prepositional phrase group identified in the corpus of freshman composition, as well as the functions they perform, and some examples taken from the corpus that illustrate those functions.

The most common bundles that hold the structure preposition + noun phrase fragment start with the prepositions *in, at, on, to, of,* and *for.* The functions of these prepositional phrases were markedly divided into two groups. In the case of the preposition *in,* for example, one group comprise those expressions indicating location, such as *in front of the, in the middle of, in the United States.* It must be explained that the expressions that indicate location are not exclusive of academic prose: they also frequently occur in conversation. The recurrent use of location markers in these freshman students' writing result from the descriptive pieces that students were instructed to produce in these courses. The bundles which function as location and temporal markers are also used as text markers in different contexts, referring to certain parts of the writing trying to guide the reader through the text. The other group of lexical bundles contained expressions used for a wide variety of functions such as *in the case of* (introducing an example), *in the form of* (indicating mode), *in an effort to* (indicating attempt), among other meanings. This peculiarity seems to be shared by other prepositions and prepositional phrases. This was the case of *at,* as in *at the end of, at the bottom of, at the top of* (indicating location), or *at the same time* (indicating simultaneity).

The most frequent lexical bundles in the noun phrase grammatical group shared some functional features with those in the prepositional phrase group. Table 5 presents noun phrase bundles, their functions, and some examples taken from the corpus.

Lexical bundles in the noun phrase group are clearly divided into those

Table 4. Frequent phrasal bundles (noun phrases) identified in freshman composition, their functions and some examples of those bundles in context.

Grammatical group	Function	Examples
Noun phrases	Location markers (used to refer to places or physical location)	the end of the …*Matt left the room and waddled down to* the end of the *hallway with all his possessions.* the other side of *On* the other side of *the table there is a secret hidden drawer…* the top of the *As evening fell in from* the top of the *sky…* the right of the *To* the right of *the man sat his date who…* the side of the …*he politely moves to* the side of the *road.* the surface of the …*casts a weak orange glow over* the surface of the *lake.*
	Temporal markers (used to refer to a point or period in time)	the end of the …*industry will reach the 35 million dollar mark by* the end of the *year 2000.*
	Text markers (used to guide the reader to certain parts of the writing)	the end of the *The occurrence of the date near* the end of the *preface seems to indicate that…* the rest of the *The* rest of the *article is also simple.*
	Special uses of lexical bundles	the other side of (introducing a different perspective) *On* the other side of *the spectrum, there are many different examples that show…* At the top of (used to emphasize the position of a certain item on a given ranking, indicating saliency) *It was at* the top of the *charts only one month after it was released.* the right of the (meaning fair action, expressing just entitlement) *English law acknowledged* the right of the *accused to retain counsel…* the rest of the (used to identify a final segment, the remains of what is being described) *The* rest of the *time, it seems they are just standing there.*

Table 5. Frequent phrasal bundles (prepositional phrases) identified in freshman composition, their functions and some examples of those bundles in context.

Grammatical group	Function	Examples
Prepositional phrases	Location markers (used to indicate place)	in the middle of …*there is a small entrance in the middle of the wall opposite the cliff.*
	Temporal markers (indicating time)	at the same time (indicating simultaneity) *trying to sing and trying to play, all at the same time.* in the middle of *He dropped dead in the middle of the game for what doctors suspected…*
	Special uses	at the same time (used to add qualities) *The image is at the same time sweeping and concentrated.* on the other hand (indicating contrast) *Brower encourages pathos in his reader. Zegerle, on the other hand, uses sarcasm.* as a result of (used as a cause and effect marker) *…women are constantly left aching and shattered into pieces as a result of the carelessness of men.* in the case of (introducing an example) *Theoretical reasoning is valuable in any study but in the case of marijuana legalization, proven information is essential…* in the form of (introducing a comparison) *In the distance, voices are heard in the form of chants* in a way that (introducing comparison and contrast) *However, we do know Mrs. Mallard in a way that her family and friends do not.*

indicating location (e.g., *the back of the, the bottom of the, the edge of the*), time (as in *at the same time*) and other phrases with varied meanings, such as expressions that indicate quantity (as in *a lot of the, a part of the, a wide range of, a wide variety of*), among other different meanings. In this grammatical group, bundles also presented some special uses, as in the case of *at the same time*. In certain examples, *at the same time* was used as a temporal marker, used to link simultaneous actions, while in other examples it was used to connect qualities that describe an issue. Other special uses include bundles which introduce examples (e.g., *in the case of*) or indicate comparison or contrast (such as *on the other hand, in the form of,* and *in a way that*).

Clausal bundles are less frequent in the corpus of freshman composition. Table 6 shows the clausal bundles identified in this corpus, their functions, and some examples of their use in context.

The most salient structures among the clausal bundles correspond to those made up of *it* +BE + adj. + clause (e.g., *it is hard to, it is obvious that*), which are expressions often used to emphasize or initiate an argument, or state a position. These type of expressions are also identified by Biber et al. (1999) as frequent in academic prose. Other expressions in this group follow the pattern, personal pronoun + (aux.) + verb + (comp.) (e.g., *I am going to*), or other verb phrases including *able* (e.g., *to be able to, will be able to*).

Some of the bundles in this grammatical category are used to convey more than one function. This is the case of *it is important to,* which is used as an emphasizer and also to introduce a suggestion.

From all the clausal bundles, the only one which is not directly related to academic prose bundles is *I am going to.* This bundle can be frequently found in the proposals that students had to write for these freshman composition courses.

5.   Conclusion

The results of this study reflect the importance of different types of analysis in the investigation of lexical bundles. When first analyzed, the lexical bundles produced by freshman students in composition courses looked structurally similar to those used in academic prose. However, a closer look showed that although the grammatical structures confirmed that similarity, the bundles used were in many cases served as temporal or location markers, which are bundles not exclusively used in academic prose. The extended analysis of the bundles in context showed that when writing for these freshman composition courses, students made an effort to produce lexical bundles that resembled bundles used in academic prose more than those bundles used in conversational language. This can be seen in the complete absence of contractions in the lexical bundles identified in this corpus, as well as in the absence of bundles starting with the pronoun *I* followed by a verb of perception (e.g., *I don't think so, I don't know what, I think it is, I know what you)* or any other bundles which occur exclusively in conversational style.

The analysis of the lexical bundles that most frequently occur in freshman composition and the examples of their use in context indicated that the instructional tasks designed for this particular composition courses influence students' use of certain bundles. This is the case, for example, of those lexical bundles that act as location and temporal markers, and those bundles that work as instructions to the readers. The use of these bundles was often directly related to the tasks in the course, as in the case of descriptions, which require the use of many location and time markers, and rhetorical analyses of texts, which call for the use of expressions that help organize the discourse, as those bundles used to guide the reader.

It cannot be predicted if the use of these lexical bundles will transfer to

Table 6. Clausal bundles, their functions, and examples.

Grammatical Group	Function	Examples
Clausal bundles	Emphasis	it is important to *It is important to get help and support the victim....* it is hard to (introducing a negative aspect of the argument) *The video is also a bit confusing; it is hard to understand what the lead singer is trying to...*
	Inference or deduction	it is obvious that *From the above evidence, it is obvious that Islam did not invent the....*
	Comparison	as if they were/as if it were *They were greener, fuller, and they smelled as if they were alive.*
	Plan	I am going to *In the introduction, I am going to draw the reader in with a story....*
	Purpose	to be able to *...they want the government to be able to limit that type of weapons.*
	Special uses	is one of the (introducing an example) *The 16 through 24-year-old group is one of the biggest buyers of music...*

disciplinary writing. Further investigation of lexical bundles in academic writing should start with the study of the use of lexical bundles in different academic disciplines in order to identify word combinations that may be discipline-bound. In addition, a corpus of students' writing in the disciplines at different university levels should be compiled in order to investigate the use of lexical bundles in students' written production across levels and disciplines, analyzing the types of bundles and the development in use that students' production may reflect.

References

Allerton, D. J. (1984). Three (of four) levels of word cooccurrence restriction. *Lingua, 63,* 17–40.

Altenberg, B. (1993). Recurrent word combinations in spoken English. In J. D'Arcy (Ed), *Proceedings of the Fifth Nordic Association for English Studies Conference.* (pp. 17–27). Reykjavik : University of Iceland.

Altenberg, B. (1998). On the phraseology of spoken English: The evidence of recurrent word-combinations. In A. Cowie (Ed.), *Phraseology* (pp. 101–122). Oxford: Oxford University Press.

Altenberg, B. & Eeg-Olofsson, M. (1990) Phraseology in spoken English: Presentation of a project. In J. Aarts and W. Meijs (Eds.), *Theory and practice in corpus linguistics* (pp. 1–26). Amsterdam: Rodopi.

Becker, J. (1975). *The Phrasal Lexicon.* Bolt Beranek and Newman Report No. 3081. AI Report No. 28.

Biber, D. (1993). Co-occurrence patterns among collocations: A tool for corpus-based lexical knowledge acquisition. *Computational Linguistics, 19,* 549–556.

Biber, D. (1996). Investigating language use through corpus-based analyses of association patterns. International Journal of Corpus Linguistics, 1(2), 171–197.

Biber, D. & Conrad, S. (1999), Lexical bundles in conversation and academic prose. In H. Hasselgard and S. Oksefjell (Eds.), *Out of corpora: Studies in honor of Stig Johansson.* (pp. 181–190). Amsterdam: Rodopi.

Biber, D. , Johansson, S., Leech, G., Conrad, S., & Finegan, E. (1999). *Longman grammar of spoken and written English.* London: Longman.

Chafe, W. (1994). *Discourse, consciousness, and time.* Chicago: The University of Chicago Press.

Cowie, A. (1988). Stable and creative aspects of vocabulary. In R. Carter and M. McCarthy (Eds.), *Vocabulary and language teaching* (pp. 126–139). London: Longman.

DeCarrico, J. & Nattinger, J. (1988). Lexical phrases for the comprehension of academic lectures. English for Specific Purposes, 7, 91–102.

De Cock, S. (1998). A recurrent word combination approach to the study of formulae in the speech of native and non-native speakers of English. *International Journal of Corpus Linguistics, 3,* 59–80.

Fraser, B. (1990). An approach to discourse markers. *Journal of pragmatics 14,* 383–395.

Fillmore, L. W. (1979). Individual differences in second language acquisition. In C. Fillmore, D. Kempler & W. Wang. (Eds.), *Individual differences in language ability and language behavior* (pp. 203–228). New York: Academic Press.

Firth, J. R. (1964). *Papers in linguistics, 1934-1951.* London Oxford University Press.

Fletcher, C. (1967). *The man who walked through time.* New York: Alfred A. Knowpf, Inc.

Hakuta, K. (1974). Prefabricated patterns and the emergence of structure in second language acquisition. *Language Learning, 24* (2), 287–297.

Howarth, P. (1998b). The phraseology of learners' academic writing. In A. Cowie (Ed.), *Phraseology,* (pp. 161–186). Oxford: Claredon Press.

Kjellmer, G. (1991). A mint of phrases. In K. Aijmer and B. Altenberg (Eds.), *English corpus linguistics.* London: Longman.

Kjellmer, G. (1994). *A dictionary of English collocations.* Oxford: Oxford University Press.

Moon, R. (1992). Textual aspects of fixed expressions in learners' dictionaries. In P. J. Arnaud & Bejoint, H., (Eds.) *Vocabulary and applied linguistics* (pp. 13–26). Oxford: Claredon Press.

Moon, R. (1998). *Fixed expressions and idioms in English: A corpus-based approach.* Oxford Claredon Press.

Nattinger, J. & DeCarrico, J. (1992). *Lexical phrases and language teaching.* Oxford: Oxford University Press.

Northern Arizona University, Composition Program. (1998). A *sense of place.* New York: Forbes.

Pawley, A. (1985). On speech formulas and linguistic competence. *Lenguas Modernas, 12,* 84-104.

Pawley, A., & Syder, F. (1983). Two puzzles for linguistic theory: Nativelike selection and native like fluency. In J. Richards and R. Schmidt (Eds.), *Language and communication* (pp. 191–226). New York: Longman.

Peters, A. (1983). *The units of language acquisition.* Cambridge: Cambridge University Press.

Renouf, A. & Sinclair, J. In K. Aijmer and B. Altenberg (Eds), *English corpus linguistics: Studies in honour of Jan Svartvik* (pp. 111–127). London: Longman.

Sinclair, J. (1991). *Corpus, Concordance, Collocation.* Oxford: Oxford University Press.

Wray, A., & Perkins, M. (2000). The functions of formulaic language: An integrated model. *Language and Communication, 20,* 1–28.

Yorio, C. (1980). Conventionalized language forms and the development of communicative competence. *TESOL Quarterly, 14* (4), 433–442.

CHAPTER 8

Pseudo-Titles in the press genre of various components of the International Corpus of English[*]

Charles F. Meyer
University of Massachusetts at Boston

Pseudo-Titles, as Bell (1988) terms them, are constructions such as *linguist* in *linguist Noam Chomsky* that occur in positions in which we normally find titles but that, unlike titles, serve not as honorifics but as a means of providing descriptive information about the proper nouns that they precede. Pseudo-titles are thought to have originated in the press reportage of American English, in a style of journalistic writing popularized by *Time* magazine that Quirk et al. (1985:276, note) term "Timestyle." However, while pseudo-titles may have originated in American English, their usage has been documented in British and New Zealand English as well (cf. Rydén 1975, Bell 1988, and Meyer 1992).

In the American media, pseudo-titles are stylistically "unmarked": they are found in almost any American newspaper, for instance, regardless of its level of formality. However, in the British media, pseudo-titles are stigmatized: their usage is prohibited in more formal newspapers such as the *Guardian* or the *Times*, and they tend to be found mainly in British "tabloids." Until recently, language usage in the New Zealand media was solidly grounded in the British tradition, but as Bell (1988:326) documents, this "traditionalist colonial foundation...has been weakening and refocussing towards the United States...." As a consequence, the use of pseudo-titles has been increasing in both the print and broadcast media in New Zealand.

The usage patterns of pseudo-titles in the British, American, and New Zealand media raise a number of questions:

(1) To what extent are pseudo-titles found in the news broadcasts and newspapers of other varieties of English, and in those varieties where they are found, are British or American norms for pseudo-titles followed?

(2) Do pseudo-titles have the same structure in these varieties that they have in British, American, and New Zealand English?

(3) What is the relationship between pseudo-titles and equivalent appositional structures, both in news broadcasts and newspapers that permit the use of pseudo-titles, and in those that do not?

To answer these questions, I studied the structure and use of pseudo-titles and equivalent appositives in one type of media English — press reportage — in seven regional components of the International Corpus of English (ICE): Great Britain, East Africa, Jamaica, New Zealand, the Philippines, Singapore, and the United States. I demonstrate that while pseudo-titles are still uncommon in British press reportage, they are very widespread in the press reportage of other varieties, even those directly influenced by British English. This finding is a reflection of the powerful influence that the American media has had on the evolution of English as an international language (see Crystal 1997: 82–95). In addition, I show that while there are general constraints on the form of pseudo-titles, in New Zealand and Philippine press reportage, innovative forms are evolving, making these varieties different from the others. This finding is significant because most studies of the influence of American English on other Englishes has focused mainly on lexical items, and such studies, as Peters (2001: 299) observes, do not present "the full linguistic bottle." The spread of pseudo-titles in press writing, therefore, not only shows that a grammatical construction can be borrowed from one variety into another but that once the construction is borrowed, the constraints on its usage can change, leading to new forms.

1.   Titles, Pseudo-Titles, and Equivalent Appositives Defined

Before any study of pseudo-titles can be conducted, it is necessary to distinguish pseudo-titles from titles and equivalent appositives. Although each of these constructions can be viewed as members of discrete grammatical categories, the boundaries between the categories are often difficult to precisely delineate.

While titles and pseudo-titles are structurally quite similar, they are semantically and pragmatically quite different. Structurally, both kinds of titles are dependent on a head: in constructions such as *President Bill Clinton* or *linguist Noam Chomsky*, neither *President* nor *linguist* can stand alone or be moved, an indication that they are closely integrated into the noun phrases that they precede. Semantically and pragmatically, however, titles and pseudo-titles are very different. Titles such as *President* or *Chancellor* have an honorific function, and are therefore markers of "respect" or "status" (Quirk et al. 1985:773). Bell (1988:330) argues that pseudo-titles have a similar function and serve to honor the person before whose name they are used by "suggesting that this person belongs to a class of human beings as exclusive as the clergy, military, or nobility." But if a construction such as *linguist Noam Chomsky* is used in a press report, it is more likely that *linguist* is being used to "describe" what Noam Chomsky is, not to honor him in any way. In this sense, pseudo-titles are very similar to appositives (e.g. *the linguist Noam Chomsky* or *Noam Chomsky, a linguist*), a construction that is exceedingly common in press reportage, particularly if one of the units of the appositive is a proper noun (Meyer 1992:99, 115–120; Biber et al. 1999:639).

Titles can be classified into various semantic classes that clearly distinguish them from pseudo-titles:

> Professional (*Doctor, Professor*)
> Political (*President, Chancellor, Senator*)
> Religious (*Bishop, Cardinal, Mother*)
> Honors (*Dame, Earl, Countess*)
> Military (*General, Corporal*)
> Police (*Commissioner, Constable, Detective-Sergeant*)
> Foreign (*Monsieur, Senorita*) (quoted from Bell 1998:329)

While someone who is a 'linguist,' for instance, would be considered a professional, *linguist* does not qualify as a title because it is not as "institutionalized" as titles such as *Doctor* or *Professor*.

Even though titles and pseudo-titles have semantic and pragmatic differences, in actual practice, these differences are not always as pronounced, largely because editors and writers in newspapers have different interpretations of what constitutes a title and what does not. As Bell (1988:332) notes, in the American and New Zealand media, most governmental designations are considered titles. Thus, in American press reportage, for instance, examples such as (1) are quite normal:

(1) Expectations are highest, of course, for the two early favorites in each party, *Gov. George W. Bush* of Texas and *Vice President Al Gore*. (ICE-USA)[1]

In certain British newspapers, however, such usages would be considered "deviant" (Bell 1988: 332). Therefore, an alternative appositive structure would be used instead:

(2)   Reports at the weekend claimed *the Prime Minister, Mr John Major,* would raise the issue with *the United States president, Mr George Bush,* at their summit meeting in Bermuda on Saturday, in the hope of softening US opposition to forced repatriation. (*Yorkshire Post* in ICE-GB)

Because titles are markers of respect, they are capitalized and pseudo-titles are not. However, practice is more mixed. In (3a), *National Security Advisor* is capitalized; in (3b) it is not.

(3)   a.   Senator Richard Lugar (R-IN) has followed up on efforts which began last month by a bi-partisan group of Senators, Representatives, and a large [group] of farm organizations by writing directly to *National Security Advisor Samuel Berger.* (*The Washington Report* January 22, 1999, http://ianrwww.unl.edu/nwga/page8.htm)

       b.   On March 14, for instance, *national security adviser Sandy Berger* went on NBC's "Meet the Press" to announce that the White House had responded "swiftly" to each charge of espionage brought to its attention. (*The New Republic,* May 24, 1999)

Because *national security advisor* is a political designation, it semantically qualifies as a title. But its lack of capitalization in (3b) suggest that in this context it is interpreted as a description of someone's job.

   This confusion is also evident in a construction such as *former Vice President Dan Quayle* (ICE-USA). This example was taken from the *New York Times,* a newspaper that expressly forbids pseudo-titles in its style manual, calling them "false titles" (Siegal and Connolly 1999: 128). In this example, *Vice President* is clearly a title. But because it is preceded by *former,* the emphasis shifts from "honoring" Dan Quayle to "describing" his former job. Constructions of this nature were common in the samples from the ICE Corpus examined, and involved some kind of adjective or noun modifier occurring before either what is clearly a pseudo-title (e.g. *spokesman* in *Army spokesman Col. Horacio Lapinid* [ICE-Philippines]) or what would in other contexts be considered a title (e.g. *Agriculture Secretary* in *acting Agriculture Secretary William Dar* [ICE-Philippines] and *Congressman* in *Makati Congressman Joker Arroyo* [ICE-Philippines]). These examples illustrate, as Bell (1988: 330) observes, that titles have "fluid boundaries" and "the ability to slide out of the category [of titles]" into the category of pseudo-titles. In the present study, examples containing a modifier before a title were classified as pseudo-titles, even if the title portion of the construction was capitalized and the construction appeared in a newspaper that normally prohibits the use of pseudo-titles.

Because pseudo-titles lack a determiner, Bell (1988) regards them as derived through a process he labels "determiner deletion." That is, the pseudo-title *Pentagon Spokesman* in example (4) is derived from a comparable construction containing the determiner *the* (example 5):

(4)   This is *Pentagon spokesman Ken Bacon* (CNN, 3–25–99)

(5)   "It will be another substantive strike, it will be severe," said *the Pentagon spokesman, Kenneth H. Bacon,* as the bombing was renewed from an armada that includes 6 warships and 400 bombers and fighters. (*New York Times,* March 26, 1999, p. A1)

However, as will be shown in 4.9, examples such as (5) were rare in the corpus, even in newspapers disallowing the use of pseudo-titles, contexts in which we would expect to find more constructions with a determiner. Moreover, there are other examples, such as (6a), that are identical in structure to (5), except that the proper noun occurs before rather than after the noun phrase containing the determiner:

(6)   "That's something that we do worry about," said *Mr. Bacon, the Pentagon spokesman.* (*New York Times,* March 31, p. A11)

Determiner deletion is also possible in examples such as (6). However, removal of the determiner yields an appositive, not a pseudo-title:

(7)   "That's something that we do worry about," said *Mr. Bacon, Pentagon spokesman.*

If (4)–(7) are considered collectively, it makes more sense to say that pseudo-titles and equivalent appositives are related not through the process of determiner deletion but through the process of "systematic correspondence" (Quirk et al. 1985: 57f), a process that captures the relationship between constructions that differ in form but that are similar in meaning.

2. Studying Pseudo-Titles and Equivalent Appositives in the International Corpus of English

Bell's (1988) study of pseudo-titles illustrates that their usage is time sensitive. In a matter of 10 years, Bell (1988:338) found a perceptible rise in the use of pseudo-titles in three of four radio stations whose broadcasts he studied in 1974 and 1984. This finding suggests that any study of pseudo-titles should be based on texts collected during a similar time frame and at least a decade after Bell's (1988) study was conducted to determine whether pseudo-title usage is continuing to increase. The various corpora included in the International Corpus of English (ICE) fulfil both these criteria.

The ICE Project was begun by Sidney Greenbaum in the late 1980s to study the evolution of English as a world language. Participating in the project are approximately twenty regional teams representing such countries as Australia, Canada, East Africa (Kenya and Tanzania), Great Britain, Hong Kong, India, Ireland, Jamaica, New Zealand, Singapore, and the United States. Each regional team began collecting in the early 1990s one million words of speech and writing divided into (ca.) 2,000 word samples representing various kinds of English: spontaneous conversations, broadcast discussions, speeches, learned and popular writing, and fiction, to name but a few of the various types of English that are being collected (cf. Nelson 1996:29 for a complete listing of text categories). Three components of ICE (Great Britain, East Africa, and New Zealand) are currently complete, and other components are presently in progress, with an interim release of the entire corpus due in the near future.

Within both the spoken and written sections of the ICE corpus are various kinds of journalistic English: news broadcasts, press reportage, and press editorials. Although pseudo-titles can be found in any kind of "hard news reportage" (Bell 1988:327), such as press reportage or news broadcasts, I decided to restrict my discussion to press news reportage, since at the time that this study was conducted a number of components had completed the press reportage section of their corpus but relatively few had finished collecting and transcribing news broadcasts. The following ICE components were included in the study: East Africa, Great Britain, Jamaica, New Zealand, the Philippines, Singapore, and the United States. I supplemented examples from these components with examples taken from other sources.

Even though each component of ICE contains 20 samples of press reportage, in many components, the same newspaper is represented in more than one sample. Since the use of pseudo-titles is sensitive to the editorial policy of a given newspaper, I included in my corpus only one sample from a given newspaper. This means that for most components, I examined fewer than 20 samples. Table 1 lists the number of newspapers from each component that were examined.

Table 1. Number of Different Newspapers Included Within the Various ICE Components

Component	Total
Great Britain	15
United States	20
New Zealand	12
Philippines	10
Jamaica	3
East Africa	3
Singapore	2

The relatively few different newspapers in East Africa, Jamaica, and Singapore reflects the fact that these countries have small populations and that in two of them (East Africa and Singapore) English is not a primary, but a second, language.

From the samples represented in Table 1, two kinds of information were obtained. First, all samples were examined to determine whether they contained pseudo-titles. Second, ten samples from ten different newspapers were subjected to a detailed linguistic analysis (described below). Since the ICE components from Jamaica, East Africa, and Singapore did not contain 10 samples from 10 different newspaper, these varieties were excluded from this part of the analysis. This left four components (USA, GB, NZ, and Philippines) for this part of the analysis.

To carry out this analysis, each pseudo-title and equivalent apposition in ICE-USA, GB, NZ, and Philippines was assigned a series of tags (see Table 2) that:

a. Identified the regional variety and sample the construction occurred in (variables 1 and 2: 'Country' and 'Sample #')

b. Specified whether the construction was a pseudo-title or an equivalent appositive (variable 3: 'Type')

c. Indicated that if the construction was an equivalent appositive, whether its 'correspondence relationship' (variable 4) to a pseudo-title involved total equivalence:

> *Durk Jager, executive vice president* (ICE-USA) → *executive vice president Durk Jager*

determiner deletion:

> the Organising Secretary, Mr Stephen Kalonzo Musyoka (ICE-East
> Africa) → Organising Secretary Mr Stephen Kalonzo Musyoka

or partial equivalence:

> Ted Shackley, deputy chief of the CIA station in Rome in the 1970s
> (ICE-GB:W2C-010 #62:10) → CIA deputy chief Ted Shackley but not
> ?deputy chief of the CIA station in Rome in the 1970s Ted Shackley

d. Noted the 'Form' (variable 5) of the construction: whether it was a simple
    NP, a genitive NP, or an NP with some postmodification.
e. Measured the 'Length' (variable 6) of the pseudo-title or unit of the
    appositive that could potentially become a pseudo-title, from values of one
    word to six or more words.

Table 2. Coding Scheme for Study of Pseudo-titles

Country	Sample #	Type	Correspondence Relationship	Form	Length
US (1)	W2C001 (1)	Pseudo-title (1)	Total Equivalence (1)	Simple NP (1)	One word (1)
Philippines (2)	W2C002 (2)	Appositive (2)	Determiner Deletion (2)	Genitive NP (2)	Two words (2)
East Africa (3)	W2C003 (3)		Partial Equivalence (3)	Multiple post-Modification (3)	Three words (3)
Jamaica (4)	W2C004 (4)		N/A (4)		Four words (4)
New Zealand (5)	W2C005 (5)				Five words (5)
Great Britain (6)	etc.				Six or more words (6)
Singapore (7)					

Coding the data this way allowed for the results to be viewed from a variety of
different perspectives. For instance, because each construction is given a
number identifying the regional variety in which it occurred, it was possible to

compare pseudo-title usage in, say, British English and Philippine English. Likewise, each sample represents a different newspaper. Therefore, by recording the sample from which a construction was taken, it was possible to know which newspapers permit pseudo-title usage, and which do not, and to determine the extent to which newspapers use pseudo-titles and equivalent appositives similarly or differently. Noting the length of each pseudo-title helped determine whether pseudo-titles were longer in some varieties than others, a hypothesis prompted by an initial survey of the data, which suggested that pseudo-titles were lengthier in the Philippine samples than in the other samples.

3.   The Distribution of Pseudo-Titles in the Various ICE Samples

Table 3 lists for each ICE component the number of newspapers that did or did not contain pseudo-titles.

Table 3.   Number of Newspapers Containing Pseudo-Titles in Various ICE Components

Country	Newspapers w/o Pseudo-Titles	Newspapers w/ Pseudo-Titles	Total
Great Britain	7	8	15
United States	1	19	20
New Zealand	1	11	12
Philippines	0	10	10
Jamaica	0	3	3
East Africa	0	3	3
Singapore	0	2	2
Totals	9 (14%)	56 (86%)	65 (100%)

Table 3 demonstrates that pseudo-title usage is very widespread: only 9 (14%) of the 65 newspaper samples investigated did not contain pseudo-titles, and seven of these newspapers were found in ICE-GB. Overall, therefore, the British norms for pseudo-title usage have had little influence world-wide, even in those varieties — New Zealand, Jamaica, East Africa, and Singapore — that have been directly influenced by British English.

The one American newspaper that did not contain pseudo-titles was surprisingly not the single American newspaper, the *New York Times*, that expressly forbids pseudo-title usage in its style manual, but the *Cornell Chronicle*. An inspection of additional articles from this newspaper outside ICE-USA revealed that this newspaper did indeed allow pseudo-titles: the 2,000 word sample in ICE-USA simply did not contain any examples, a consequence in this case of the relatively small size of the sample. Not only did the *New York Times* contain borderline examples of pseudo-titles, such as *former Vice President Dan Quayle* (cf. 1.0), but it and one British newspaper from ICE-GB forbidding pseudo-titles, the *Guardian*, contained pseudo-titles in sports reportage. Commenting on the inclusion of pseudo-titles in the sports reportage of the *New York Times*, Siegal and Connolly (1999:334) note that this "exception" to the editorial policy of the paper has its roots in "tradition" and is not intended to cover all cases where a pseudo-title could potentially be used but only "sports positions" (e.g. *Red Sox Manager Pat Agneau*); other kinds of pseudo-titles, such as *suspended Braves pitcher Leigh Dann*, are prohibited. The acceptance of pseudo-titles in sports reportage suggests that the prohibition against pseudo-title usage does not always extend to less formal kinds of writing.

Although one of the British-influenced varieties, East Africa, did contain newspapers with pseudo-titles, there were cases clearly illustrating a mixture of British and American styles. Example (8) begins with a pseudo-title, *Lawyer Paul Muite*, but two sentences later contains not another pseudo-title, but instead an equivalent appositive, *a lawyer, Ms Martha Njoka*, that has very marked characteristics of British newspaper English: a title, *Ms*, before the proper noun (American newspapers, with the exception of the *New York Times*, use only the name) and no punctuation following the title to mark it as an abbreviation (American usage would mandate a period).

(8)   *Lawyer Paul Muite* and his co-defendants in the LSK contempt suit wound up their case yesterday and accused the Government of manipu- lating courts through proxies to silence its critics...Later in the after- noon, there was a brief drama in court when *a lawyer, Ms Martha Njoka,* was ordered out after she defied the judge's directive to stop talking while another lawyer was addressing the court. (ICE-East Africa)

4.   The Use and Structure of Pseudo-Titles and Equivalent Appositives in the Various ICE Samples

Figure 1 plots the frequency of pseudo-titles and appositives in the four ICE varieties that were subjected to detailed linguistic analysis: ICE-USA, Philip- pines, NZ, and GB. As Figure 1 demonstrates, there were significant differences between the distributions of pseudo-titles and equivalent appositives in the four varieties. Because of the stigma against pseudo-titles in British newspapers, overall the British samples contained far fewer pseudo-titles than equivalent appositives. In contrast, ICE-Phil , NZ, and USA contained more pseudo-titles than equivalent appositives. Further statistical tests were conducted to pinpoint specific differences in Figure 1, and it was found that ICE-GB differed from the other three varieties, that ICE-USA differed from ICE-NZ and Phil, and that ICE-NZ and Phil did not differ from each other.

These findings suggest an interesting evolutionary process for pseudo-titles. As pseudo-titles entered British press writing, they met resistance, an aversion to the intrusion of an "Americanism" into the British press. This resistance is not unique but has typified the relationship between American and British English for quite some time. The stigma against pseudo-titles was transferred to

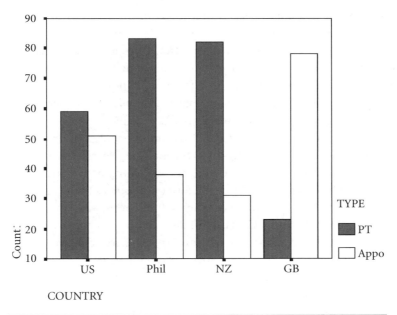

Statistical Test [2]	Value	Degrees of Freedom	Significance Level
Chi square	65.686	3	$p = .000$
Likelihood Ratio	67.832	3	$p = .000$

Figure 1. The Frequency of Pseudo-Titles and Equivalent Appositives in the ICE Varieties

another British-influenced variety: New Zealand English. However, the stigma is breaking down. Bell (1988:338) documents a rise in the use of pseudo-titles, particularly in the broadcast media. And while at the time he conducted his study (1984 and earlier) he still found pseudo-title usage split between the "popular" and "elite" media in New Zealand, this study demonstrates that this dichotomy may no longer exist, at least in press reportage: only one in 12 New Zealand newspapers examined did not contain pseudo-titles. In fact, the greater incidence of pseudo-titles in ICE-NZ and ICE-Phil than in ICE-USA suggests that as this construction has been borrowed from American English into other varieties, its popularity has been increasing. And an examination of the form of pseudo-titles in the various varieties illustrates that while there are general constraints on pseudo-title usage common to all varieties, ICE-NZ and ICE-Phil exhibited some notable differences.

Because ICE-GB contained more equivalent appositives than pseudo-titles, it was expected that this variety would contain more appositives related to pseudo-titles by the correspondence relationships of exact equivalence and determiner deletion than the other varieties, since a logical alternative to a pseudo-title such as *popular novelist Martin Amis* is an exactly equivalent appositive (*Martin Amis, popular novelist*) or an appositive with a determiner (*the popular novelist Martin Amis*). Figure 2 plots the frequencies for the correspondence relationships in the four ICE varieties.

Figure 2 demonstrates that ICE-GB did indeed contain more instances of appositives related to pseudo-titles by exact equivalence or determiner deletion than the other varieties: ICE-USA, Phil, and NZ contained virtually no appositives related by exact equivalence, and fewer appositives than ICE-GB related by determiner deletion. However, these differences were not statistically significant.[3] Even though ICE-GB contained more instances of appositives representing each correspondence relationship, these greater frequencies merely reflect the greater number of appositives in general in ICE-GB (see Figure 1). For each variety, the trends are similar: the fewest number of instances in the category of total equivalence, the most instances in the category of partial equivalence, and an intermediate number of instances in the category of determiner deletion.

These findings add further support to the claim made in 1.0 that Bell's (1988) notion of determiner deletion is not viable, since if pseudo-titles were really derived through the process of determiner deletion, we would expect greater numbers of them in the samples in ICE-GB. Even if the seven samples in ICE-GB without pseudo-titles (and the one sample in ICE-NZ) are compared

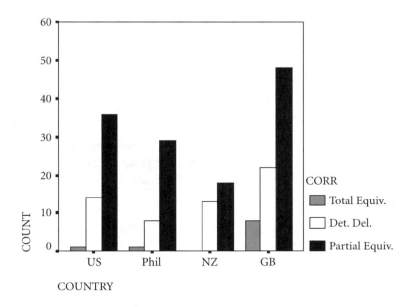

Figure 2. The Frequency of the Three Correspondence Relationships in the ICE Varieties

Statistical Test	Value	Degrees of Freedom	Significance Level
Chi square	3.849	3	p = .278
Likelihood Ratio	3.924	3	p = .270

with the other samples containing pseudo-titles, the differences were still not statistically significant.

In each of the varieties, as Figure 2 illustrates, the correspondence relationship with the highest frequency was the category of partial equivalence. There are purely linguistic reasons why most appositives were in this category. There are two types of constructions in this category that inhibit conversion to a pseudo-title: those containing some kind of postmodification (9a) (Bell 1988: 336)[4] and those containing a genitive noun phrase (10a).

(9) a.   Ted Shackley, deputy chief of the CIA station in Rome in the 1970s (ICE-GB:W2C-010 #62:1)

     b.   ?deputy chief of the CIA station in Rome in the 1970s Ted Shackley

(10) a. the bureau's litigation and prosecution division chief Osias
          Baldivino (ICE-Philippines)

      b. ?*bureau's litigation and prosecution division chief Osias Baldivino

In (9a), conversion to a pseudo-title creates an unbalanced noun phrase (9b),
since the postmodifier beginning with *of* places too much weight at the start of
the noun phrase. The only way a pseudo-title can be created from (9a) is by
using only part of the second unit of the apposition (e.g. *CIA deputy chief Ted
Shackley*). Likewise, conversion of an appositive with a genitive noun phrase
(10a) to a pseudo-title is quite unacceptable (10b) unless the genitive is removed (e.g. *litigation and prosecution division chief Osias Baldivino*).

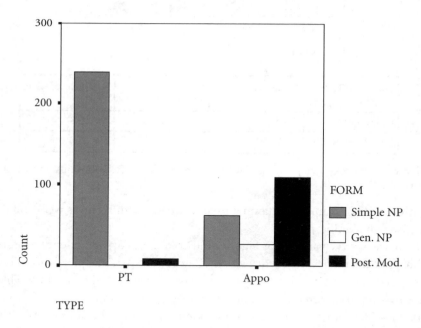

Statistical Test	Value	Degrees of Freedom	Significance Level
Chi square	215.488	2	p = .000
Likelihood Ratio	246.965	2	p = .000

Figure 3. The Form of Pseudo-Titles and Equivalent Appositives in the ICE Varieties

Because of these constraints on pseudo-titles, they have, as Figure 3 illustrates, a much more limited range of forms than equivalent appositives. The differences in form in Figure 3 are largely a consequence of the fact that the structure of a pseudo-title is subject to the principle of "end-weight" (Quirk et al. 1985:1361–2). This principle stipulates that heavier constituents are best placed at the end of a structure, rather than at the beginning of it. A pseudo-title will always come at the start of the noun phrase in which it occurs. The lengthier and more complex the pseudo-title, the more unbalanced the noun phrase will become. Therefore, pseudo-titles typically have forms (e.g. simple noun phrases) that that are short and non-complex structures. In contrast, an equivalent appositive consists of two units, one of which corresponds to a pseudo-title. Because this unit is independent of the proper noun to which it is related — in speech it occupies a separate tone unit, in writing it is separated by a comma from the proper noun to which it is in apposition — it is not subject to the end-weight principle. Consequently, the unit of an appositive corresponding to a pseudo-title has more forms of varying lengths.

Of the 247 pseudo-titles in Figure 3, only eight contained some kind of postmodification (e.g. *MILF Vice Chairman for Political Affairs Hadji Murad* [ICE-Philippines]), and these eight instances were restricted to the samples taken from either ICE-NZ or ICE-Philippines. As was noted earlier in this section, it was these two varieties that exhibited the greatest use of pseudo-titles. This trend, along with fact that these two varieties are using forms not in the other varieties, suggests a change in both the use and form of pseudo-titles in ICE-NZ and ICE-Philippines. However, more than eight instances are needed to document any evolution in the form of pseudo-titles. A better measure is to look not at their form but their length.

Figure 4 lists the length of pseudo-titles in the four ICE varieties. Figure 4 documents significant differences in the length of pseudo-titles in the four varieties: both ICE-NZ and Phil had more pseudo-titles that were lengthier than 5 words than either ICE-GB and USA. Table 4 provides a more detailed breakdown of the length of pseudo-titles in the varieties. ICE-GB had no pseudo-titles lengthier than three words, with most being either two (11a) or three words (11b) in length:

(11) a.   Tory leader Cllr Bob Blackman (ICE-GB:W2C-009 #54:3)

b.   Conservative housing spokesman Cllr Irwin Van Colle
(ICE-GB:W2C-009 #13:1)

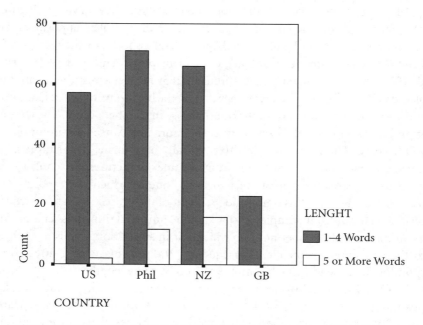

Statistical Test[5]	Value	Degrees of Freedom	Significance Level
Chi square	12.005	3	p = .007
Kruskal Wallis	11.956	3	p = .015
Likelihood Ratio	15.688	3	p = .001

Figure 4. Length of Pseudo-Titles in the Various ICE Varieties

Table 4. Specific Lengths for Pseudo-Titles in the ICE Varieties

Country	One Word	Two Words	Three Words	Four Words	Five Words	Six or More Words	Total
US	7 (12%)	22 (37%)	20 (34%)	8 (13.6%)	2 (3%)	—	59 (100%)
Phil	8 (10%)	33 (40%)	26 (31%)	4 (5%)	5 (6%)	7 (8%)	83 (100%)
NZ	10 (12%)	15 (18%)	28 (34%)	13 (16%)	12 (15%)	4 (5%)	82 (100%)
GB	4 (17.4%)	11 (48%)	8 (35%)	—	—	—	23 (100%)
Total	29 (12%)	81 (33%)	82 (33%)	25 (10%)	19 (8%)	11 (5%)	247 (100%)

Although ICE-NZ, Phil, and USA also had many pseudo-titles that were two or three words long, ICE-NZ and Phil had significantly more pseudo-titles that were lengthier than five words (12a-f), making these two varieties quite distinct from the other two varieties:

(12) a. Salamat and Presidential Adviser on Flagship Projects in Mindanao Robert Aventajado (ICE-Philippines)
       b. Oil and Gas planning and development manager Roger O'Brien (ICE-NZ)
       c. Time Magazine Asia bureau chief Sandra Burton (ICE-Philippines)
       d. corporate planning and public affairs executive director Graeme Wilson (ICE-NZ)
       e. Autonomous Region of Muslim Mindanao police chief Damming Unga (ICE-Philippines)
       f. Wesley and former New Zealand coach Chris Grinter. (ICE-NZ)

5.   Prospects for the Future Development of Pseudo-Titles

At the end of his discussion of pseudo-titles, Bell (1988: 341–3) offers a number of predictions about the future development of pseudo-titles in the various national varieties of English. Since the present study was conducted on texts published 10–15 years after those analyzed by Bell (1988), it is possible to test whether Bell's (1988) predictions have been fulfilled.

One prediction that Bell (1988: 342) makes is that pseudo-titles will spread to other registers of English, possibly even conversational English. Because only press reportage was investigated in this study, this prediction is difficult to test. But a search of the entire ICE-GB found pseudo-titles in the categories of broadcast interviews, sports commentaries, news broadcasts, and skills/hobbies.[6] Whether pseudo-titles will ever find their way into spontaneous dialogues is highly questionable, primarily because they serve no honorific function. It is quite common for us to address people as *President* or *Professor* because these are titles of respect. But it would be quite another matter to walk up to an individual and say, "Hello, former radio broadcaster Franco Gupta." Conceivably, a pseudo-title could be used when talking about someone, as in "Yesterday I spoke with former radio broadcaster Franco Gupta." But there is little communicative need for such structures because equivalent appositives of this type (e.g. *a former radio broadcaster, Franco Gupta*) are extremely uncommon in speech (Meyer 1992:116).

Bell (1988:341) also predicts that the "staccato, formulaic nature" of the pseudo-title will increase, and that many pseudo-titles, such as *Prime Minister*, will become acceptable as full titles. Because all ICE corpora are relatively short, it is not possible to determine whether a given pseudo-title is formulaic. For instance, following the U.S. invasion of Panama, Manuel Noriega was continually referred to in the American press as *Panamanian dictator Manuel Noriego*. But to discover usages such as this, one would need a huge monitor corpus, such as the Bank of English, containing millions of words of text covering an extended period of time. However, because three of the components studied — ICE-East Africa, GB, NZ — are complete, it is possible to determine the extent to which in the spoken and written language of a given variety, an expression such as *Prime Minister* has fully moved into the category of titles.

Table 5. The Frequency of *Prime Minister* as a Title, Pseudo-title, and Appositive in Three ICE Varieties

	Title	Pseudo-Title	Appositive	Total
Great Britain	4	0	21	25
New Zealand	15	5	9	29
East Africa[7]	12	13	22	47

Table 5 lists the number of times *Prime Minister* was used as a full title 13a), a pseudo-title (13b), or an equivalent appositive (13c).

(13) a. Prime Minister Obed Diamini (ICE-East Africa)
      b. former prime minister Sir Robert Muldoon (ICE-NZ)
      c. the Prime Minister Mr John Major (ICE-GB:S2B-012 #10:1:A)

Prime Minister is well established as both a full title and pseudo-title in ICE-NZ and ICE-East Africa. However, in ICE-GB it occurred very infrequently as a full title, most frequently in an appositive construction, and never as a pseudo-title. These findings are consistent with other findings in this study: that of all the varieties analyzed, British press English is the most conservative and the most resistant to change.

The larger explanation for this finding lies in another of Bell's (1988:342) predictions, namely that "as long as the prestige media within a country hold to determiner deletion, the rule will keep its social force." This study has demonstrated quite strongly that the British-based stigma against pseudo-titles has virtually disappeared world-wide, even in those varieties, such as East African, Jamaican, New Zealand, and Singapore English, that are British influenced. There still exist isolated newspapers — the *New York Times* in the United States, the *Press* in New Zealand — that still follow the British model. But outside Great Britain, pseudo-titles are quite common — so common, in fact, that they were used more frequently in the New Zealand and Philippine samples than in the American samples, even though pseudo-titles originated in American English. And in the New Zealand and Philippine samples new types of pseudo-titles are evolving that are longer than pseudo-titles in the other varieties.

Notes

* I wish to thank Dr. Jie Chen, Computing Services, University of Massachusetts at Boston, for help with the statistical tests discussed in this paper.

1. Examples taken from ICE components are identified simply by reference to the particular component. Full citations are given for examples taken from sources outside the ICE components.

2. Two statistical tests were applied to the results discussed in this section: chi square and likelihood ratio. The likelihood ratio test (which is sometimes refereed to as the "log likelihood" or G^2 test) is considered more reliable for lower frequencies, as is the case for the data in this paper (cf. Dunning 1993 for details).

3. It is not possible to obtain valid statistical results for tests such as chi square when frequencies fall below 5, as was the case with the category of exact equivalence in ICE-USA, Phil, and NZ. To increase frequencies, I therefore combined the results for the categories of exact equivalence and determiner deletion, since these categories represent very similar stylistic choices (e.g. *Dan Quayle, former Vice President* or *Dan Quayle, the former Vice President*).

4. Bell (1988:336) cites other linguistic criteria favoring or disfavoring conversion to a pseudo-title not investigated in this study, such as the articles *a* and *the* favoring conversion.

5. A third statistical test, Kruskal Wallis, is included here because this test is less sensitive to low cell frequencies (e.g ICE-USA had only two instances of pseudo-titles lengthier than five words).

6. Because ICE-GB is fully tagged and parsed, it is relatively easy to search the whole corpus and find instances of pseudo-titles. However, ICE-East Africa and ICE-NZ exist only in lexical form. Therefore, these components were excluded from this analysis, since it was not possible to automatically search them for pseudo-titles

7. Because ICE-East Africa is longer than the other corpora (ca. 1,300,000 words), the figures in Table 6 list number of occurrences per one million words.

References

Bell, A. 1988. "The British Base and the American Connection in New Zealand Media English." *American Speech* 63: 326–44.

Biber, D., Johansson, S., Leech, G., Conrad, S. and E. Finegan 1999. *Longman Grammar of Spoken and Written English*. Essex: Pearson Education Limited.

Crystal, D. 1997. *English as a Global Language*. Cambridge: Cambridge University Press.

Dunning, T. 1993. "Accurate Methods for the Statistics of Surprise and Coincidence." *Computational Linguistics* 19(1). 61–74.

Meyer, C. F. 1992. *Apposition in Contemporary English*. Cambridge: Cambridge University Press.

Nelson, G. 1996. "Markup Systems." *Comparing English Worldwide: The International Corpus of English,* S. Greenbaum (ed.), 36–53. Oxford: Clarendon Press.

Quirk, R., Greenbaum, S., Leech, G. and Svartvik, J. 1985. *A Comprehensive Grammar of the English Language*. London: Longman.

Rydén, M. 1975. "Noun-Name Collocations in British Newspaper Language." *Studia Neophilologica* 67: 14–39.

Peters, P. 2001. "The Influence of American English on Australian and British English." *Who's Centric Now? The State of Postcolonial Englishes*, B. Moore (ed.), 297–309. Oxford: Oxford University Press.

Siegal, A. M. and Connolly, W. G. 1999. *The New York Times Manual of Style and Usage*, Revised and Expanded Edition. New York: Times Books.

CHAPTER 9

Pattern grammar, language teaching, and linguistic variation

Applications of a corpus-driven grammar

Susan Hunston
University of Birmingham

1. Word behaviour and variation

This paper is about pattern: an approach to language which maintains the generalising characteristics of grammatical descriptions while prioritising the behaviour of individual lexical items. 'Pattern grammar' can therefore be described as a new approach to language description, although it incorporates and reinterprets some aspects of traditional grammar. As will be argued in this paper, awareness of pattern is important to language teaching because it can facilitate the development of both accuracy and fluency. Pattern is also an important site of investigation with regard to variation, because it represents a link between lexis, grammar and meaning. Identification of the significant patterns in a given variety, or register, of English helps to indicate the meanings that are prevalent in that variety or register. In addition, a single meaning is often able to be expressed in a number of lexis-pattern combinations, and it is important to know how variation between those combinations correlates with variation in register.

Although some traditional grammars pay scant attention to lexis, some features have long been recognised as restricted to particular lexical items. These include transitivity and the complementation behaviour of verbs. The availability of large, electronic corpora allows studies of these behaviours to be carried out more extensively and in greater detail, and to take account of variation between registers.

It is well known, for example, that many words, especially verbs and adjectives, are followed by finite or non-finite clauses i.e. that-clauses, wh-clauses, to-infinitive clauses, and '-ing' clauses. There is significant variation in the distribution of these clauses, between registers and between the verbs and adjectives that control them (Biber et al 1999: 754–759). For example, verbs followed by that-clauses are particularly frequent in conversation. The most frequent verb with this complementation pattern in conversation is *think*, with *say, know* and *guess* also occurring frequently (ibid: 668). In academic prose, on the other hand, the 'verb + that-clause' combination is less frequent, but 'adjective + to-infinitive clause' combinations are relatively common, particularly with adjectives that indicate degrees of certainty, such as *certain, liable* and *(un)likely* (ibid: 754). A few verbs occur with all four kinds of complementation clause, but most verbs occur with only one or two patterns (ibid.: 755).

Biber et al also consider clauses that complement nouns (1999: 647–656). They note that noun complementation clauses are rare in conversation, but more frequent in news reportage and in academic prose. News texts show a high incidence of to-infinitive complementation clauses, especially *chance to, attempt to, decision to, plan to* and *bid to*. Academic texts include a relatively high proportion of that-clause noun complementation, especially *fact that, possibility that, doubt that, belief that* and *assumption that*.

Complementation by a finite or non-finite clause, however, is only one of the behaviours that distinguishes one lexical item from another. Rudanko (1996), for example, discusses verbs that occur with each of the prepositions *in, to, at, on, with* and *of* followed by an '-ing' clause. Levin (1993) distinguishes classes of verbs that share aspects of behaviour such as the occurrence of various participants in the process as subject.

The work to be presented in this paper draws on the lexicographical work undertaken during the compilation of the *Collins CoBUILD English Dictionary* (1995), which allowed the behaviour of each lexical item in that dictionary to be described in some detail. In particular, the tendency of individual verbs, nouns and adjectives to control certain clause types, or prepositional phrases, was noted. These behaviours, along with the occurrence of verbs as intransitive (no object), transitive (followed by an object), or ditransitive (followed by two objects), are coded in the dictionary as a sequence of items such as 'verb and noun group' (**V n**), 'adjective, preposition *of* and noun group' (**ADJ *of* n**), or 'noun and that-clause' (**N that**). Such sequences are known as patterns. The concept of 'pattern' will be described in the next section. Here it might be noted that patterns subsume much of what has been described by others as transitivity, complementation clauses, and prepositional phrases governed by verbs, but that they are able to indicate the range of behaviours of a given item more precisely. Two arguments will be presented here: that 'pattern' is an important concept in language teaching, and that the study of pattern variation in different registers is both feasible and desirable.

2. Pattern grammar

'Pattern grammar', then, is an approach to the grammar of English which prioritises the behaviour of individual lexical items (see Francis et al 1996; 1997; 1998; Hunston & Francis 1998; 1999). It has its roots in the pioneering work of Hornby (1954), but takes its theoretical stance from Sinclair's (1991) observations that

i.   words tend to occur in more-or-less typical phraseologies;
ii.   meaning and patterning are connected;
iii.   grammar and lexis cannot be treated as distinct phenomena in a description of English (Hudson 1984: 3–4 makes a similar point).

To this we might add that, when observing raw corpus data, traditional grammatical categories (such as 'direct object', 'indirect object', 'noun clause' and 'extraposed clause') might be unnecessary or even unhelpful (Hunston & Francis 1998; 1999).

A pattern is a sequence of grammar words, word types or clause types which co-occur with a given lexical item. An item may be said to control or 'have' a pattern if the pattern occurs frequently and is dependent on the item in question. Patterns are observable through concordance lines, though intuition is also involved in deciding on dependency. Below are sets of concordance lines for the verb *decide*, showing the patterns this verb controls.[1] (For reasons of space, only five lines for each pattern are shown: this masks the comparative frequency of the patterns).

V that

```
when Bartoli was a free agent, he decided all he had to do was play a
   jobs. The letter reads: 'I have decided it is necessary to draw your
s postwar 'economic miracle". MITI decided that the computer industry ha
on World War II until in college I decided that I wanted to become a Mar
with infertility treatment, Lorna 'decided that it really didn't matter
```

V wh

```
another face, for a while. I must decide if I want my old one, or a nic
   pregnancy" not Profet's list to decide what's best for her. Willi
are in Minnesota as tourists. They decided what they wanted to do and wh
   to sent short messages and Glen decides whether or not he's going to
 A trial is set for December 4 to decide who will get permanent custody
```

V wh to-inf

of the issues facing charities when deciding how to utilise their investm
    would be. When you're a teenager, deciding what to do with your life, y
who, before Royan last week, had not decided whether to start Almox Ratina
up to the state attorney general to decide whether to appeal the judge's
        demolished." The bank must now decide whether to sell the building,

V to-inf

        So the churchwardens have decided no longer to pay the quota, a
    Register office wedding. People decide to marry at a register office
the parents. <M01> And what did you decide to study? <M02>I-
ovulatory problems). When a couple decides to have a child, it is a decisio
    availability of the plants. So he decided to start his own nursery, from

be V-ed

        blabbered.' The itinerary was decided at the highest level. The Hom
cus race in Santa Cruz County that was decided by 25 votes. There were, you
    interpreters, the matter may be decided for you by the coupling.
        Allende's election itself was decided in the Chilean congress again
        1), 7-5, 6-3. The match will be decided tomorrow," he said of the dou

it be V-ed that

of the Battle of Britain. So it was decided that the celebrations would be
    babes. For some reason, it was decided that the latest from the Mexican
completely done by now, but it was decided that rather than put Brett in da
give up his life so easily. It was decided that the only place to treat him
out from monetary union it has been decided that eight different coins will

To show the range of words that might control one pattern, below are
concordance lines showing some of the adjectives occurring in the pattern *it
v-link ADJ that* (referred to in Biber et al 1999 as an extraposed that-clause).
(Again for reasons of space, only a maximum of two lines for each adjective are
shown.)

    ill Constable Jones, Mr Casey said It is **apparent** that fate intervened th
orses. Elegance being a key factor, it was **appropriate** that Joanne
all I can tell you." From his tone it was **clear** that Dick Ryle had had
        in Mecca to perform the haj. It is **clear** that the revolution in mas
National Union of Students said that it is **crucial** that universities give a
    only to add the fateful words: 'But it is **essential** that we end it in such
e Woodgate Valley Country Park, and it was **fitting** that two of the city's
    health clinic, or any hospital. It is **important** that the woman
is sewn up is not so important; but it is **important** that North Korea should
        impossible. At the same time it is **inevitable** that those at home,
ters to Stick Letters <p> I suppose it was **inevitable** that this passionate
    him to act so out of character? It was **ironic** that Penelope's insistence
    co-operation, however he said it was **likely** that Germany would have t
is a lethal muscle wasting disease. It is **likely** that any child with this
ll enjoyment of this exquisite poem, it is **necessary** that the reader should
    a camera attached and working. It is **obvious** that the chance of a
which it had been contracted here, it was **obvious** that that was not what
        <M02> And we asked them and it was **overwhelming** that- the the
portant parts of every relationship. It is **possible** that your partner's mil
s a template for building proteins — it is **possible** that the FraX protein h
    exchange transactions in London. It is **revealing** that the Socialists wh
st past the end of the year. Indeed it was **significant** that the Jakarta
    n euthanasia is a guess at best. It is **surprising** that, following an
others. <p> Some doctors have said it is **suspicious** that the pills named
s ever as simple as presented. While it is **true** that vertical integration
Europe will require a high-wire act. It is **true** that Malcolm Rifkind, the

```
et to him, but he couldn't help it. It was typical that Robyn would have
  who said: 'In a civilised society, it is unacceptable that women are
        in this Year of Remembrance. It is unfortunate that the article made
anti-government protests. He said it was unfortunate that a number of
More recent work has suggested that it is unlikely that family boundary
        to testify. In retrospect, it is unlikely that a US court would
```

Below are individual examples of words and their patterns (in each case the word with the pattern is underlined; in the coding, the symbol for the word with the pattern is in capitals):

i. *Crowds of near hysterical men jostled their way through to try to find news of their wives and families.* **V** *way* **prep/adv**

ii. *He instructed family members in nursing techniques.* **V** n *in* n

iii. *Japan's industrial output increased by 2%.* **V** *by* **amount**

iv. *The mood in Japan is changing and candidates want to identify themselves with reform.* **V pron-refl** *with* n

v. *I can be very rude to motorists who hoot at me.* **V** *at* n

vi. *It's an honour to finally work with her.* **it** v-link **N** to-inf

vii. *He was too high on drugs and alcohol to remember them.* **ADJ** *on* n

viii. *Do they have a chance of beating Australia?* **N** *of* -ing

ix. *We played that record all night long.* n **ADV**

x. *...a thinly disguised attack* **ADV** -ed

xi. *There'd be no telling how John would react to such news as this.* **DET** n *as* n

xii. *She let the dogs into the house and fed them.* v **PRON**

2.1 The non-randomness of pattern

It appears that the co-occurrence of lexis and pattern is not random, but is associated particularly with meaning (as noted also by Rudanko 1996). This association is not, however, predictive. As will be seen below, two words with similar meanings may not share a pattern (though Hunston and Francis 1999 present some evidence that patterns change over time so that words with similar meanings become more like each other in this respect). Furthermore, words that share a pattern rarely all share a single element of meaning. Rather it is the case that the words sharing a pattern can be grouped so that the members of each group share an aspect of meaning. In Francis et al (1996; 1997; 1998) the groups are termed 'meaning groups'. Below are two examples of patterns and the meaning groups associated with them: 'verb followed by *into*' and 'noun followed by *at*'.

V *into* n (from Francis et al 1997: 122)

1. something becomes something else: *change, convert, develop, escalate, evolve, form, grow, merge, turn*
    With her care, he <u>grew</u> into a normal, healthy child.

2. something breaks or divides into pieces or groups: *break, crumble, divide, separate, shatter, smash, split*
    The plane hit the ground and <u>broke</u> into three pieces.

3. one person or thing collides with another: *bang, bump, crash, run, slam, smash*
    The spokesman said both vehicles <u>crashed</u> into a burned-out car.

4. someone enters a place: *book, break, check, cram, crowd, dive, move, pack, pile, push*
    Then we all <u>crowded</u> into a small restaurant and ordered a meal.

5. someone or something disappears or is not noticeable: *blend, fade, fade away, melt, merge, vanish*
    <u>Does</u> the new housing stick out like a sore thumb or <u>blend</u> into its surroundings?

6. pressing something or making a hole in something: *bite, dig, drill, eat, sink*
    He <u>bit</u> into the bread and chewed slowly.

7. someone investigates something: *dig, inquire, look, probe, research*
    The team <u>has been researching</u> into the genetic cause of the disease for more than six years.

8. someone becomes involved in something: *break, enter, get, go, plunge, rush, tumble, venture, walk*
    I'd like to <u>get</u> into management.

9. someone or something starts being in a different state or starts doing something: *break, burst, burst out, come, descend, dissolve, erupt, fall, fly, get, lapse, launch, plunge, retreat, sink, slide, slip*
    She <u>burst</u> into tears.

10. someone puts on different clothes: *change, slip*
    I <u>changed</u> into my suit.

N *at* n/-ing (from Francis et al 1998: 137–139)

1. emotions and attitudes: *amazement, anger, anxiety, awe, bewilderment, bitterness, concern, delight, despair, disappointment, disbelief, disgust, dismay, displeasure, distress, embarrassment, exasperation, excitement, frustration, fury, glee, grief, guilt, horror, joy, jubilation, laughter, outrage, rage, relief, resentment, revulsion, sadness, satisfaction, shame, shock, surprise, terror, thrill*
    Large crowds later took to the streets to express their <u>anger</u> at yesterday's killings.

2. attempts to do or get something: *attempt, bash, chance, crack, effort, go, shot, stab, tilt, try*
    Mr Downer said that he may one day get another <u>chance</u> at the leadership.

3. looking at someone or something, physically or metaphorically: *glance, glimpse, look, peek, smile*
    The island is bigger than a first <u>glance</u> at the map indicates.

4. someone is good or experienced at a particular activity: *dab hand, expert, genius, master, novice, old hand, past master, whizz, wizard*
    Dickens was a <u>genius</u> at creating characters of great depth and this film is peppered with them.

5. critical comments: *dig, protest, side-swipe*
    It's a none-too-subtle <u>dig</u> at the officials of the Brisbane and Canberra clubs.

3. Applications to language teaching

In considering the applications of pattern to language teaching, four topics will be discussed briefly: accuracy, fluency, the place of patterns in language pedagogy, and the issue of consciousness-raising.

3.1 Accuracy

Patterns are important to language production in terms of both accuracy and fluency. Even advanced learners tend to have imperfect control over patterns; in fact, in the case of very advanced learners, pattern use is perhaps the greatest source of a sense of non-idiomaticity in English. Below are some examples, with the kind of advice the teacher might offer, based on the association of pattern and meaning.

Teachers … discourage students to try to use the target language to express their own ideas.

The verb *discourage* is not used with this pattern (though its opposite *encourage* is). The correct pattern is 'verb + noun + *from* + -ing', so the phrase should read *discourage students from trying.…* The teacher could point out that *discourage* is similar in meaning to *stop* and *prevent*, which have the same pattern.

Criminals will find it difficult to evade from being arrested.

The verb *evade* is not used with this pattern (though *escape* is). The most likely alternative is *evade arrest* (with the pattern 'verb + noun'). The pattern 'verb + -ing' is also possible (*evade being arrested*) but is much less frequent. The better-known verb *avoid* also has these two patterns.

Not all undergraduates are given the privilege to stay in university accommodation.

The noun *privilege* is rarely used with this pattern (though the pattern '*it* + link verb + noun + to infinitive', as in *It's a privilege to meet you*, is common). Much more frequently found is the pattern 'noun + *of* + -ing' (*the privilege of staying*). The nouns *advantage, benefit, distinction, gift, honour, luxury* and *pleasure* are also used with this pattern.

Teachers have the objective to help learners acquire natural English.
Again, the noun *objective* does not have this pattern. It does have the pattern 'noun + *of* + -ing' (*the objective of helping*), along with *aim, function, purpose* and *role*.

Along with accuracy, however, goes creativity, and it would be contentious to suggest that a pattern not typically used by native speakers is necessarily infelicitous. Different geographical varieties of English have in some cases different pattern-word combinations. For example, in standard Singapore English the verb *forget* has the pattern 'verb + noun + prepositional phrase/adverb', as in *She forgot her books at home*. In British English, *forget* does not have this pattern, though many other verbs, such as *leave*, do. Intuition is sometimes a poor guide to what can be attested to occur. For example, a teacher coming across the sentence *She mistook him as her brother* might object that the verb *mistake* does not have the pattern 'verb + noun + *as* + noun' and that the sentence is therefore in error. In terms of meaning, however, this pattern does fit well with the verb (by analogy with *She wrongly identified him as her brother*), and indeed the Bank of English corpus contains seven examples of this pattern with *mistake*.[2] This suggests that the usage is rare rather than wrong.

3.2 Fluency

Control over patterns can be said to aid fluency as well as accuracy. This is because if a word with its pattern has been learnt the learner can produce, not just one word, but a series of words, a phrase, together. A single mental effort produces a whole string of language. For example, here is a native speaker of English talking about his addiction to cigarettes:

My nan sometimes <u>says to me that</u> I <u>get really moody</u> when I <u>don't have a cigarette</u> and I <u>keep snapping at her</u> she says but I <u>try not to do it</u> but I just <u>keep doing it</u> and then she <u>gives me a cigarette</u>.

Each of the verbs in this short extract has a pattern, which translates into a recognisable phrase:

say	**V** *to* **n that**	*says to me that*
get	**V adj**	*get really moody*
have	**V n**	*don't have a cigarette*
keep	**V — ing**	*keep snapping; keep doing*
snap	**V** *at* **n**	*snapping at her*
try	**V to-inf**	*try not to do*
do	**V n**	*do it; doing it*
give	**V n n**	*gives me a cigarette*

Together, these phrases, which are not fixed lexically but are not random either, make up a large proportion of the utterance. The speaker has produced a novel utterance by putting together patterns belonging to the individual words that are used. So, although a learner may never have heard or said *keep snapping at her* before, it can be produced without hesitation by putting together the pattern of *keep* (*keep snapping*) with the pattern of *snap* (*snapping at her*).

One way of interpreting fluency is as what has been called 'pattern flow'. When a word that is part of a pattern has a pattern of its own, the result is flow from one pattern to the other. It is possible to show this diagrammatically, as in the example below.

```
I tend to  think that it'd be wrong    to  arm the    police because...
V....to..inf
          V.....that
                  it...be..ADJ......to-inf
                          V............n
```

In this example, the lexical items *tend, think, wrong* and *arm* demonstrate a typical behaviour. This gives the sequence *I tend to think that it'd be wrong* a sense of naturalness and familiarity, such as might be associated with a fixed phrase that is chosen by the speaker as a single item, rather than being constructed from the raw materials of lexis and grammar. Yet the sequence is not frequently met (there are no instances in the Bank of English corpus). It is not a single choice but might be seen as a series of choices, each arising from the one before.

3.3 Patterns and Pedagogy

One important question is how an approach to lexis and grammar as pattern relates to current models of language teaching. It seems clear that patterns fit most closely with views of language that prioritise lexis — what is sometimes called the lexical approach (Willis 1990; Lewis 1993). If a syllabus is composed of lexical items instead of structures or notions, patterns will be what is taught about a word, because knowing a word means, among other things, knowing the patterns a word has.

The next question to be addressed is what teaching method is most appropriate to patterns. It is probably obvious that no one could set out to teach one pattern per lesson (though some patterns, such as **V to-inf** and **V -ing** have been part of the teaching repertoire for years). In fact, patterns sit uncomfortably with what has been called the PPP model of teaching. They accord much better with task-based learning, as discussed by Long and Crooks (1992) and by Willis and Willis (1996), among others. In Willis and Willis's approach, students perform a task which leads into a period of language focus, in which awareness is raised of aspects of the language used, such as tense use, pronouns, phraseology and so on. Patterns are ideally suited to this awareness-raising approach. The next section gives some examples of exercises based on patterns. The point of these exercises is partly to raise awareness of the individual patterns in focus, but a more general purpose is to make the learner aware that patterns, in general, are important, so that the learner can notice patterns wherever they are met, not only when the teacher draws attention to them.

3.4 Consciousness-raising

Exercises designed to raise learners' awareness of pattern can involve pieces of language taken out of context. Such exercises have the benefit of traditional parsing exercises in that they encourage learners to identify the parts that make up a sentence, but because they require recognition of surface features only they make far fewer demands in terms of metalanguage. They also direct attention to specific items such as individual prepositions as well as to general categories such as 'noun'. Here is one such exercise, with the instructions to learners given first:

Here are two sets of sentences. Each sentence from the first set matches one from the second set in that the word in bold has the same pattern. Match up the two sets. (For example, sentence 1c matches 2a because in both the verb is followed by *of* and a noun — *died of a heart attack* and *complained of a headache.*)

(1) a. They've just **banned** bikes from the city
    b. He's much more **familiar** with those kinds of issues than I am.
    c. She **died** of a heart attack.
    d. So you didn't come to a **conclusion** as to how many different sentences there were.
    e. I felt perhaps they would you know **give** more attention to the girls.

(2) a. She **complained** of a headache.
    b. Let me just **introduce** you to the gentleman sitting behind you.
    c. My mum's never **hidden** anything from me.
    d. Please give him some **advice** as to what to do.
    e. Presumably the bank was also **happy** with the budget.

Alternatively, an exercise might be set in the context of another language task. The next example is based on a reading text used by Willis and Willis (1996) and quoted here. It is possible to create various exercises based on this text. Below are suggestions for ways of drawing attention to just one pattern — 'verb + noun + past participle' (**V n — ed**), used with the verb *LEAVE*. The exercises begin with examples from the reading text and then introduce other material taken from the Bank of English corpus.

Auto-pilot
The flight ran several times a week taking holiday-makers to various resorts in the Mediterranean. On each flight, to reassure the passengers all was well, the captain would put the jet on to auto-pilot and he and all the crew would come aft into the cabin to greet the passengers.
Unfortunately on this particular flight the security door between the cabin and the flight deck jammed and <u>left the captain and the crew stuck in the cabin</u>. From that moment, in spite of efforts to open the door, the fate of the passengers and crew was sealed.

Look at the underlined phrase *left the captain and the crew stuck in the cabin*. We can divide it up as in the table:

Now divide up these sentences and add them to the table:

a. The masked men left her bound and gagged.
b. A serious operation left her confined to a wheelchair.
c. A childhood illness has left her crippled.
d. The war left 300,000 homes destroyed.
e. The bitter winds left many fishermen frozen to their seats.
f. An earthquake killed around 170 people and left thousands deprived of shelter.

Look at what you have written in Column 1. What kind of things do these words describe?
Look at what you have written in Column 4. What kind of things do these words describe?

Column 1	Column 2	Column 3	Column 4
The security door	left	the captain and the crew	stuck in the cabin.

4. Applications to the study of variation

The work on identifying patterns to date has been done manually,[3] most of it by lexicographers compiling the *Collins COBUILD English Dictionary* (1995). The patterns of around 20,000 words are given in that dictionary and/or in the two major volumes of the 'pattern grammar' series. Now that this ground-word has been done, it is a tractable problem to automate the identification of patterns in running text. That is, a program can be written which, on encountering a word, can check what patterns that word may have, and thus can identify the elements of the pattern in the text (Mason and Hunston 2001). There are various possible applications of this. Firstly, and most obviously, the comparative frequency of patterns with individual lexical items can be calculated. This would extend the work done in Biber et al (1998) which compares, for example, the frequency of *begin* followed by a to-infinitive and followed by an '-ing' clause. Secondly, the relative frequency of different patterns in various registers can be calculated. This would extend the work described in Biber et al (1999) on complementation clauses, allowing a more complete picture of verb, noun and adjective behaviour to emerge.

Finally, the connection between pattern and meaning opens the possibility of quantifying ways of expressing meanings in different registers via the concept of 'local grammar' (Barnbrook and Sinclair 1995; Hunston and Sinclair 2000). A local grammar is a grammar that seeks to account for, not the whole of a language, but one meaning only. One example is a grammar of definitions (Barnbrook and Sinclair 1995), another is a grammar of evaluation

(Hunston and Sinclair 2000). A grammar currently being written is that for 'cause and effect' (Allen 1999). Below are some examples of analysed expressions of cause and effect. In each case, a sentence expressing causality is parsed into semantic elements ('cause', 'effect' and 'observer'). The parsing can be done because a pattern is recognized along with one of a number of verbs or nouns which use that pattern to express causality. In the first example, for instance, identification of the verb *lead* with the pattern 'noun$_1$ + verb + noun$_2$ + to-infinitive' is followed by a mapping of the meaning elements on to the pattern (where 'noun$_1$' = 'cause'; 'noun$_2$ + to-infinitive' = 'effect'), allowing the analysis to be made.

Personal problems at home led her to misbehave at school.
Personal problems at home = CAUSE
Her … misbehave at school = EFFECT
IDENTIFYING PATTERN = noun…*led*…noun….to-inf
POSSIBLE VERBS: *cause; compel; drive; force; impel; induce; lead; push; tempt*

The libel case arose from John Pilger's film 'Cambodia'.
The libel case = EFFECT
John Pilger's film 'Cambodia' = CAUSE
IDENTIFYING PATTERN = noun…*arose from*…noun
POSSIBLE VERBS: *come; follow; result; stem*

Drugs are certainly the cause of much crime but a large part of this is because of their illegality.
Drugs = CAUSE
Much crime = EFFECT
IDENTIFYING PATTERN = noun…*be*…the *cause* of…noun
POSSIBLE NOUNS: *agent; benefit; cause; consequence; effect; fruits; generator; implications; legacy; outcome; product; result; root; secret; source*

The effect of radiation is to shift the transition from ductile to brittle behaviour to a higher temperature.
Radiation = CAUSE
Shift the transition…to a higher temperature = EFFECT
IDENTIFYING PATTERN = the *effect* of…noun…*be*…to-inf
POSSIBLE NOUNS: *effect; result*

> *The final exam determines whether you can sit for university entrance or not.*
> The final exam = CAUSE
> Whether you can sit for university entrance or not = EFFECT
> IDENTIFYING PATTERN = *determine* ... wh
> POSSIBLE VERBS: *decide, determine, define, dictate, influence*

> *Kelly attributes her coping ability to growing up in a big family.*
> Kelly = OBSERVER / SOURCE
> Her coping ability = EFFECT
> Growing up in a big family = CAUSE
> IDENTIFYING PATTERN = noun....*attribute*...noun...*to*...noun/-ing clause
> POSSIBLE VERBS: *ascribe; assign; attach; attribute; credit; impute; put down*

Once a complete grammar of cause and effect is available, all instances can be identified in a large corpus, and the frequency of instances in different registers can be calculated.

An example may be given from a less complex meaning-type than cause and effect (less complex in terms of the range of patterns used): the meaning 'abstain from an action' (see Francis et al 1996:619–620). Typical realisations of this meaning include:

> 'verb + -ing', with verbs such as *avoid* and *(not) bother*, as in *avoided doing the washing-up*;
> 'verb + to-infinitive', with verbs such as *(not) bother, fail, forget* and *refuse*, as in *failed to do the washing-up*;
> 'verb + about + -ing', with verbs such as *forget* and *(not) bother*, as in *forgot about doing the washing-up*;
> 'verb + from + noun or -ing', with verbs such as *abstain, desist, flinch, recoil, refrain* and *shrink*, as in *refrained from house-work/doing the washing-up*;
> 'verb + out of + noun or -ing', with verbs such as *drop, get* and *opt*, as in *opted out of doing the washing-up*.

Two corpora — a corpus of British spontaneous spoken English and a corpus of issues of the *Guardian* newspaper — have been compared with respect to the occurrence of each of these patterns with all their verbs (not just the ones listed above) with this meaning. The results suggest that:

i.   This meaning is expressed through these verbs and their patterns more frequently in the *Guardian* than in spoken English. In the Guardian corpus there are 436.4 instances per million words, taking all the patterns together. The comparable figure for the spoken corpus is 85.

ii. Overall, the patterns with prepositions are less frequent than those with non-finite clauses. The total frequency per million words over both corpora is 135.4 for patterns with prepositions and 386 for patterns with clauses. In both corpora, the patterns with a to-infinitive are more frequent than any other group.

iii. The patterns with prepositions are especially infrequent in spoken English. For example, the verbs with *from* occur a total of only 3.7 times per million words. Many of the target verbs are not found in those patterns at all in the spoken corpus. An exception to this general rule is the expression *GET out of*, which occurs 34.3 times per million words in the spoken corpus. In the Guardian corpus, most of the verb-pattern combinations are found. Some of them are infrequent, but the relatively large number of verbs pushes up the overall frequency. The verbs with *from*, for example, occur a total of 36.4 times per million words.

iv. These verb-pattern combinations are much more frequent in the Guardian than in the spoken corpus: '*avoid* + -ing'; '*decline* + to-infinitive'; '*fail* + to-infinitive'; '*refuse* + to-infinitive'; '*refrain* + *from* + n/ing'; '*opt* + *out of* + n/ing'.

v. These verb-pattern combinations are much more frequent in the spoken corpus than in the Guardian corpus: '*(not) bother* + -ing'; '*forget* + to-infinitive'; '*(not) bother* + *about* + n/ing'; '*get* + *out of* + n/ing'.

5. Conclusion

Pattern grammar is an approach to the description of English which prioritises the behaviour of individual lexical items as observed in an un-parsed corpus, and which consequently owes little to pre-corpus theories of grammar. Patterns are an important aspect of language for learners, particularly in the context of a lexical syllabus and of a consciousness-raising approach to grammar teaching.

Patterns are a significant aspect of the study of variation. Examples have been given in this paper of pattern differences between regional varieties and registers. More significantly, patterns are an essential component of Local Grammars, and can be used to quantify the occurrence and expression of particular meanings in different registers.

Notes

1. Concordance lines and examples are taken from the Bank of English corpus, currently standing at over 400 million words, and jointly owned by HarperCollins publishers and the University of Birmingham.

2. All examples appear to be from native speakers. Three examples occur in Australian newspapers, suggesting a possibility that the pattern may stem from a regional variety. The other examples come from books published in Britain (1), books published in the US (1), and a British tabloid newspaper (1).

3. 'Manually' here means that the researchers examined the concordance lines and collocational information for each word in turn, or for each pattern in turn. To this extent the search was computer-assisted, but was not automatic.

References

Allen, C. 1999. A local grammar of cause and effect. Unpublished MA dissertation, University of Birmingham.

Barnbrook, G. and Sinclair, J.M. 1995. "Parsing CoBUILD Entries". In *The Languages of Definition: The Formalization of Dictionary Definitions for Natural Language Processing*, J.M. Sinclair, M. Hoelter and C. Peters (eds), 13–58. Luxembourg: Office for Official Publications of the European Community.

Biber, D., Conrad, S. and Reppen, R. 1998. *Corpus Linguistics: Investigating Language Structure and Use*. Cambridge: CUP.

Biber, D., Johansson, S., Leech, G., Conrad, S. and Finegan, E. 1999. *Longman Grammar of Spoken and Written English*. London: Longman.

Francis, G., Hunston, S. and Manning, E. 1996. *Collins CoBUILD Grammar Patterns 1: Verbs*. London: HarperCollins.

Francis, G., Manning, E. and Hunston, S. 1997. *Verbs: Patterns and Practice*. London: HarperCollins.

Francis, G., Hunston, S. and Manning, E. 1998. *Collins CoBUILD Grammar Patterns 2: Nouns and Adjectives*. London: HarperCollins.

Hornby, A.S. 1954. *A Guide to Patterns and Usage in English*. London: OUP.

Hudson, R. 1984. *Word Grammar*. Oxford: Blackwell.

Hunston, S. and Francis, G. 1998. "Verbs observed: a corpus-driven pedagogic grammar". *Applied Linguistics* 19: 45–72.

Hunston, S. and Francis, G. 1999. *Pattern Grammar: A Corpus-driven Approach to the Lexical Grammar of English*. Amsterdam: Benjamins.

Hunston S. and Sinclair J.M. 2000. 'A local grammar of evaluation'. In Hunston S. and Thompson G. (eds.) *Evaluation in Text: Authorial Stance and the Construction of Discourse*, 75–101. Oxford: OUP.

Levin, B. 1993. *English Verb Classes and Alternations: A Preliminary Investigation*. Chicago: The University of Chicago Press.

Lewis, M. 1993. *The Lexical Approach: The State of ELT and a Way Forward.* Hove: LTP.

Long, M. H. and Crooks, G. 1992. "Three approaches to task-based syllabus design" *TESOL Quarterly* 26: 27–56.

Mason, O. and Hunston S. 2001. "The automatic recognition of verbs patterns: a feasibility study". Paper read at the COMPLEX conference, University of Birmingham, 2001.

Rudanko, J. 1996. *Prepositions and Complement Clauses: a Syntactic and Semantic Study of Verbs Governing Prepositions and Complement Clauses in Present-day English.* New York: State University of New York Press.

Sinclair, J. 1991. *Corpus Concordance Collocation.* Oxford: OUP.

Willis, D. 1990. *Lexical Syllabuses.* London: HarperCollins.

Willis D. and Willis J. 1996. "Consciousness-raising activities". In *Challenge and Change in Language Teaching,* J. Willis and D. Willis (eds), 63–76. Oxford: Heinemann.

PART II

Exploring dialect or register variation

CHAPTER 10

Syntactic features of Indian English

An examination of written Indian English

Chandrika K. Rogers (formerly Balasubramanian)
Northern Arizona University

1. Introduction

While there have been numerous studies identifying phonological aspects of Indian English, there have been few empirical studies on the syntax of Indian English.

The aim of this study is to analyze approximately 800,000 words of Indian English in 11 different registers (described below) for the patterns of occurrence of three syntactic features. The features examined include:

a. Stative verbs in the progressive
b. Patterns of occurrence of the present and past perfect
c. Prepositional verbs

The reason for choosing these particular syntactic features is the regularity and frequency with which they are identified in the literature as characteristic features of Indian English. A corpus-based approach has been adopted for this study, and a certain feature will be identified as characteristic of Indian English if it is found to differ consistently (judged by its frequency of occurrence) from British and American English. My main source of comparison of Indian English with British and American Englishes is Biber et al. (1999).

Researchers of Indian English (Hosali, 1991; Kachru, 1976) make the claim that the use of stative verbs in the progressive is a feature of Indian English. Hosali claims that "there are certain features of English usage which are widespread in India" (p. 65), and that the use of stative verbs in the progressive is one example. The illustration she provides is "Are you having a cold?" Kachru (1976) claims that the "be + ing" verb constructions in Indian English seem to "violate the selectional restriction applicable to such constructions in the native[1] varieties of English, where members of the sub-class of verbs such as *hear* and *see* do not occur in the progressive tenses" (p. 17). A possible reason for their occurrence in Indian English, Kachru explains, is that the progressive form is permissible in Hindi. One wonders, however, that without empirical support, how such a claim may be made of Indian English in general, where there are so many Indian languages (other than Hindi) influencing it. Also without empirical support, several other researchers (Bakshi, 1991; Lukmani, 1992; Verma, 1980) mention the same feature as being characteristic of Indian English. Some examples that appear in the literature include the following:

1. a.   I am not understanding the lesson
    b.   They were now knowing one another.

Schmied's work is notable and different from other work on Indian English because it is largely empirical. He conducted a study of the syntactic features of Indian English on the Kohlapur Corpus, an untagged written corpus of Indian English compiled in 1976. On the use of the progressive constructions in Indian English, he states: "To tackle the question of whether 'Indians' tend to overuse the progressive form, a broader retrieval form has been applied... And indeed, although we have taken into account a certain error margin, the construction's frequency in the Kohlapur corpus exceeds that in the LOB corpus by far" (p. 224). From Schmied's statement, however, it is not clear whether he is referring to all progressive forms, or to occurrences of stative verbs in the progressive only.

Use of the present or past perfect in place of the simple past tense is another feature that researchers often identify as characteristic of the English spoken in India. This is explained by Verma (1980), as follows: "In English, the present perfect establishes a link between the past and the present. It is not used in the environment of the simple past. In Indian English, this distinction is neutralized" (p. 80). Examples of this use (Shekar & Hegde, 1996; Verma, 1980) include the following:

2. a.   I have worked there in 1960
    b.   I have read this book yesterday.
    c.   I had been there last year.

With reference to the use of prepositions, researchers comment that Indian English contains "errors" of three types: prepositions are deleted where essential, prepositions are inserted where inessential, and "wrong" prepositions are used (Hosali, 1991; Bakshi, 1991). The following are examples of sentences to illustrate Indian patterns of preposition use:

3. a. She said she would neither resign nor bow <u>down</u> to their demands.
   b. The next course will commence <u>from</u> Monday, 8 January.

That speakers of Indian English do sometimes use features that differ from British or American English is not debated. What is being questioned, however, is whether any features are used consistently enough to warrant their being called characteristics of any register of Indian English. Sahgal and Agnihotri (1985) echo this opinion:

> Verma (1980) claims that certain syntactic patterns have become so well established in IndE that they get passed on from one generation to the next, acquiring the status of stable dialectal innovations. He also claims that these patterns differ systematically in a rule-governed way from the native varieties of English. The frequency with which educated Indians use these patterns in their actual behavior, is, however, an empirical question. (p.117)

It is this empirical question that this paper attempts to answer. The significance of this study is that it is one of the first empirical investigations of what grammatical features are actually used in Indian English, and the extent to which they occur across different registers.

2. The Corpus

A corpus was specifically compiled for this study because no complete and adequate corpus of Indian English exists for a syntactic study of this kind. The only exisiting comparable corpus, the Kohlapur Corpus, is untagged and now is over 30 years old.

The corpus used for this study currently has only a written component. A spoken component, however, is being added to it. Currently the corpus consists of approximately 800,000 words in 11 different registers. The different registers and the number of words in each are provided in Table 1 below. Gathering texts for 9 of the registers entailed downloading material from the Internet. Materials mainly included articles from Indian newspapers and magazines. Newspapers and magazines from different parts of India were chosen in order to get as wide a representation as possible of the different language backgrounds in India. In order to have a reasonable basis of comparison, I tried to include as many of the registers as possible from other well-known corpora such as the Brown Corpus, and the Kohlapur Corpus. Texts were chosen only if I was sure they were written by Indians in India. Once the texts were chosen, all names and any other forms of identification were removed from them, and they were then saved as text files. Appendix A describes each of the registers briefly.

Texts from the tenth register came from email messages written by speakers of Indian English both to me and other speakers of Indian English. The resulting sample includes a range of topics. All personal names and any other identifying factors were removed from the emails, and they were then saved as text files.

Texts for the eleventh register contributed about 96,000 words of Indian fiction in English to the corpus. This fiction section included 27 short stories originally written in 7 different languages. The short stories were all taken from the Journal of Indian Literature, published in India. The stories were photocopied from the journal and scanned into a computer. The scanned versions were then checked for accuracy, and compared to their hard copies to make necessary corrections. The versions on the computer were then also saved as text files. The list of short stories, their authors, and other information about the authors and their native languages is provided in Appendix A.

A limitation of the current collection of fiction is that all the short stories were originally written in an Indian language and subsequently translated into English either by the author or by a translator. It will be necessary to add fiction originally written in English[2] to the present collection, and to compare the results of the present study with the results obtained by conducting a similar analysis of fiction originally written in English. With the fiction added, the entire corpus is represented in Table 1 below.

With all registers, once the files were saved as text files, they were all tagged using Biber's tagger. All analysis was conducted on the tagged versions of the texts.

A limitation of the corpus as it currently exists is that the sub-corpora are of different sizes. In order to perform a thorough register analysis of the different registers of Indian English represented in the corpus, it would be beneficial to have sub-corpora of comparable sizes. However, it would be very difficult to greatly increase the size of certain sub-corpora like Emails. The corpus is currently being expanded to make the different sub-corpora as equal as possible. In any future studies on this corpus, any difference in size between sub-corpora that might still exist due to practical limitations will have to be noted.

Table 1. The Corpus

Register	Number of words
Regional News	135,254
Business	92,980
Entertainment	76,751
Features	93,619
Interviews	93,076
Letters to the Editor	10,513
Editorials	63,129
Sports	60,250
Travel	84,535
Email	8,009
Fiction	96,000

3. Methodology

To conduct the necessary analysis of the three syntactic features under investigation, two different computer programs were written. The first program was used to analyze the first two features, and the second, to analyze the third feature.

In order to determine the frequency of occurrence of stative verbs in the progressive, the first computer program generated KWIC concordance lines for all instances where the six stative verbs that were under investigation (*have, know, want, like, hear,* and *look*) occurred as finite progressive verbs. In order to determine the patterns of occurrence of the present and past perfect, the first computer program was then modified slightly so that it would generate KWIC lines for all occurrences of the past or present aspect of any verb.

In order to determine what prepositional verbs occurred in written Indian English, the second computer program generated a list of all the prepositional verbs that occurred in the texts being analyzed, and a frequency of each of the verbs.

4. Results and discussion

This section provides details on the methods of analysis and then the results obtained from the analysis of the three features in question.

4.1 Stative verbs in the progressive

The verbs examined for this study are the following: *have, know, want, like, hear,* and *look.* These verbs were chosen (from a long list of other stative verbs) for their frequency of occurrence in different registers (Biber et. al, 1999).

Biber et al. (1999) note that the traditional distinction between stative and dynamic verbs, namely that the progressive aspect "occurs freely" with dynamic verbs, while "stative verbs have been described as not occurring in the progressive" (p. 472), is not altogether true. Both classes of verbs may or may not occur in the progressive. Celce-Murcia also cautions that it is incorrect to say that stative verbs never occur in the progressive. Indeed, Celce-Murcia explains that "many stative verbs have nonstative counterparts that are active in meaning and that may occur with the progressive" (p. 72). The salient distinction between them is the frequency with which the two classes of verbs occur in the progressive. In British and American English, the verbs examined in this study occur in the progressive less than 2% of the time.

The computer program generated KWIC entries for all finite progressive occurrences of the verbs under examination. A thorough examination of the KWIC entries indicated that finite progressive occurrences were rare, as indicated in Table 2 below.

Table 2. Stative verbs in the Progressive

Verb	Finite progressive occurrences
Having	4
Knowing	1
Wanting	0
Liking	0
Hearing	1
Looking	2

Examples of sentences with these occurrences include the following:

4. a. "Are you hearing me, dearie?" (Fiction)
   b. She was looking like a new bride. (Fiction)
   c. She was looking so young and so beautiful. (Entertainment)
   d. They were all knowing one another very well. (Travel)
   e. The city was having a Nawabi time. (Travel)
   f. Few selected international carriers are also having their flights to the city.

Given their low occurrence in the progressive, the present analysis of written Indian English (including fiction, which contains a fair amount of dialog) therefore suggests that stative verbs do not occur in the progressive any more frequently than they do in British or American English. An analysis of spoken Indian English, might, however, reveal interesting differences.

4.2 Progressive form of non-stative verbs

Reading some of the short stories for pleasure spurred me to conduct a more detailed analysis of the fiction component of the corpus. I noticed that the progressive form seemed to occur more frequently than one might have expected. Given this observation, and Schmied's observation of the frequency of progressive use in Indian English, I was surprised to note the infrequency with which stative verbs occurred in the progressive, since I was expecting to find several. I therefore performed a preliminary analysis of all progressive verbs forms — whether stative verbs or not. This analysis revealed interesting facts. On studying the KWIC entries of all the progressive verb forms, and going back to the stories to examine the occurrences more carefully, I noticed that progressive verb forms seemed to be used in situations where you "normally" might find the simple present or simple past. These situations involved narration and they occurred in several different stories. While it would take a more thorough analysis to make more detailed conclusions, what I can conclude at this stage is that the frequency of occurrence of the progressive in general in Indian English is perhaps greater than the corresponding frequency in British or American English. These conclusions suggest the value of comparing the proportion of progressive verb forms with simple verb forms in Indian English and British and American English. It would also be interesting and necessary to conduct a discourse analysis and determine whether the more frequent use of the progressive performs a discourse function of some sort in different registers. Examples of sentences in which the progressive occurred instead of (possibly) the simple present or simple past include:

5. a. I say, "Dear wife, if I keep this paper aside now, will I have the opportunity of even glancing at it? Don't you know that this chariot called our family is moving on smoothly only because I am sweating all the time with the hard work?" (The Masquerade)

   b. How lonely I was, except the company of the laughter; it was tumbling like huge rocks from the Sethani's apartment and hitting my brain. (The Profession)

c.   Holding my head in my hand, I was sitting on my bed for a long
time. My mind was bubbling with laughter, but there was no smile
on my face. (The Profession)
d.   Those four were sitting with their eyes glued to the television screen.
(The News)
e.   With eyes closed, she was recalling something that happened six
weeks ago. (Pankajam's Dream)

4.3 Patterns of occurrence of the present and past perfect

Biber et al. (1999) note that in British and American English, the present perfect describes a situation that continues to exist up to the present time. Adverbials indicating duration are usually used with the present perfect to mark the beginning point of the duration, but not the end. Situations that no longer exist, or an event that took place at a particular time, therefore, do not use the present perfect, but the simple past.

Biber et al. explain that past perfect verb phrases often occur in dependent clauses, and often have accompanying adverbials of time. Based on their corpus analysis, Biber et al. claim that 70% of past perfect verb phrases have accompanying adverbials, or occur in dependent clauses. These patterns are true of both standard British and American English.

With both the present and past perfect, the patterns I looked for included any differences from the patterns described by Biber et al. The "Indian" present perfect would therefore include instances of the present perfect being used for situations that took place at a particular time, or to indicate situations that no longer exist. Similarly, the "Indian" past perfect would include instances of the past perfect being used in independent clauses and without accompanying adverbials of time.

The computer program generated KWIC entries for the past and present occurrences of any verb. Because of the large size of the output, every fifth sentence containing the present or past perfect was examined to ascertain if it contained any deviation from the patterns described by Biber et al. Sentences that did contain any deviation (which I called "Indian") were marked and then studied further. To determine whether the instances I counted as "Indian" were truly "Indian", after studying the KWIC entries, I went back to the texts and looked at a larger context to make sure that my initial analysis was correct. In some cases, I found that I had initially been wrong, and those sentences were eliminated from my final counts. Table 3 below provides total counts and normed

Table 3. Past and present perfect in Indian English

Register	Total Pres. Perf.	"Indian" Present Perf.	# in 100	Total Past Perf.	"Indian" Past Perf.	Count in 100
Reg. News	39	1	2.56	26	1	3.84
Business	81	2	2.46	16	0	0
Enter.	40	1	2.5	15	3	20
Sports	41	0	0	15	0	0
Travel	55	2	3.63	8	3	37.5
Editorials	81	3	3.70	26	1	3.84
Interviews	122	3	2.45	25	3	12
Features	55	1	1.81	11	0	0
Letters	35	2	5.71	4	1	25
Email	48	3	6.25	5	3	60
Fiction	262	7	2.67	359	9	2.51
Total	859	25	–	510	25	–

(per 100 instances) counts of "Indian" patterns of past and present perfect. Given the counts in the table above, a few points should be noted:

Out of the three "Indian" past perfect instances in the Travel section, two came from the same text by the same author.

Most of the occurrences of "Indian" past and present perfect in fiction occurred in direct speech. This is interesting in light of the fact that in fiction, direct speech represents spoken language.

Emails had a higher proportion of "Indian" patterns of past and present perfect relative to the other registers. This is also interesting given that Email is a register that approximates some registers of spoken language in its degree of informality.

What can be concluded from these results is that overall, the frequency of the "Indian" present and past perfect is not sufficient to say that any pattern is characteristic of written Indian English. More importantly, however, the results of the current study direct my next inquiry to a thorough analysis of spoken Indian English. Also, the present results point out the need to perform a thorough register analysis of Indian English and determine whether certain features are characteristic of certain registers.

Examples of "Indian" instances of the present and past perfect include the following sentences. Following the sentences within parentheses are the short stories the sentences came from.

6. a.   I had tried to get two tickets but could not. (Fiction)
   b.   I had thought you were sleeping since then. (Fiction)

    c.   He has married an hour after coming to the village. (Fiction)

    d.   Her mother has left some letters for her when she died due to complications at childbirth. (Entertainment)

    e.   He has found someone else a week after we broke up. (Email)

4.4 Prepositional verbs and patterns of preposition use

In order to determine if differences exist between British and American English and Indian English regarding patterns of preposition use, I decided to examine all prepositional verbs in my corpus that occur in the grammatical pattern NP + Verb + Preposition + NP. I restricted my analysis to this pattern for simplicity. The computer program for this analysis generated a list of all the prepositional verbs with their accompanying prepositions. From this list I was able to identify the most common (based on frequency of occurrence) prepositional verbs in Indian English and compare these with Biber et al.' s findings in British and American English. Several differences were found, and these are outlined below:

a.   A similarity is that in British and American English and in Indian English, the prepositional verbs *go for, come from, deal with, enter into,* and *ask for* are common.

b.   Prepositional verbs from the semantic domains of communication, existence, and mental prepositional verbs (such as *talk to, speak to, think about, depend on*) which are common in British and American English were rare in my corpus.

c.   The prepositions most commonly accompanying prepositional verbs were found to be different in British and American English and in Indian English. Biber et al. claim that in British and American English, *to* is the most common preposition occurring as part of a prepositional verb. In the Indian corpus, however, *to* was found to occur infrequently. The same was the case with the prepositions *in, on, of,* and *at.* The preposition *from,* however, is not found frequently in British and American English, but is very common in Indian English in all the registers examined.

d.   With specific reference to fiction, several prepositional verbs (*care for, come from, burst into, fall into, live with, laugh at,* and *look after*) occurred more than 40 times per million words of Indian fiction. All these verbs, however, are said to occur less than 10 times per million words of British or American fiction.

These preliminary results of this analysis of prepositional verbs indicate that with regard to prepositional verbs, or perhaps preposition use in general, there are marked differences between British and American English and Indian English. I did not, however, attempt to perform a register analysis (besides an initial examination of fiction), which would be a necessary next step to determine exactly where the differences lie. Further, a thorough analysis of spoken Indian English is also necessary.

5. Conclusion

Based on these results obtained from this study, therefore, we can conclude that there seem to be no differences between British and American English on the one hand, and *written* Indian English on the other, with regard to the patterns of occurrence of the present and past perfect. This conclusion can also be extended to the occurrence of stative verbs in the progressive. My preliminary analysis of Indian English fiction, however, has raised important questions about the frequency of occurrence of the progressive verb form in general (as opposed to the progressive form of stative verbs in particular). An analysis of the proportion of progressives to the proportion of simple tenses in Indian English is therefore a next logical step.

This study has also confirmed that with regard to prepositional verbs, and perhaps the use of prepositions in general, written Indian English does differ from British and American English. Further research is needed to confirm the present conclusion, and also to determine whether spoken Indian English shares these differences.

Appendix A

Registers in the Corpus

I tried to include as many of the registers included in the Kohlapur corpus as possible. Included in my corpus are the following registers: Regional News, Business, Email, Entertainment, Features, Interviews, Letters to the Editor, Editorials, Sports and Travel. These registers were chosen to have as much variety in the language represented as possible. Below is a brief description of each of the registers. Also outlined below are certain criteria for choosing or not choosing certain materials.

While I have tried to have more or less the same number of words in each register, this has been a bit difficult. The two registers that have markedly fewer words than the others are Letters to the Editor and Email. I hope to remedy this situation by continuing to add to the corpus.

Regional News

Included in this register are news items from all over India. Articles were chosen if they were written by Indians in India. Articles were not chosen if they were written by foreign correspondents to the newspapers. Further, even if the articles were identified as having been written by people in Pakistan, they were not chosen. This is because of my inability to recognize if the authors were Indian or Pakistani, and the only language included in this corpus is that produced by Indians.

Business

This section includes business news from all the newspapers and the magazine *India Today*. Business news ranged from news regarding the status of the Reserve Bank of India to the price of washing machines. Articles included in this section came from the business sections of the newspapers and magazines examined.

Entertainment

This is a large section containing mostly news from the film world in India. The section contains articles on films being produced, reviews of films already produced (which can be compared to fiction), and also any articles on any film personalities. The language tends to be more informal than that used in sections such as Regional News or Business.

Features

This is a section that contains articles both from magazines and newspapers. The articles are on diverse subjects, from child-bearing issues to gardening, from religion to tips on doing laundry. While a lot of these articles come from *Femina*, several newspapers (particularly the Sunday editions) do have sections labeled "Features", too.

Interviews

This is an interesting section providing the corpus with some spoken English (the transcribed version). The interviews come mainly from the Rediff collection, but several come from the film magazine, *Filmfare*. I made sure the interviewees and the interviewers were both Indian (mostly names I recognize) before selecting a particular interview to be a part of the corpus.

Letters to the editor

This section tends to contain more informal language than does a register like "Regional News." The letters are by Indians all over India to the editors of the various newspapers, and deal with various issues of relevance to the common person. If the letters were chosen from one of online-only publications, I made sure that the person writing the letter lived in India, and not anywhere abroad. As far as possible, all names were deleted.

Editorials

This section contains articles by the editors of the various newspapers examined. The nature of the writing is such that an issue is raised by the editor, followed by reactions or responses by other people, who know something about the issue. Once again, editorials were chosen only if the participants lived in India, and all names were deleted.

Sports

This section contained sports news from all the newspapers chosen. Once again, I made sure that the news items concerned sports events in India. Even if the article dealt with the performance of an Indian team abroad that article was not included. This is because I didn't want to include anything by a foreign correspondent.

Travel

This section includes travel information and information about restaurants and Indian food mainly from two online publications — the *Restaurant Guide* and the *India Travel Guide*. I made sure that the articles from both these online publications were by Indians who currently lived in India.

Email

This section contains personal email messages. This register was included because it makes an interesting connection between written and spoken language, and given the informality of the register, I am curious to see if it contains any features that a more formal register does not. In order to get as large a collection of email messages as possible, and messages on a wide variety of subjects, I requested friends and family to forward me their own messages. Any names present were deleted. While several of the friends and family the messages were collected from live in the US at the moment, they have lived here for less than a year.

Fiction

This section included approximately 96,000 words of Indian English fiction — short stories. All the stories appeared in a journal named "Indian Fiction," published in India. The authors of all the stories are Indians who live in India. Like Emails, fiction, too, makes an interesting addition to the current corpus, as it contains a lot of dialog. It therefore has some representation of spoken language, and it would be interesting to see if it contains any features that the more formal written registers do not. The table below provides details on the individual stories in this collection of fiction.

Name of story	Author	# of words	Original language	Translation by	Info on author/translator
Empty Handed	K. S. Duggal	1854	Punjabi	Author	Fiction writer in Urdu, Hindi, Punjabi, English
The Skeleton	Ram Sarup Anakhi	2162	Punjabi	Author	Punjabi fiction writer
I'm no Gaznavi	Gurbachan Bhullar	3023	Punjabi	Rana Nayar	Translator, teaches at Punjabi univ.
Sukritam	M. T. Vasudevan Nair	3714	Malayalam	V. Ravindran	Translator
Junk	Anand	5027	Malayalam	K. M. Sherrif	Translator, teaches at Narmada College

Text	Krishna Baldev Vaid	2171	Hindi	Author	Hindi novelist
The Golden Bracelet	Sriramana	5888	Telugu	Syamala Kallury	Translator
Pankajam's Dream	R. S. Sudarshanam	5280	Telugu	Author	Novelist & short story writer
The Masquerade	Madhuranthakam Narendra	5050	Telugu	Author	Short story writer
Mother	Uma Maheshwara Rao	2355	Telugu	C. L. L. Jayaprada	Translator, teaches at Andhra University
What is my Name?	P. Satyavathi	1758	Telugu	V. Vijayalakshmi	Translator
No Devotion, No Salvation	Ashapurna Devi	2500	Bengali	Bhaskar Roy Barman	Poet, writer, translator
The Transfer of Land	Amar Mitra	4229	Bengali	Dipendru Chakrabarti	Novelist & essayist
Sin	Asfar Ahmed	3680	Bengali	Bhaswati Chakravarty	English critic, translator
The Musician	S. Muknopadhyaya	6426	Bengali	Bhaswati Chakravarty	English critic, translator
Stain	Amiya B. Mazumdar	5090	Bengali	Asim Kumar Mukherjee	Translator, teaches at R. K. College
The Profession	Ismat Chughtai	4336	Urdu	Abul Farooque	Urdu short story writer
Sunlight on the Staircase	Ram Lall	5331	Urdu	M. Asaduddin	Writer, translator, teacher
Harambe	Joginder Paul	1570	Urdu	K. K. Khullar	Novelist, short story writer

Strange Faces	Jilani Bano	2566	Urdu	M. Asaduddin	Writer, translator, teacher
Shadowlines	Surinder Prakash	4512	Urdu	M. Asaduddin	Writer, translator, teacher
Vultures	Ali Imam Naqvi	1691	Urdu	M. Asaduddin	Writer, translator, teacher
The News	Salam Bin Razak	2216	Urdu	Author	Short story writer
Portrait	Sughra Mehdi	958	Urdu	Author	Novelist & short story writer
The Domestics of Teen Batti	Ali Imam Naqvi	2878	Urdu	M. Asaduddin	Writer, translator, teacher
The Golden Dream	Poornachandra Tejaswi	2834	Kannada	Bageshri	
Bail Saheba	Vivek Shanbhag		Kannada	Manu Chakravarty	
The Mediators	Shantinath Desai	6894	Kannada	Author	

Number of words from each of the Indian languages represented:

Hindi:	2,171
Urdu:	26,103
Bengali:	21,925
Punjabi:	7,039
Telugu:	20,331
Malayalam:	8,741
Kannada:	9,728
	96,038

Notes

1. Traditionally, the distinction between "native" and "non-native" was used to differentiate people who speak English as a first language (such as people from Britain and America, for

example) from people who do not. Thus, this distinction tended to exclude people from countries like India. However, this distinction has lost its popularity because it has become clear that it is extremely difficult to define what "non-native" is. For countries like India and Singapore today, it is difficult to draw boundaries between "native" and "non-native" because, as Graddol, Leith & Swann put it, "some (notionally) non-native speakers become familiar with English from an early age and use the language routinely" (p. 13). For detailed discussions on the native/non-native distinction, see D'Souza (1997), Crystal (1995), and Graddol, Leith, & Swann (1996).

2. Since this study was conducted, another study studying fiction originally written in English by Indians has also been done. The latter study analyzed the second set of Indian fiction for the same three features under examination in the present study. The latter study revealed that the original English fiction did not differ from the translated fiction in any substantial way with respect to the three grammatical features examined. This indicated that perhaps due to the fact that the translation was done by Indians, it did not effect the results.

References

Baskhi, R. N. 1991. Indian English. *English Today*, 7, 3: 43–46.

Biber, D., Johansson, S., Leech, G., Conrad, S., & Finegan, E. 1999. *Grammar of Spoken and Written English*. London: Longman.

Celce-Murcia, M. & D. Larsen-Freeman. 1983. *The Grammar Book: An ESL/EFL Teacher's Course*. Boston: Heinle and Heinle.

Crystal, D. 1995. *The Cambridge Encyclopedia of the English Language*. Cambridge: Cambridge University Press

D'Souza, J. 1997. Indian English: Some myths, some realities. *English World Wide, 18, 1*: 91–105.

Graddol, D., Leith, D., & Swann, J. 1996. *English: History, diversity and change*. London: Routeledge.

Hosali, P. 1991. Some Syntactic and Lexico-Semantic Features of an Indian Variant of English. *Central Institute of English and Foreign Languages Bulletin* 3, 1–2: 65–83.

Kachru, B. B. 1965. The Indianness in Indian English. *Word*, 21, 3. 391–410.

Kachru, B. B. 1983. *The Indianization of English: The English language in India*. Delhi: Oxford University Press.

Kachru, B. B. 1986. *The alchemy of English: The spread, functions and models of non-native Englishes*. Oxford: Pergamon Press

Kachru, B. B. 1976. *Indian English: A sociolinguistic profile of a transplanted language*. ERIC Document Reproduction Service No. ED132 854.

Schmied, J. 1994. Syntactic Style Variation in Indian English. In *Anglistentag 1993 Eichstatt: Proceedings*: 217–232.

Shekar, C., & M. N. Hegde. 1996. Cultural and linguistic diversity among Asian Indians: A case of Indian English. *Topics in Language Disorders,* 16, 4: 54–64.

Verma, S. K. 1980. Swadeshi English: Form and Function. *Indian Linguistics* 41, 2: 73–84.

CHAPTER 11

Variation in academic lectures
Interactivity and level of instruction

Eniko Csomay
San Diego State University

1. Background

Most studies investigating academic language have restricted their focus to written discourse (e.g., Biber, 1988, 1995; Conrad, 1996; Grabe, 1987; Grabe and Kaplan, 1997; Johns, 1998; Leki 1992; Swales, 1990). The majority of the comparatively few studies that have dealt with academic spoken language took a linguistic approach to the rhetorical, lexical, and topical analyses of academic lectures (Chaudron and Richards, 1986; DeCarrico and Nattinger, 1988; Dudley-Evans, 1994; Hansen, 1994; Nattinger and DeCarrico, 1992; Olsen and Huckin, 1990; Young, 1994). The impetus for these linguistic analyses has been to find out why second language learners may have listening comprehension difficulties with academic lectures (Waters, 1996).

Missing in these studies so far is a comprehensive linguistic description of academic lectures. That is, most of the research done has relied on limited data collected in experimental settings and from pre-arranged data-sources. What is needed to describe the linguistic characteristics of academic lectures is a quantitative, empirical investigation through naturalistic studies "that look at academic listening as it actually occurs in real rather than experimental settings" (Waters, 1996:26). Moreover, besides a linguistic description for register analysis, we need descriptions of the linguistic variation within lectures, for example, among lectures exhibiting "interactive vs. non-interactive styles, addressed to small or large groups; presented to undergraduates or post-graduates; technical or non-technical fields" (Flowerdew, 1994:296).

From the point of view of register analysis, lectures are especially interesting because they can be considered as a register at the interface of an oral/literate continuum[1]. While lectures are highly informational in purpose, as is academic prose, they are delivered under on-line production duress. These two situational features create a 'hybrid' register that could be positioned on a continuum between academic prose, having high informational load, and face-to-face conversation, exhibiting features of spoken discourse (Csomay, 2000).

An equally important point to emphasize is that academic lectures (see 2.2 below for definition of lectures) are not homogeneous. In fact, there are important differences among lectures in the extent to which they are interactive or informational. For example, lower division instructional classes (generally first and second year students) may have less dense information delivered than in upper division (generally third and fourth year students) or in graduate courses. At the same time, lecturers differ in their teaching styles: some lecturers involve their audience in a dialogue while others tend to deliver their lectures without engaging in verbal interaction with their audience (DeCarrico and Nattinger, 1988; Nattinger and DeCarrico, 1992). Considering these points of variability, and the fact that lectures exhibit characteristics of both academic prose and conversation, as discussed above, they are especially interesting from a theoretical point of view in terms of register variation study.

1.1   Outline of the present study

The aim of the present study is to investigate major patterns of variation within lectures focusing on level of instruction and interactivity (e.g., Does level of instruction impact the linguistic features of academic lectures? How does interactivity influence the linguistic feaures?). Adopting a corpus-based, quantitative approach to analyzing transcripts of naturally occurring academic lectures helps achieve this goal.

The following section describes the corpus and the methods of analysis. Based on Biber's (1988) study of variation across speech and writing, I identify 23 linguistic features associated with academic prose and conversation. These linguistic features are clustered into five parameters: (1) informational focus, (2) involved production, (3) explicit discourse or elaborated reference, (4) abstract style, and (5) on-line informational elaboration. These parameters serve the basis for the statistical analysis comparing the variation within lectures classified by degrees of interactivity (low, medium, high) and by level of instruction (lower division, upper division, graduate). Finally, I discuss the implications of the study and point to further research in this area.

2. Methodology

This section describes the design of the study and the analytical procedures. I used a corpus-based analysis, which required decisions about the corpus of texts, operational definitions of the text categories, and a careful selection of linguistic features for analysis.

2.1 Corpus

A total of 176 academic lectures were selected from the T2K-SWAL Corpus,[2] a 2.7 million word corpus of spoken and written academic discourse collected at four universities in the United States (Biber, et al., 2001). All lectures were audio-recorded with a tape-recorder placed at the front of the classroom near the lecturer. Following the recording, tapes were transcribed based on pre-defined transcribing conventions, and the texts were tagged for grammatical features using Biber's grammatical tagger.

Texts were classified according to two situational parameters: level of instruction (low division, upper division, graduate) and interactivity (low, medium, high). These categories are described further in 2.2. Table 1 shows the distribution of texts according to the two categories.

Table 1. Distribution of lectures and number of words based on level of instruction and interactivity

Level and Interactivity	Low level (1–200)		Upper level (3–400)		Graduate level (500-up)		Total	
	Number of Lectures	Number of Words	Number of Lectures	Number of Words	Number of Lectures	Number of Words	Number of Lectures	Number of Words
High Interactivity	15	108,108	23	144,232	23	220,324	61	472,664
Medium Interactivity	20	133,824	25	177,715	16	126,804	61	438,343
Low Interactivity	19	113,586	24	141,577	11	82,641	54	337,804
Total	54	355,518	72	463,524	50	429,769	176	**1,248,811**

2.2 Definitions

"Academic lectures" in the present study is a cover term for various kinds of teaching taking place in university classrooms. Two parameters — interactivity and level of instruction — were used to classify academic lectures and investigate linguistic variability within them.

The analysis was based on a preliminary categorization of interactivity taking the normed counts of turn-taking patterns in a lecture. Accordingly, lectures containing fewer than 10 turns per one thousand words were classified with low interactivity, those lectures having more than 25 turns per a thousand words were labeled as high interactivity lectures, and finally, the ones in between were put into a medium interactivity group. Although satisfactory as an operational definition for the present purposes, a more precise way to define interactivity is needed for future research. I return to this need in the conclusion.

The level of instruction was defined by the course number available for each lecture. Accordingly, 100 and 200 level courses (generally taken by first and second year students), were considered as lower division 300 and 400 level courses (generally taken by third and fourth year students), were considered upper division, and classes with course numbers indicating 500 and above, were classified as graduate level courses.

2.3 Feature groups and linguistic features selected for analysis

Biber's (1988) analysis of variation across speech and writing served as the basis for the linguistic investigation. Given the situational analysis outlined in the previous section, the most appropriate dimensions for academic lectures are those containing linguistic features relating to the informational load apparent in the academic context, and those reflecting the on-line situation and planned nature of academic lectures (Csomay, 2000). For the purposes of the present study, selected grammatical features in four dimensions (see below for details), especially relevant to academic lectures, are discussed in detail. In this study, the different linguistic groups are called 'feature groups' instead of dimensions for two reasons: (a) they are not a complete set of linguistic features as presented in Biber's 1988 & 1995 work, and (b) the linguistic features associated with the two groups in Dimension 1 are discussed separately. Accordingly, the five feature groups identified in the present study are: (1) informational focus, (2) involved production, (3) explicit discourse or elaborated reference, (4) abstract style, (5) on-line informational elaboration.

In Dimension 1, among other linguistic features Biber (1988, 1995) associated the high frequency of nouns, attributive adjectives, prepositions, and passive constructions "with communicative situations that require a high informational focus and provide ample opportunity for careful integration of information and precise lexical choice" (Biber, 1988:104). These grammatical features will comprise the first feature group in this study called 'informational focus'.

On the other extreme of the scale in Dimension 1, present tense, private verbs, *that-* deletions, contractions, demonstrative pronouns, first- and second-person pronouns, *be* as copula were the major features representing a "fragmented, generalized packaging of content with an affective, interpersonal focus" and "on-line production circumstances" (Biber, 1995:145). In this study, these features constitute the second feature group called 'involved production'.

In Dimension 3, called 'Situation-dependent versus elaborated reference', besides phrasal coordination, and pied-piping constructions such as *a car in which he sat,* two types of relative clauses showed elaborated reference: wh-relative in object and subject positions. These features together indicated "referentially explicit discourse" (Biber, 1995:156). They will make up the third feature group in this study, called 'explicit discourse'.

Abstract information, as in Dimension 5 (called 'Abstract versus non-abstract information') is represented by an array of conjuncts, agentless- and by-passives, past participial adverbial clauses, and past participial (passive) postnominal clauses. These passive constructions were characteristic of academic prose; more specifically, they were "especially prominent in the academic subregister of technical and engineering prose" (Biber, 1995:165). Three passive constructions (agentless- and by- passives and past participial (passive) postnominal clauses) are considered in the fourth feature group here, called 'abstract style'.

Finally, selected from Dimension 6 (called 'On-line informational elaboration marking stance'), the present study will contain the following grammatical features in the fifth feature group, called 'on-line elaboration': three types of dependent clauses (*that-* complement to verb including *that* deletion, *that-* complement to adjective, and *that-*relative and wh-relative in object positions), demonstratives (pronouns and determiners), existential *there.* Informational spoken registers (e.g., spontaneous, public and prepared speeches) showed the highest number of these features while other spoken registers (e.g., face-to-face conversations) were "unmarked" (Biber, 1995:166).

2.4 Analytical procedures

After the texts were run through a grammatical tagger, I developed Delphi Pascal computer programs to count and display the characteristic linguistic features in the present study. First, a program was developed to determine the degree of interactivity in the lectures. The second program was designed to do counts of all the linguistic features specified in the previous section (2.3). After analyzing these general patterns, a third program was developed to select and write out relevant excerpts from lectures.

2.5 Counts and statistical procedures

Lectures averaged between 6,000 and 10,000 words. All turn-taking and linguistic feature counts were normed to 1,000 words (total count of a given feature divided by the number of words in that lecture, multiplied by one thousand). This procedure compensates for differences in the length of lectures, which would otherwise provide unequal opportunity for the turn-taking patterns and linguistic features to occur.

To identify the statistically significant differences among lecture categories Factorial Analysis of Variance measures were used applying SPSS 9.0 statistical software. Further, to identify specific differences among levels (lower division, upper division, graduate), and among degrees of interactivity (low, medium, high), Tukey HSD post-hoc tests were computed.

3.   Interactivity and level of instruction

As outlined earlier, the primary goal of the present study is to investigate the major patterns of variation within lectures by focusing on level of instruction and interactivity. A two-way analysis of variance tests the significance of the two main effects — interactivity and level of instruction — as well as the interaction between these two variables as predictor variables for the combined scores of the various linguistic features in the five feature groups.

As Table 2 shows, four of the five feature groups showed statistically significant differences. In three feature groups the differences were related to the degree of interactivity while in one feature group, they were related to the level of instruction. On the other hand, no statistically significant differences were found in the way the grammatical features appear in the different levels of

Table 2. Two-way ANOVA results on the five feature groups

Feature Group	Source	SS	df	MS	F
Informational Focus	Level	2782.969	2	1391.485	1.135
	Interactivity	36005.895	2	18002.947	14.685**
	Level*Interactivity	4803.593	4	1200.898	.980
	Error	204738.99	167	1225.982	
Involved Production	Level	5517.884	2	2758.942	1.286
	Interactivity	76550.152	2	38275.076	17.834**
	Level*Interactivity	12385.528	4	3096.382	1.443
	Error	358403.25	167	2146.127	
Explicit Discourse	Level	3.464	2	1.732	.600
	Interactivity	1.484	2	.742	.257
	Level*Interactivity	10.567	4	2.647	.916
	Error	481.698	167	2.884	
Abstract style	Level	9.076	2	4.538	.542
	Interactivity	61.320	2	30.660	3.662*
	Level*Interactivity	17.173	4	4.293	.513
	Error	1398.097	167	8.372	
On-line Elaboration	Level	663.845	2	331.922	3.556*
	Interactivity	369.460	2	184.730	1.979
	Level*Interactivity	849.220	4	212.305	2.275
	Error	15586.539	167	93.333	

* $p < .05$; ** $p < .01$

instruction or in the varied interactivity patterns in one feature group called 'explicit discourse'.

More specifically, the turn-taking patterns had a statistically significant impact on the grammatical features associated with informational focus, involved production, and abstract style. The level of instruction had a significant impact on the linguistic features associated with on-line elaboration. In the following subsections, the three feature groups showing differences related to turn-taking patterns are discussed first, followed by the discussion of the feature group where the level of instruction had an impact.

3.1   Differences related to interactivity patterns and Informational focus

The scores for informational focus differ depending on the degree of interactivity in academic lectures. Low interactivity lower division and low interactivity graduate classes have the highest mean scores for informational focus while high interactivity classes have the lowest for this feature group in all three divisions. Further, the mean scores (Table 3 below) for classes in all three divisions with medium interactivity fall in between ones with high interactivity and low interactivity. The post hoc test results (Table 7, Appendix) show that the strongest difference (p < .01) in informational focus lies between high interactivity classes, and ones with low or medium interactivity.

Table 3. Mean scores for informational focus by degree of interactivity and level of instruction

Interactivity		Level of instruction			
		Lower division	Upper division	Graduate	Average
Low interactivity	Mean	332.27	326.94	333.24	330.81
	s	39.62	39.56	33.61	
Medium interactivity	Mean	310.74	325.95	303.11	313.26
	s	29.68	33.43	30.32	
High interactivity	Mean	288.85	301.53	291.65	294.01
	s	31.50	35.59	37.37	

Extracts 1 and 2 illustrate the linguistic differences in informational focus between high and low interactivity classes. Italicized bold words illustrate *nouns*, italicized underlined words illustrate *adjectives*, regular (non-italicized) bold words are **passive constructions** and regular (non-italicized) underlined words are examples of prepositions in the following extracts.

Informational focus — high interactivity lecture

> **Extract 1**
> 1: *We're gonna get there. Do you see what, what I, I wanna make this clear on how we did this first. It is clear right?*
> 2: *It has whole* **numbers** *that you're not in any* **trouble** *then you can put it in there.*
> 1: *That's right. And so here we have, and and of course, there's always some* **way**, in *the* **group** *who'll ask me, what if, you have nine point five, and so you say,*

*OK, I have uh, well, I'll just have to refine, my <u>true</u> **limits** <u>to</u> whatever **degree** <u>of</u>*
***precision** that I need. And I can do this, to infinity if I have to. And so, and then*
*we change. See one, just a little **bit**. [WOB]*
2: So you can fill it in however you want to?
*1: No. You have to follow these **directions**.*
*2: You just you can change them to **infinity**.*
1: And it's not, we can, not if we want to, we can if we have to.
2: Oh.

(Solus51)

Informational focus — low interactivity lecture

Extract 2
*1: So that's our our <u>final</u> **formula** and then this uh **VIJ**, this **Einstein coefficient**,*
*this <u>actual</u> **work** here was done <u>by</u> **Einstein** originally, a very clever **way of***
***research** [a few unclear syllables] the **way Einstein** presented this. Um, it's it's just*
*a **constant** and we'll come back to what that **number** is or what it should be <u>in</u> a*
*a **moment** or two. OK, so that's uh that's the (**reduction**) **rate** going up. Now once*
*the **electron** is in the uh <u>upper</u> **state** it can fall <u>back down</u>. The first we'll say is the*
*<u>spontaneous</u> **return** which is just left <u>on</u> its own the **electron** will probably decay*
*<u>back down to</u> a lower **state** and the **energy rate** <u>of</u> **return** <u>of</u> [incomplete word]*
***photons** <u>back into</u> the **beam** <u>from</u> this uh **drop** <u>down</u> will go <u>by</u> **MJ** which is the*
***number** <u>of</u> **particles** that are <u>in</u> the <u>upper</u> **state** J.. uh each uh **energy jump** of*
*course is (H. Nu) and uh we'll say that there's a **constant**...*

(Aslgg44)

The varying font styles show specific examples of the grammatical features
associated with this feature group. In the second extract (Extract 2) there are
clearly more nouns, prepositions, and attributive adjectives. A specific example
of a very dense informational package could be reflected for example, in
prepositional phrases with (multiple) 'of' constructions, or nouns premodified
by nouns (noun-noun) constructions. While both constructions can be found
in low interactivity lectures (Extract 2: "the energy rate of ... return of
[incomplete word] photons", or "actual work here was done by Einstein" or
"energy rate" or "energy jump") neither of them is present in high interactivity
lectures (Extract 1).

Classes with low interactivity have fewer turns than classes with high
interactivity. One speaker tends to hold the floor in these situations while, as
the extract shows, the text is denser in informational features. The focus in
these less interactive lectures seems to be information transmission, most
probably from the lecturer, while in more interactive classes knowledge may be

constructed in a different way. In high interactivity classes, where more turns are taken by participants, students may have more opportunity to be engaged in verbalizing their thinking while constantly evaluating and reformulating their understanding of the issues raised. Possible reasons for the difference in the degree of interactivity may relate to the lecturers' varying pedagogical purposes in the two types of lectures (interactive versus non-interactive). Other reasons for less interactive lectures displaying more informational focus may relate to varying classroom practices in different disciplinary areas, or to varying class-sizes.

3.2 Differences related to interactivity patterns and Involved production

Involved production features, as discussed in an earlier section (see 2.3), express direct interaction together with personal attitudes and feelings. More involved production is characterized by grammatical features related to more fragmented discourse, resembling a conversational style. The mean scores for each inter-activity and level are shown in Table 4 below. The post hoc test results (Table 7, Appendix) show that the difference in involved production lies between high interactivity classes, and ones with low or medium interactivity.

Table 4. Mean scores for involved production by degree of interactivity and level of instruction

Interactivity		Level of instruction			
		Lower division	Upper division	Graduate	Average
Low interactivity	Mean	295.02	307.45	292.40	298.29
	s	49.02	54.10	42.15	
Medium interactivity	Mean	318.43	301.04	332.61	317.36
	s	33.38	49.03	34.63	
High interactivity	Mean	354.11	336.82	361.72	350.88
	s	47.39	43.29	53.66	

Interestingly enough, this difference is the exact reverse of the ones reported in the previous section. That is, classes with high interactivity display the most of the grammatical features present in this feature group versus classes with low interactivity. Recalling the fact that both this feature group (involved production) and the one discussed earlier (informational focus) originate from Biber's

(1988, 1995) single dimension (Dimension 1), the results are not surprising. In fact, these results support the ones reported in Biber (1988, 1995) in that there is a strong relationship in the way these two sets of grammatical features in Dimension 1 relate to each other. The findings of the present study support the idea that lectures vary providing strong evidence for not only the variation in methods of delivery (degree of interactivity) but also the variation in which information is conveyed in these varied settings.

Discussing involved production in more detail it is noteworthy that both lower division and graduate lectures show a progressive change in the way the grammatical features are present. That is, low interactivity lectures exhibit the least number of grammatical features associated with this feature group followed by medium and then high interactivity lectures. In upper division classes, the distribution of the grammatical features associated with this feature group is noticeably different. While there is a large difference between classes with medium and high interactivity, almost no difference is present between classes with medium and low interactivity. What is more interesting is that in the upper level, classes with medium interactivity have fewer of the involved production features than those with low interactivity.

The three extracts below illustrate the differences in the way the grammatical features are present in the lectures with varying interactivity patterns. Extract 3 is from a high interactivity graduate class, Extract 4 is from a medium interactivity graduate class, and finally, Extract 6 is from a low interactivity graduate class. Bold italicized words show *present tense*, bold regular (non-italicized) words show **private verbs**, italicized underlined words with a single line show *first and second person singular pronouns*, italicized underlined words with a double line show *contractions*, capitalized non-italic words show DEMONSTRATIVE PRONOUNS, capitalized italic words show *BE AS COPULA*, and finally, words in parentheses denote [*that0*] deletion.

Graduate — high interactivity class

> **Extract 3**
> 2: How open **ARE** those two conferences to student papers? When they, **do** the call for papers **do** they
> 1: very. They never know *you're* a student.
> 2: Right.
> 1: And, um, *I* presented papers when *I* was getting my Master's degree. Um, and, if *you* **write** a good abstract, it, yeah.
> 2: And, if *you're* **presenting** a paper *you* **can** get funding, to go. But just to go for yourself *you* **don't**. But if *you* **can** BE on a panel, **present** a paper.

*1: Not much, but it **helps**. Yeah. Even if you **don't** go this year, it's something to keep in mind for next year, the call for papers usually **comes** out in, April or, March actually. And then it's due in, May or something really early, you **have to plan** almost a year ahead.*

2: yeah.

1: But

*2: But it's worth it. And you could prob-I mean, I **don't** know what this (dinners) ARE like but if it's like other things in the disciplines that I've been involved in, the papers that have been known in this class I **think** could probably be made into conference presentations. And THAT's a great (bee-line).*

2: What journal is the main triple A.L., (in)?

*1: You **don't** get a particular journal with your membership. Applied linguistics, is, somewhat affiliated with it. And then there's an international, applied linguistics, organizational journal. But there's no journal, there's not like a, triple A.L. journal. OK.*

Graduate — medium interactivity class

Extract 4

*1: There's this, end, but, it's just, I **guess**, along the way, it was like, it was just reaching a level of absurdity. You **can't**, you can't replicate, the experience of the other.*

*2: Ever. You **can't**. [4 sylls], but you can never, you can never experience it, so, I **guess** just taking it kind of, appreciation IS wrong, the wrong word but that.*

*1: Some criticism [3 sylls] from, came to from, a number of the African American natives and others as well, who felt that you **know** here you could go.*

*2: And sometimes that **has to be** good enough. You know. It has. You **can't** recreate it and you **don't** want to recreate it. And then I just kind of **want** to go back further and **say**, when they interviewed her, ...*

(Polgn203)

Graduate — low interactivity class

Extract 5

*1: ...the story **goes** like this, when Duke recruited McD., they presumably offered him something other than just a mere position because he had been at Harvard and nonetheless he left Harvard and went to Duke and according to this story the faculty remaining at Harvard made a joke about this. and the joke was that McD. thought he was getting a University and Duke thought they were getting a professor and they were both disappointed*

2: nasty

*1: I had anticipated uh having doctor K. here given that he **has** some connection with Duke so that he would give this story but such IS life. he **doesn't** he **isn't** here today. uh McD. was a very unusual psychologist uh he had been educated in*

England but spent most of his career in this country. he was very interested in strange kinds of behavior and in particular he was very interested in extra sensory perception and things such as that and continued that line of work.

(Pslgg116)

Noticeably, there is a gradual progress in the way the different grammatical features are used in the three different classes with varying turn-taking patterns. In the highly interactive class (Extract 3), most of the grammatical features associated with this feature group are present. That is, first and second person pronouns are exhibited in the text as much as present tense, contractions, or *be* as copula. In Extract 4, these features are also present, however, fewer in number. Finally, in Extract 5, not only hardly any of the grammatical features mentioned above are present, but the types are also limited to contractions, present tense, and *be* as copula.

Having a closer look at the extracts, a clear difference can be seen in the way the language varies in the classes with different interactivity patterns. Although these differences may be due to the number of turns taken in the given class, they may reflect other patterns apparent in classrooms, for example, varying themes, communicative goals, or diverse methods of delivery. While the communicative purpose may be the same in all three instances (information transmission), the theme and the way in which the information is conveyed vary. In Extract 3, the teacher and the students are discussing professional issues related to conference proceedings in a very informal, collegial manner. In Extract 4, the topic of discussion is also about professional matters. Evaluative comments are given on whether the research in question could be replicated. Here, the teacher prompts the issues to be discussed and the students evaluate these issues. Finally, the discussion in Extract 5 also centers around professional matters. A biographical story is told about a psychologist. Here, the teacher takes the floor, tells the story and provides the evaluative comments. The linguistic differences in these classes may be attributed to these other, non-linguistic factors present in the classrooms.

3.3 Differences related to interactivity patterns and Abstract style

The third feature group contains three types of passive constructions. As Biber (1995: 165) suggests, abstract style is "especially prominent in the academic sub-register of technical and engineering prose", and "all spoken registers are marked by the absence of this". Apparently, in academic lectures the degree of interactivity makes a difference in the way the grammatical features are present in this feature group. The mean scores for each division are in Table 5. The post hoc test results (Table 7, Appendix) show a statistically significant difference in abstract style between medium, and high interactivity classes, where medium interactivity classes have a higher number of the grammatical features associated with this feature group.

Extract 6 is taken from a medium interactivity lecture and displays a high number of passive constructions associated with abstract style. In the extract below, underlined are the <u>agentless passives</u> in this feature group, bold italicized are the ***post-nominal passives*** and finally non-italicized are the by-passives.

Abstract style — medium interactivity

Extract 6
1: So this is a very important replacement. It is a fiber but it<u>'s not going to be used</u> as a structural fiber. It<u>'s going to be used</u> as a replacement for (sphagnum) peat moss. OK? What about leaf-derived fibers? Let's get some examples of leaf-derived fibers. We'll talk about these and then we'll talk about how they<u>'re related</u> to one another. [clears throat] Any of you have any idea of a leaf-derived fiber?
2: M [two unclear syllables]
1: what's that?
2: M fiber? Like hemp?
1: hemp fiber, we're gonna talk about hemp fiber. Hemp <u>is</u> actually <u>derived</u> from stem. We're gonna get there. OK I'm just gonna put some names of some fibers up here. Then we'll look at how they<u>'re related</u>. Cos they all <u>are are</u> basically <u>derived</u> where or processed in in in quite the same way. Leaf-derived fibers. Has anybody ever heard of this? Sisal? OK? Not talking about the guy who just died. OK. Like Sisal [sic] and Ebert? Thumbs up, it

(Bolui142)

The extract above (Extract 6) displays a few of the passive constructions in question. It is possible that some major disciplinary areas express the topic of discussion differently from others. The text extract above is from a Botany lecture in an upper division class with medium interactivity. Further examples from various disciplinary areas may show a variation in the way this feature group is represented. Alternatively, the reason for a high number of linguistic features associated with abstract style can be explained by the possible, constant repetitions occurring in class while the teacher explains or clarifies a concept. This happens to be the case in Extract 3 (e.g., they are related, they are derived, it's going to be used). Although insightful as it is, the frequency counts in this study do not exclude the possibility of lexical repetitions. Hence, the counts are

Table 5. Mean scores for abstract style by degree of interactivity and level of instruction

Interactivity		Level of instruction			
		Lower division	Upper division	Graduate	Average
Low interactivity	Mean	7.56	7.10	6.93	7.19
	s	2.17	3.11	3.96	
Medium interactivity	Mean	7.67	8.29	7.32	7.76
	s	3.33	2.89	2.33	
High interactivity	Mean	5.71	6.83	6.46	6.33
	s	2.65	3.40	1.97	

equally high if one lexical item is repeated several times or many different lexical items of the same grammatical type are present in texts. Alternatively, a lexical distribution plot, which I will return to in the conclusion, could overcome this problem.

3.4 Differences related to level of instruction and On-line elaboration

As noted in Section 2.1.3 of the paper, the group of grammatical features associated with this parameter is most common in registers focusing on information while "produced under real-time constraints" (Biber, 1995: 166) such as spontaneous and prepared speeches, or public conversations. Instead of variation depending on turn-taking patterns, level of instruction relates to this feature group. Table 6 displays the mean scores for on-line elaboration features. Post hoc test results indicate a statistically significant difference between undergraduate and graduate classes in the way the grammatical features are present in this feature group.

Extracts 7 and 8 are from high interactivity undergraduate class sessions. All grammatical features underlined constitute the feature group in discussion. In the extracts below, the following notations are used: *that* verb complement, **demonstrative determiner**, *demonstrative pronoun*, existential 'there', wh- or that- relative object position, **that adjective complement**.

Lower division — high interactivity

> **Extract 7**
> 1: *let's take I'm going to let me [unclear word] college graduates and non-college graduates. let's take people who make more than fifty thousand a year. [W. O. B.]*

Table 6. Mean scores for on-line elaboration by degree of interactivity and level of instruction

Interactivity		Level of instruction		
		Lower division	Upper division	Graduate
Low interactivity	Mean	45.07	50.24	47.26
	s	11.99	9.57	6.56
Medium interactivity	Mean	45.63	47.42	55.09
	s	6.71	8.41	12.86
High interactivity	Mean	51.55	47.63	54.58
	s	8.02	6.92	12.34
Average	Mean	47.41	48.43	52.31

and let's say that uh thirty-eight percent of college graduates make more than fifty thousand a year. and of people who are not college graduates let's say that twenty-two percent make more than fifty thousand a year. again, then between college graduates and making more than fifty thousand dollars a year there is a positive correlation. why? because percentage wise, more college graduates than non-college graduates belong to this group. [unclear words] notice I'm not comparing college graduates with each other, I'm not comparing this thirty-eight with the other sixty-two percent, so it's going to have positive correlation. this doesn't have to be more than fifty percent. it just has to be higher than people who don't belong to this group or things that don't belong to this group or (whatever). OK? if that's positive correlation what would negative correlation be? it would be the opposite. it's where this number is smaller than this number.

(Humplleldhg119)

Upper division — high interactivity

Extract 8
2: share cropping?
*1: share cropping, no. **That's** a different kind of economic arrangement.*
2: building homes for guests.
1: OK. [W. O. B.] What guests, [one unclear syllable] add what, for what purpose?
2: [three unclear syllables]
*1: one of the cooperative efforts of **this this** (saroan) is to build [incomplete word] temporary shelters, they're used to house guests that are attending funerals. What else? Also along the lines of things that are done at a funeral. … What needs*

to be done at a funeral? a (Tiraga) funeral? …
2: there's lots of cooking.
1: cooking. all the labor associated with the funeral activities is performed by a (saroan). The (saroan) of the deceased. [W. O. B.] And then what other cooperative effort, economically [incomplete word] economical effort is done by the work group? Which I've already mentioned in part. What are they cooperating with, one of the other, (with) respect to?
2: [unclear words] of the meat?

(Anlui 123)

Extract 9, taken from a high interactivity graduate class, demonstrates a radically different pattern.

Graduate level — high interactivity

Extract 9

*2: Even getting, uh I guess there were, I-I-I would agree with that, I saw **that** too but, I think [thatØ] it's just that you're at such a p- we're at such a point now where you're just completely bombarded and and it just doesn't, you know before, remember the big clanky old answering machines and stuff, and um, we just thought that at this point, I don't think that the phone really commands as much attention as it used to because of telemarketing, you know all kinds of things.*
1: Mhm.
2: [4 unclear syllables] on the phone all day.
*2: Yeah but I think [thatØ] if you think of it in terms of the cell phone, I mean [thatØ] I- I sort of agree that **this** may be written at an earlier time but, you put this phone in context of cell phones, I think [thatØ] it's just as applicable. I mean [thatØ] you [1 unclear syllable] down the highway, like you said [thatØ] in Europe all the time but, I go to meetings, I drive down the highway I see people with cell phones all the time.*

(Mglug76)

Contrasting Extracts 7, 8 and 9 illustrates the striking difference between highly interactive classes from undergraduate and graduate levels. Although all three classes are highly interactive (based on the turn-taking patterns), there is a striking difference in the way the grammatical features associated with on-line production are used. In the extract of the lower division class (Extract 7), there are more demonstrative determiners used than in the other two instances. Determiners used in this extract denote anaphoric reference, i.e., reference to the immediate context, and reflect the singular nouns used following the determiners. Although there are demonstratives used in the graduate lecture

(Extract 9), they are mainly demonstrative pronouns rather than demonstrative determiners, denoting a different type of discourse. Demonstrative pronouns characterize conversations while a demonstrative determiner denotes singular nouns following them.

Even more striking is the high number of verbs taking *that* complement clauses in the graduate class versus in the undergraduate class. As can be seen in Extract 9, they are extensively used in the graduate classes. The most commonly used verbs in spoken registers with *that* deletion are also the ones that mark stance. Whether being able to take and state your stance in graduate classes is due to generally smaller class-sizes of this division remains an area to investigate further. At the same time, the difference in language use may relate to a diverse atmosphere triggered by power relations between teacher and student in undergraduate versus graduate divisions. Students in the graduate classes may experience a more collegial atmosphere. Alternatively, pedagogical goals and approaches to transmitting information may differ in the two settings. This may be reflected in the way students may be exposed to different types of questions, triggering more or less elaborate responses. The difference in language use, in fact, seems to support this claim.

The extract from a lower division class shows the way the teacher talks. While explaining some concept to the students, the teacher asks some (rhetorical) questions that s/he immediately gives the answer to without waiting for the students to work out the answers. In contrast, the student is talking in the graduate class (Extract 9), hence using the grammatical structures mentioned above. The prompt to which the student is responding in the graduate business management class is "How did you like the poem?". Through this question, the students are suggested to give an opinion, an evaluation of the poem read. In contrast, the prompts in the upper division class are, "What needs to be done?", and "What guests, add what for what purpose?". The questions posed in the upper division class require phrasal or simple clause answers whereas the question posed in the graduate class seems to trigger careful thought expressed as a more elaborated answer. The two types of prompts seem to generate qualitatively different answers reflecting contrasting attitudes to displaying knowledge.

From the point of view of the quality of the "discussion", the lower division class seems to be very similar to the upper division class. The answer in the upper division class simply responds to a display question, generating a pseudo-interactional pattern, while in the graduate class, a genuine discussion seems to be present. In the latter case, a genuine answer is expected of the student expressing his/her attitudes, feelings, and stance towards the topic of discussion.

Further investigation of the verbs taking *that* complement clauses may indicate further diversity between the two levels, suggesting ways discourse varies in the two settings, and shedding light on the nature of the differences in the discourse between undergraduate and graduate classes.

4. Conclusion

In sum, both degree of interactivity and level of instruction have an impact on the linguistic features present in lectures. Three of the feature groups are affected by interactivity (informational focus, involved production, and abstract style). On the other hand, level of instruction has an impact on the way grammatical features are present in on-line production circumstances.

The way the different feature groups cluster indicates that (a) academic lectures constitute a register that, although planned and informational in purpose, is delivered under time-constraints and in a spoken mode (Csomay, 2000), and (b) there is a variation in the way the discourse is patterned in classes of different levels. Low interactive classes reflect features of academic prose, hence, the informational focus tends to be highest in these classes. Highly interactive classes resemble oral discourse most in terms of their involvement. Lectures classified with high interactivity differ significantly from classes with medium interactivity. Graduate classes show the highest number of grammatical features characterizing on-line production circumstances, characterizing discourse with an informational focus delivered under on-line production circumstances.

These results suggest that the way classes are held on this level may be very different from the way the classes are held in the graduate level. One explanation may relate to the way displaying knowledge is required through phrasal and single clausal responses in undergraduate classes versus a more reflective approach on graduate levels.

5. Implications and further research

The present study was carried out to investigate major patterns of variation within lectures by focusing on level of instruction and interactivity. Patterns showed that low interactivity lectures exhibited more informational features while high interactivity lectures had more conversation-like features. Compared to other levels, graduate lectures exhibited the most frequent use of the linguistic features associated with on-line elaboration marking stance. This finding suggests distinct types of interaction between the two divisions. The question-answer patterns, for example, indicated a qualitatively different discourse in these two settings, where the diversity is reflected in the verbs taking *that* complement clauses that is associated with on-line production circumstances marking stance. The difference in interaction between the two levels may be due to smaller class-sizes, varying pedagogical goals, a difference in power relations, or a more collegial atmosphere in the graduate classes.

Given the findings of the present study, various areas need further exploration. First, as indicated earlier, there is a need for a more empirical measure of interactivity. In the present study, the frequency of turn-taking was considered; whether taken by the teacher or the student was not considered. Further, one-word feedback utterances or backchanneling were also counted as turns. I am currently developing a computer program to count the number of turns as well as the turn-length for each turn. The means and standard deviations of turn-length for each lecture will be computed. These measures are both important for defining interactivity. First, lectures with a lower mean turn-length are more interactive than the ones with longer average turns. In addition, for a given mean turn-length, the larger standard deviations show less interactivity, reflecting the situation where some turns are very long while others are very short (i.e., minimal responses).[3]

Second, additional grammatical and lexical features need to be examined for more refined analyses of the various feature groups. Further exploration of the frequency and distribution of lexical items could also shed light on the different ways lectures are patterned in terms of their vocabulary.

Third, the non-linguistic characteristics of academic lectures such as the perceived purpose of lectures need to be investigated in greater detail. This analysis could give insights as to why particular lectures or particular levels of instruction are more or less interactive in nature, and how those differences correspond to systematic patterns of linguistic differences represented by the various grammatical and lexical features present in them.

Appendix

Table 7. Tukey HSD scores (mean difference) by degree of interactivity

Feature groups		Degree of interactivity	
		Medium	High
Informational focus	Low	15.68*	35.36**
	Medium	—	19.67**
Involved production	Low	- 15.80	- 50.26**
	Medium	—	- 34.45**
Abstract information	Low	- .58	.81
	Medium	—	1.39*

$*$ p < .05; $**$ p < .01

Notes

1. In this study 'oral' refers to stereotypical speaking such as conversation, and 'literate' refers to stereotypical writing as in academic prose (Biber, 1988, 1995).

2. I would like to thank the Educational and Testing Services (ETS) for the permission to use the corpus for research purposes.

3. For example, two lectures with identical turn-taking patterns (e.g., five turns each) can display varying turn-length measures (number of words in each turn).

	Turn-length (number of words) for each turn (5 turns)	Total	Mean	Standard Deviation
Lecture 1	2, 140, 2, 3, 3	150	30	61.49
Lecture 2	30, 30, 30, 30, 30	150	30	0

References

Biber, D. 1988. *Variation across Speech and Writing.* New York: Cambridge University Press.
Biber, D. 1995. *Dimensions of Register Variation.* New York: Cambridge University Press.

Biber, D., S. Johansson, G. Leech, S. Conrad, E. Finegan. 1999. *Longman Grammar of Spoken and Written English*. New York: Longman.

Biber, D., R. Reppen, V.Clark, J. Walter. (2001). Representing spoken language in university settings: The design and construction of the spoken component of the T2K-SWAL Corpus. In R.Simpson and J.Swales (eds.) *Corpus Linguistics in North America*. pp. 48–57. Ann Arbor MI: University of Michigan Press.

Chaudron, C. and J.C. Richards. 1986. The effect of discourse markers on the comprehension of lectures. *Applied Linguistics* 7/2:113–127.

Conrad, S. 1996. Academic discourse in two disciplines: professional writing and student development in biology and history. Unpublished Doctoral Dissertation: Northern Arizona University.

Csomay, E. 2000. Academic lectures: An interface of an oral/literate continuum. *NovELTy*, 7/3: 30–47.

DeCarrico, J., and J.R. Nattinger. 1988. Lexical phrases for the comprehension of academic lectures. *ESP Journal*, 7:91–102.

Dudley-Evans, T. 1994. Variations in the discourse patterns favored by different disciplines and their pedagogical implications. In J. Flowerdew (ed.) *Academic Listening: Research Perspectives*. pp. 146–158. New York: Cambridge University Press.

Flowerdew, J. 1994. *Academic Listening: Research Perspectives*. New York: Cambridge University Press.

Grabe, W. 1987. Contrastive rhetoric and text-type research. In U. Connor & R.B. Kaplan (eds.) *Writing across Languages: Analysis of L2 Texts*. pp. 115–138Reading, M.A.: Addison-Wesley Publishing Co.

Grabe, W. and R.B. Kaplan. 1996. *The Theory and Practice of Writing*. New York: Longman.

Hansen, C. 1994. Topic identification in lecture discourse. In J. Flowerdew (ed.) *Academic Listening: Research Perspectives*. pp. 131–145. New York: Cambridge University Press.

Johns, A. 1997. *Text, Role, and Context: Developing Academic Literacies*. New York: Cambridge University Press.

Leki, I. 1991. Twenty-five years of contrastive rhetoric: Text analysis and writing pedagogies. *TESOL Quarterly* 25:123–43.

Nattinger, J.R. and J. DeCarrico. 1992. *Lexical Phrases*. New York: Cambridge University Press.

Olsen, L.A. and T.N. Huckin. 1990. Point-driven understanding in engineering lecture comprehension. *ESP Journal*, 9/1:33–47.

Ruetten, M.K. 1986. *Comprehending Academic Lectures*. New York: Macmillan.

Swales, J. 1990. *Genre Analysis*. New York: Cambridge University Press.

Waters, A. 1996. *A Review of Research into Needs in English for Academic Purposes of Relevance to the North American Higher Education Context* [TOEFL Monograph Series MS-6]. Princeton, NJ: Educational Testing Service.

Young, L. 1994. University lectures — macro-structure and micro-features. In J. Flowerdew (ed.) *Academic Listening: Research Perspectives*. pp. 159–176. New York: Cambridge University Press.

Young, L. and B. Fitzgerald. 1982. *Listening and Learning: Lectures*. Rowley, MA: Newbury House.

PART III

Exploring historical variation

CHAPTER 12

The textual resolution of structural ambiguity in eighteenth-century English

A corpus linguistic study of patterns of negation

Susan M. Fitzmaurice
Northern Arizona University

1. Introduction: a corpus of eighteenth-century English

This paper examines a language variety in which two grammatical systems appear to coexist. I am interested in how speakers construct negative infinitive clauses in the context of the co-existence of two historical systems for the formation of negative clauses. Our case involves the grammatical practice of English speakers in the one hundred or so years between 1660 and 1760, a period in which the role of auxiliary verb *do* as pivotal in the construction of interrogatives and negatives was gradually being regularized. The question for investigation in this paper is whether the language of early eighteenth-century speakers suggests the presence of ambiguity caused by the co-existence of phrasal and clausal negation systems, and if so, whether these writers exploit apparent structural opportunities for ambiguity in the expression of negation (negatives with and without *do*) in order to create unambiguous negative constructions. The recent rise in present-day American English in the use of constructions such as negative split infinitives alongside infinitives negated in the main clause raises the question of whether constructions such as the split negative infinitive were used by speakers for the unmistakable expression of negation. The variety under investigation is represented by the personal writing of people who lived and wrote in late seventeenth and early eighteenth century London. The sample used for the present study is part of a larger corpus designed to provide a basis for the investigation of the linguistic influence of a highly prestigious network of men led by Joseph Addison on the construction of the standard modern English that is formalized in the prescriptive grammars of the second half of the eighteenth century. The corpus consists of sizeable samples (about 40,000 words per genre) of the personal letters, essays, fiction and drama written by Addison and his cohort, as well as figures who were peripheral to this group and figures who were complete outsiders though they were contemporaries of one or more members of the group. The corpus includes both women and men in order to afford the examination of sex differences in language in a range of registers practiced at the time. Every attempt has been made to include examples of every genre or style produced by a writer to facilitate the study of idiolect — the extent to which a writer's individual style shows up across registers — and to allow the in-depth study of registers that are part of the literary and linguistic practice of the period. Thus the writing of Matthew Prior, diplomat and poet, includes satirical dialogues — a highly popular form of philosophical discourse in the seventeenth century — in addition to more usual registers represented by letters and essays. Some figures have very little variety in their writing; Sarah Churchill, Duchess of Marlborough, is represented by her letters only while Lady Mary Wortley Montagu's writing is register-rich, including letters, essays, drama, and fiction. By including in the corpus the writing of figures peripheral to and outside the central Addison network, it is possible to compare the writing of the central group with that of people not associated with them, and to assess the extent to which the corpus as a whole represents a cluster of idiolects rather than a homogeneous and continuous variety. The sample searched for the present study consists of almost 500,000 words of prose. The prose belongs to a single genre — the private letters of a central figure in the publication of the *Spectator* periodical, Joseph Addison, and members of his circle. The letters are all from attested correspondences. Some were transcribed from existing edited collections while others were transcribed from manuscript sources.[1] The letters of central figures in the network were readily available in good edited collections — the letters of Alexander Pope, Jonathan Swift, Richard Steele, Joseph Addison and Lady Mary Wortley Montagu have been the subject of editorial interest since their own lifetimes. Letters of figures just as central to the network but whose literary work received less attention in the twentieth century — poets George Stepney and Matthew Prior — exist only in manuscript. Included in the sample are the letters of figures more peripheral to the circle, like John Dryden (peripheral because he died in 1700) and Daniel Defoe (who had no connection to what we might call the inner circle dominated by Addison and Steele).[2] In addition, I have included the letters of complete outsiders for the purposes of comparison; poet and playwright Aphra Behn was known to Dryden but died in 1688 before most of the circle reached maturity. Sarah Churchill, Duchess of Marlborough, although a contemporary of many of the key figures, was not connected to any of them as far as I am aware.[3] The letters selected for study were written over a 100-year period, between 1650–1762. Table 1 lists the writers, their dates of birth and death, and the number of words collected for this study. The birthdates of the writers place them into three time zones or generations, a sizeable central generation that clusters around Addison, and two smaller, peripheral generations on either side. Thus Dryden and Behn, both born before 1650, belong to the first time zone, and Pope and Lady Mary Wortley Montagu, both born in the late 1680s, occupy the third zone. Addison and his cohort, all born in the 1660s and 1670s, inhabit the central time zone.

Table 1. The Sample Corpus

Name	Dates	Text length (words)
Dryden, John	1631–1700	23,422
Behn, Aphra	1640–1688	16,459
Stepney, George	1663–1707	20,103
Defoe, Daniel	1660–1731	45,166
Churchill, Sarah	1660–1744	50,776
Prior, Matthew	1664–1721	20,903
Swift, Jonathan	1667–1745	47,924
Congreve, William	1670–1729	29,733
Wortley, Edward	1672–1761	25,428
Addison, Joseph	1672–1719	52,472
Steele, Richard	1672–1729	47,142
Pope, Alexander	1688–1744	41,666
Montagu, Lady Mary Wortley	1689–1762	41,121
Range	1631–1762	462,315 words

2.   Background to the study

2.1   The Context: Present-day American English

I have been studying the role of the infinitive marker as part of the continuing grammaticalization of semi-auxiliaries in present-day American English such as *have to*. In the course of conducting this research, I have noticed that split infinitives provide an interesting example of the way in which the infinitive marker *to* could be isolated from its verb (Fischer, 2000, Fitzmaurice, 2000a). It has become clear that infinitives split by negatives are appearing in a range of spoken contexts in American English. The utterances in (1), transcribed from recent television broadcasts, illustrate one such context (Fitzmaurice, 2000b):

(1) a. We will send enough troops to not let Macedonia shut down its borders. (William Cohen, NBC Today, April 5, 1999)
    b. You have to learn to not let it start. ('The Puzzle Place', PBS TV, March 16,1999)

(2) a. We will send enough troops not to let Macedonia shut down its borders
    b. You have to learn not to let it start

In the attested utterances in (1), the placement of *not* after the infinitive marker *to* directly adjacent to the verb that falls within its scope results in an emphatic effect. The source of this effect is arguably the purposive force invested in the infinitive marker as it is split from the main verb by *not*. The alternative and much more usual construction of negative infinitives is illustrated by the (unattested) examples in (2). Because the anchor of the modern English verbal system is the auxiliary, and because the auxiliary is central to the construction of sentence forms like negatives and interrogatives, the variability in the placement of *not* in negative infinitives does not result in a change of meaning. However, in a system in which the main verb rather than an auxiliary might be used to construct a negative sentence, and which thus allows negation to be expressed phrasally (and locally) rather than clausally (and globally), it is possible for the placement of *not* to give rise to ambiguity of reference.

Given that the construction of negative infinitives with *to* preceding *not* and the verb being negated in modern English results in the impression of the emphatic, unmistakable expression of negation, it is tempting to consider whether this split negative infinitive pattern has ever been used as a means to avoid ambiguity of scope in historical varieties in which mixed systems such as the one mentioned were productive. Work on the history of infinitive *to* (Fischer (1997, 2000), Van Gelderen (1998)) has examined the occurrence in earlier stages of English, particularly Middle English, of this kind of negative split infinitive, but this work has not examined the discourse function of or pragmatic motivation for this construction. In addition, the question of the continuity or otherwise of the construction in English has not been considered in any detail (though see Fischer, 1992; and Rissanen 1999 for brief comment). This study therefore addresses the question of whether, and if so, to what extent, the *to not V* pattern is attested in earlier periods in the history of the English language. Our candidate period for this investigation is the late seventeenth and early eighteenth centuries.

2.2 Historical background: Negation in the seventeenth and eighteenth centuries

In late seventeenth and early eighteenth-century British English, it was possible to construct negative declaratives in two ways (Tieken-Boon van Ostade 1987). An older system of phrasal negation, in which the negator's scope extended only to the lexical category immediately adjacent to it (Ellegard 1953), was gradually receding in favor of a system of clausal negation, in which the negator's scope extended across the domain of the clause, aided by the anchor of a key structural category, the auxiliary (Rissanen 1999, Denison 1993). More specifically the recessive combination of finite verb plus adjacent *not* (as in (3b) gradually lost ground to the regularizing combination of operator (modal, *have* or *be* auxiliary) and *not* (3a):

(3) a. ... they <u>do not</u> know that they are a band of prostitute pensioners gapeing and (those that can talk) prateing for better Translations. (Lady Mary Wortley Montagu, An Expedient to put a stop to the spreading Vice of Corruption [c 1737])

   b. They <u>embellish not</u> the heart to make it worth the god; their whole care is outward, and transferred to the person. (Mary Manley, *Atalantis*, 1719).

In (3a), *not* is anchored by its attachment to dummy auxiliary *do* with the result that it has scope not only over the verb *know*, but over the entire complement of the verb. By contrast, in (3b), *not* has scope only over the verb it follows, namely *embellish*. The effect of these different rules is basically the same: both sentences are negative. There may not appear to be any practical or communicative consequences of the difference between the two systems. However, the negation of infinitive verb complements requires that the negator be understood to have scope over the infinitive verb complement, rather than the matrix verb. Consider (4a) as a case in which the reader may not be able to decide immediately whether *not* negates the matrix verb *stayed* (as in 4a[i]) or whether it negates the infinitive complement governed by *stayed* (as in 4a[ii]):

(4) a. Leonora <u>stayed not to make</u> him any reply, only tipped him upon the arm, and bid him follow her at a convenient distance to avoid

observation (William Congreve, *Incognita*, 1694).

4a^i =Leonora did not stay [to make him any reply]. = V not [to V]

4a^{ii} =Leonora stayed [to not make him any reply].

The analysis offered in (4a^i) has the entire verb phrase (including the embedded infinitive) within the scope of *not*. By contrast, (4a^{ii}) restricts the scope of *not* to the infinitive complement. The insertion of the purposive phrase 'in order' immediately before the infinitive marker *to* helps to resolve the ambiguity encountered by the modern reader; the infinitive complement is adverbial in structure and clearly purposive in force. This example attests the practice of applying the *do*-less negative rule at the phrasal level and reading *not* as if it were placed in the matrix clause (i.e. notionally raising it in order to read its scope correctly). The example in (4b) looks very similar to that in (4a), except that the object of the matrix verb *admonished* — the pronoun *him* — is explicit.

(4) b. His Wife <u>admonished him not to think</u> of Revenge, but to take care of his Stock and his Soul: (Pope, A Full and True Account of A Horrid and Barbarous Revenge by Poison on the Body of MR. EDMUND CURLL, Bookseller [c 1716])

4b^i =his wife did not admonish him [to think of revenge…]

4b^{ii} =his wife admonished him [to not think of revenge…] = V [not to V]

The analyses offered in (4b^i) and (4b^{ii}) present the matrix verb either as being negated or as not being negated. These interpretations do not differ except in degree of force; it is possible to understand the scope of *not* in (4b^i) to include both the matrix verb *admonish* as well as the infinitive complement. This reading would apply the *do*-less negative rule at the same time as allowing for *not* to govern the infinitive. The analysis in (4b^{ii}) may be marginally preferable merely because of the rhetorical balance created by the second infinitive introduced by the adversative conjunction *but*. This example is different from (4a) because both readings admit the negation of the infinitive complement, and because the second infinitive clarifies the relation of object to the complement.

These examples illustrate the nature of the ambiguity or vagueness that arises when two systems are in use in a variety at the same time. Interpreting these constructions requires in part a practical understanding of which system of negation is operating in a particular instance — the auxiliary-based, sentential (global) system of present-day English, or the phrasal-based (local) one. The difference between the two pivots on the development and regularization of modals and dummy *do* as full-blown auxiliary verbs. To explore the extent to which speakers compensate for the co-existence of the two systems, this study examined the relationship of the recessive *do*-less and the regularizing *do*-support negation rules in the late seventeenth and early eighteenth centuries as a context for the syntax of negative infinitive VPs.

3.   The study

The question for investigation is: Does the use of negation with infinitive VPs in late seventeenth and early eighteenth century English appear to exhibit any signs of pressure from the flux in the auxiliary system? I approach the answer to this question by examining first the extent to which the recessive *do*-less negative construction (as illustrated in (3b) above) co-occurs with the rule involving dummy auxiliary *do* (as illustrated in (3a) above). The present study provides a salient context for the examination of the grammatical patterns used in constructing negative infinitives. One motivation for this investigation is the speculation that writers adopt split negative infinitives (as illustrated in (2a) above) in order to avoid the possible ambiguity presented by the mixture of phrasal and clausal rules of negation. The overarching concern of this study then is to ask to what extent if any the retreating *do*-less negation rule interacts with the syntax of infinitive VPs.[4]

The constructions for investigation include a baseline set and a secondary set. The baseline set consists of main and subordinate clause negative declaratives, with two major variants described below. The first consists of an auxiliary verb plus *not* or the contraction *n't*. The second consists of a main verb plus *not* without auxiliary support.

auxiliary [do/modals/perfect/progressive] + *not/'nt* (e.g. 3a)
main verb + *not* (e.g. 3b)

The secondary set consists of post-predicate negative infinitive constructions. The two salient variants are captured by the structural descriptions below. Note that the first consists of *not* immediately followed by the infinitive marker *to* and the infinitive verb. The second consists of the split negative infinitive, that is, it consists of the infinitive marker *to* followed by *not* and the verb.

(V NP) not to V   e.g. she begged him not to scold the children
(V NP) to not V   e.g. she begged him to not scold the children

This study deployed the techniques of corpus linguistics in order to address the question. The techniques and materials of corpus linguistics allow the investigation of constructions that are complementary at the same time as those that potentially interact with one another. The texts were tagged using a program developed by Douglas Biber, and key constructions were searched to produce KWIC (Key Word in Context) concordance files for each search conducted. The files were checked and erroneous instances discarded. The instances were counted and the frequency counts normalized to occurrences per 10,000 words for ease of presentation and interpretation.

4. Findings

4.1 Clausal negation patterns with *not*.

The proportion of negatives with *do* relative to *do*-less negative declaratives overall is represented in Figure 1 below. Figure 1 displays the overall variation in use across speakers, from the oldest to the youngest in the sample. John Dryden, the oldest member of the group, is the most vigorous user of the recessive pattern. This is not to say that he does not have any instances of negatives constructed with *do*-support; he does, but at a mere 6.39 instances per 10,000 words compared with a total of 22.63 instances of *do*-less negatives per 10,000 words, he may be said to prefer the recessive system. By contrast, the person closest to him in age, Aphra Behn, does not appear to favor the old

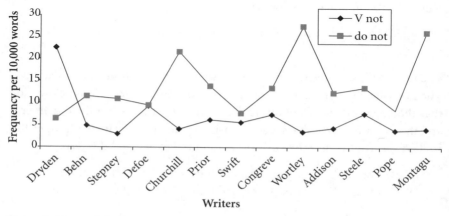

Figure 1. Do- and do-less negatives

system. Her use of *do*-support (11.54 per 10,000 words) compares well with Steele (13.58), Stepney (10.94), Prior (13.86), and Congreve (13.45), and is notably ahead of younger men like Swift (7.72), Pope (8.4) and Defoe (9.52 instances per 10,000 words). The most vigorous adherents to the regularizing rule with *do*-support are not necessarily the youngest members of the sample; Sarah Churchill, Duchess of Marlborough (1660–1744) and the youngest member of the group, Lady Mary Wortley Montagu, are both frequent users, but the most regular exponent of the new rule is Edward Wortley Montagu, an exact contemporary of Addison and Steele. Sarah Churchill and Edward Wortley are not literary figures at all, and the only texts that represent them (their letters) are for the most part the work of communication rather than the occasion for literary expression. Their frequencies suggest that these speakers are both modern and that they tend to the vernacular (rather than to the formal) in their practice.

Figure 2 presents an opportunity to compare the syntax of negation in main and subordinate clauses. Dryden exhibits a greater preference for main clause *do*-less negatives than for subordinate clause ones, and for *do*-supported negatives in subordinate clauses than for the same constructions in main clauses. This pattern is also evident in the language of Defoe, Swift and Pope. While Addison, Behn and Wortley also seem to prefer *do*-supported negatives in subordinate clauses over *do*-supported negatives in main clauses, they differ from the writers mentioned in using *do*-less negatives more frequently in subordinate clauses than in main clauses. The others — Prior, Congreve, Montagu, Stepney and Churchill — clearly prefer *do*-supported negatives in main clauses than the same constructions in subordinate clauses, and all (except for Sarah Churchill) use the recessive pattern more frequently in main clauses than in subordinate clauses.

The interpretation of the trends presented in Figures 1 and 2 is aided by a closer examination of the guise assumed by the *do*-less pattern, that is, by considering the choice and range of lexical verbs that speakers select for use with the negative without *do*-support. After all, it seems clear that the *do*-less negative system varies with respect to whether it is productive or merely residual when we look at the verbs that appear to attract the auxiliary-less negative, from the most frequent to the least frequent (Table 2).

The verb *have* is by far the most frequently occurring main verb in the negative. *Have* and *know* occur in the *do*-less negative pattern in the letters of every speaker in the group, and *doubt* appears in the texts of all except for Sarah Churchill, Edward Wortley and Lady Mary Wortley Montagu. Indeed, Lady

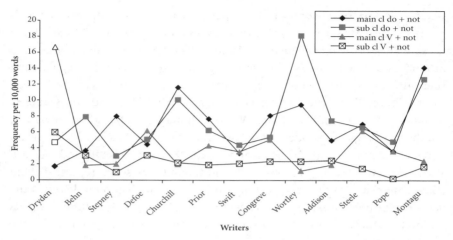

Figure 2. patterns of negation in main and subordinate clauses

Table 2. Verbs most frequently used in *V* + *not* pattern

Have	know	doubt	question	make	come	care	seem	understand	want
93	53	34	8	5	4	3	2	2	1

Mary Wortley Montagu's choice of verb is restricted to the pair *have* and *know*, while her husband adds to this pair only *seem* and *come*. George Stepney's verb choice is limited to the three most frequently occurring verbs, *have, doubt* and *know*; Steele adds to these central verbs a single instance of *inquire*; Prior adds *stay* to the central trio, and Addison adds to the three core verbs his personal favorite, *question*. In fact, Addison accounts for the total number of occurrences of *question* in the *do*-less pattern. The low users of the *do*-less pattern are also the most stereotypical users. That is, they do not use the pattern productively, but restrict their choice of verbs to a very small set which they use repeatedly.

Some of the major contributors to the range and variety of verbs used in the *V* + *not* pattern are not surprising; the most senior writer, Dryden, and Daniel Defoe, one of the oldest members of Addison's generation, are low *do*-negative users and so we might expect them to demonstrate more variety and range in their control of the recessive system. And indeed, as might be expected, the most prolific user of the recessive rule, Dryden, is also the most productive. He uses 27 different verbs at least once each in the *V* + *not* pattern, including *pretend, remember, flatter, go*, and *merit*, and Defoe uses thirteen different verbs in the pattern. Dryden's near contemporary, Aphra Behn, follows the trend characteristic of the younger speakers. She uses only five different verbs, including *have* and *doubt*; she also has *follow*, *come* and *suffer*.[5] Other verbs that occur once in the *do*-less pattern include *converse, give, live, value, find, please, like, desire, discover, remember, pay, despair, say, continue, answer, deal, render, drink* and *break*.

The analysis of the baseline set of constructions indicates that the *do*-less negative rule is indeed recessive and unproductive, and that the formation of negative sentences with *do*-support is well established in the language of this sample.

4.2 Negative infinitives

It is relevant to note at the outset that there were no occurrences at all of negative split infinitives in the sample. This finding seems to confirm Rissanen's view that the split infinitive rarely occurs in English between the end of the fifteenth century and the end of the eighteenth century (1999:290).[6] Table 3 illustrates the relative frequency and distribution of negative infinitives in the sample corpus examined. The table is organized to reflect the range of negative infinitive patterns encountered in the sample. The categories are based on the typology offered by Biber *et al.* (1999:693ff.) to capture the major structural descriptions of post-predicate infinitive clauses in present-day English. The discrimination between different types of infinitive clause patterns allows the close study of the varying relationship between negator (*not*) and both the matrix verb that governs the infinitive, and the infinitive verb itself.

The table indicates that the most frequently occurring infinitive clause pattern consists of the governing verb, a NP that functions both as object of the governing verb and as subject of the infinitive complement, *not* and an adjacent infinitive verb, such as the expression, *I asked him not to answer the question*. By contrast with PDE, in which the infinitive pattern consisting of a governing verb such as *want, try* or *seem* and *to* plus infinitive verb is the most frequently encountered verb pattern in conversation, fiction, news and academic discourse (Biber *et al.* 1999:698), the pattern's negative counterpart shows up in the historical English sample five times less frequently. More frequent than this pattern is a comparative or degree type of construction, in which the negative infinitive functions as a dependent component of a lexical phrase headed by the adverbs *so* or *as*. This is related to the negative infinitive governed by an adjective, which occurs slightly less frequently than the degree construction. The remaining negative infinitive patterns are variants of the more frequent

Table 3. Distribution of Post-predicate negative infinitive patterns (frequencies normalized to occurrences per 100,000 words)

	V+NP+ not to	so/as X as not to	V+Adj not to	V+ not to	be Ved not to	V (NP) conj. not to	V+for NP not to	V Adj (for X) not to
Dryden	12.8	0	4.26	4.26	4.26	0	0	0
Behn	12.15	6.07	0	0	0	0	0	0
Stepney	24.87	9.97	9.97	4.97	4.97	4.97	0	0
Defoe	22.14	2.21	4.42	0	4.42	0	0	0
Churchill	9.84	1.96	0	1.96	0	0	0	0
Prior	23.92	4.78	9.56	9.56	0	0	0	0
Swift	6.25	2.08	4.17	0	0	0	2.08	0
Congreve	16.81	3.36	6.72	3.36	0	6.72	0	0
Wortley	7.86	7.86	3.93	3.93	3.93	0	0	3.93
Addison	11.43	1.9	0	1.9	3.81	0	0	0
Steele	16.97	8.48	6.36	2.12	0	0	0	2.12
Pope	16.8	19.2	4.8	2.4	0	2.4	0	0
Montagu	9.72	4.86	9.72	2.43	2.43	0	4.86	0
Totals	191.56	72.73	63.91	36.89	23.82	14.09	6.94	6.05

ones. Negative passive infinitives occur more frequently than variants of the NP and adjective constructions with the additional apparatus of *for*. In addition, the construction in which a governing verb precedes an optional NP and a conjunction occurs sufficiently frequently for me to note it. Below I give examples of each type, and discuss them in more detail, both in terms of their relation to one another, and with respect to whether the scope of the negative in these patterns is ambiguous.[7] Figure 3 illustrates the relative frequency with which these patterns occur in the sample in graphic form.

4.2.1 *V NP not to*

The following examples illustrate some ways in which the pattern occurs in the sample.

(5) a. for yt reason ye Elr had injoynd Count Harrack not to converse wth ym upon these matters, but to conferr only with himself & his Feld Marshall, (Stepney)

   b. and I hope there will not a day appear to our lives end wherein there will not appear some instance of an Affection not to be excelled but in the Mansions of Eternity to which We may recommend Our selves by our behaviour to each other Here. (Steele)

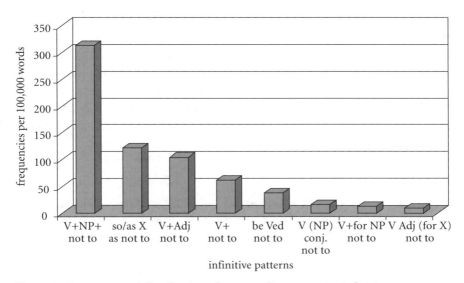

Figure 3. Frequency and distribution of post-predicate negative infinitives

    c.   Adieu, my Lord, I have conjured Monsr de Torcy not to write to you upon this Subject and I begg of you not to remember I have written, if you think proper to refuse what I so earnestly implore however short my stay here may be. (Prior)

The controlling verbs in (5a) — *enjoin* — and (5c) — *conjure, beg* — are speech act verbs that are typical controlling verbs of post-predicate infinitives. *Beg* occurs no fewer than seven times in this pattern in the sample as a whole; *conjure* and *advise* occur three times, and *bid* occurs twice. Other speech act verbs used in this pattern are *address, beseech, relate,* and *charge*. Steele's extremely complex string of negatives in (5b) includes a pair of clauses in each of which the subject is existential *there* and the main verb is a verb of probability, *appear*, in the first (main) clause as a verb governing the prepositional phrase, and in the second (relative) clause as the controlling verb (5b) without subject raising. The sentence may be construed thus: 'I hope that the day when an affection that can only be surpassed in heaven (which our behaviour on earth guarantees our entry) appears before the end of our life'. Note that the negatives cancel one another out to result in a markedly tentative expression of regard for the addressee.

    Every speaker uses this pattern more frequently than the others (except for Pope who seems to prefer the intensive/comparative negative infinitive). Note that the examples in (5) are cases in which the NP may be analysed as a subject in the subordinate clause raised to object in the matrix clause. The presence of the NP provides a block to interpreting the scope of the negator as including the matrix verb. The NP provides an effective barrier, ensuring that the domain of *not* includes the following infinitive. This pattern would seem to be a candidate for alternative formulation as 'V NP to not', that is, in which *not* might split the infinitive marker *to* from its verb. Such a variant in the historical sample would provide for the unambiguous expression of emphatic negation. As already noted, however, this variant does not occur at all.

4.2.2   *V so X as (not) to Y*

(6) a.   This I should have acquainted you with about a fort night ago had I not bin so much taken up as not to have had a spare-moment, and that I knew my Intelligence of this kind would have bin of no Use to You. (Addison)

   b.   Tis not unlike the happy friendship of a stay'd man and his wife, who are seldom so fond as to hinder the business of the house from going on all day, or so indolent as not to find consolation in each other every evening. (Pope)

Characteristic of this pattern is the use of *be* as the verb preceding the adjectival subject complement that governs the infinitive clause. The most remarkable feature of the pattern is the use of the intensifier *so* (with its variant *so much*), and the comparative *as* which requires a second instance immediately before the negator. This pattern appears to be characteristic of the historical and social variety of English encountered in the sample as it occurs in the language of every speaker except for Dryden. In the same way that the first pattern (*V NP not to*) has a built-in barrier to the extension of *not*'s scope to the matrix verb, the intensifier/comparative construction also has material (X) that serves to block the application of negation to the controlling verb.

4.2.3   *Adj not to*

(7) a.   I have really thought it tedious not to have heard from you. (Congreve)

   b.   … and certainly you can never be too careful not to offend probability, in supposing a man not to discover his own wife (Congreve).

   c.   I hear it said as from some of my acquaintances as if I were resolved not to leave the University in a future Parliament, I neither said nor wrote anything of this kind to any body. (Prior)

Adjectival predicates controlling infinitive clauses belong to a range of semantic domains. Examples (7a, b) illustrate the most common type of adjective, that is, adjectives expressing evaluation (*tedious, careful*). Other notable adjectives with an evaluative function in negative infinitives in the sample are *criminal*, and *ignorant*. Example (7c) illustrates the use of an adjective expressing degree of certainty (*resolved*). The sample also includes adjectives expressing the speaker's personal affective stance (*be pleased, ingrateful* [sic], *sorry, unreasonable*). The adjective is pivotal in this construction pattern in separating the matrix verb from the negator. The consequence is that *not* is adjacent to the infinitive verb, and thus presents no danger of confusion.

4.2.4 *V not to*
This pattern is the most vulnerable to difficulty of interpretation in a variety in which two different systems are in use. In this pattern the controlling verb is immediately adjacent to *not* and is thus in danger of being analyzed as falling within the scope of *not* if the system of negation understood to be operating is the recessive system which allows post-verbal *not*. Consider the following examples from the sample:

(8) a. And that you will please not to make so much a stranger of me an-
         other time. (Dryden)
     b. I come before a couple of Gentlemen who have greater fortunes than
         myself and have endeavoured not to fall short of either of them in
         my friendship to Your self: (Addison)
     c. I don't much like a Thing I heard of the Gentleman that R. begins
         not to think well of, that Hee professes much to bee for the Protes-
         tant Succession, but is not att all persuaded there is any Danger of
         the P. of W., (Churchill)

In most cases it is not difficult to make a judgment about the most likely interpretation of the combination of verb and *not*. Indeed it is possible to make probabilistic statements about the role of the auxiliary system in the construction of negative infinitives on the basis of the writer's preference for *do*-supported or *do*-less negation. So the extent to which a writer uses *do* or another auxiliary in constructing the negative will shape judgment of the likely interpretation of a negative infinitive. For instance, Dryden is notable for using *do*-less negatives most often, but the fact that he uses auxiliaries other than *do* (much more frequently) suggests that negative infinitive constructions might well not be ambiguous in his language. Indeed, the cotext in example (8a) offers additional guidance, so that *not* belongs with *to make* rather than with the matrix verb *please*. In this case, the controlling predicate, *please*, is sufficiently conventional for Dryden's expression not to be understood as occurring in the negative.

A regular *do*-supported negative user like Sarah Churchill or Edward Wortley is even less likely to construct infinitives governed by matrix verbs that are not negated using *do*. So Sarah Churchill's (8c), in which we have a *do* negative (*don't much like*) co-occurring with a negative infinitive (*not to think*), should not present difficulty. However, the fact that Addison uses markedly few instances of the *do*-less negative is useful information as we negotiate the meaning of (8b), which is straightforwardly a negative infinitive rather than a negated controlling verb.

It is interesting that not all the speakers in the sample use this pattern; it is absent from Defoe's corpus and from Behn's corpus. Because they are two of the earliest figures whose language is represented, it is tempting to suppose that the absence of this pattern indicates some awareness of the interpretative difficulties that it poses. The problem with jumping to such a conclusion is that although Defoe might justifiably be judged thus on the basis of the extent to which he uses the recessive rule for the formation of negative declaratives, Behn's evident preference for the regularizing rule with *do*-support does not endorse such an interpretation. Jonathan Swift's language also exhibits no instances of this construction; actually as a sparse user of negative infinitives compared with the other people in the sample, the lack of this pattern is not surprising. The distribution of the pattern across the sample does not indicate then that speakers appear aware of possible structural ambiguity in this pattern.

4.2.5   The minor patterns
The remaining four patterns appear sparsely and unevenly across the speakers in the sample. None of them presents difficulties in interpreting the scope of *not*.

4.2.5.1   *Be verb-ed not*. The passive form of the first pattern (without agent) seems somewhat formulaic in its appearance. Defoe favors the construction, possibly because the avoidance of the agent expresses negative politeness. The result is an obsequious tone. Addison also uses the construction more frequently than his contemporaries.

(9)   a.   yet I humbly refer to your Lordship my former entreaty that your
           Lordship will be pleased not to communicate to my Lord the favors I

have received from your Lordship, least perhaps it may cool the inclination my Lord T-----r has been pleased to express of doeing something for me. (Defoe)
  b. besides, as a father, I hope I may be allowed not to Love in a less Exalted and Sublime Manner, but a greater; (Defoe)

The construction presents no opportunity for confusion of meaning; if the controlling predicate were to be negated, the passive *be* provides an anchor for *not* because it functions as an auxiliary. Consequently, the negative infinitive governed by a passive verb does not appear ambiguous.

4.2.5.2 *X Conj not to.* This construction occurs very seldom; it is worth noting for its role in creating rhetorically measured balance at the level of the clause.

(10) Only to give the Audience some light into the Character of Maskwell, before his appearance; and not to convince Mellefont of his Treachery; (Congreve)

4.2.5.3 *for NP not to.* This is a variant of the pattern that occurs most frequently in the sample, namely, *NP not to.* The variant itself appears only in the idiolect of one person, Jonathan Swift.

(11)   a. It is a point of wisdom too hard for me, not to look back with vexation upon past management. (Swift)

4.2.5.4 *V Adj (for X) not to.*

(12) ...it is impossible for any one who thinks and has any publick Spirit, not to tremble at seeing His Country in its present Circumstances, in the hands of so daring a Genius as Yours (Steele).

Example (12) illustrates how the material intervening between controlling predicate and negative infinitive — here a complex NP — acts as an effective barrier to interpreting the negative as applying to anything other than the infinitive clause.[8]

5. Conclusion

This study of the patterns of variation in the construction of negative declaratives and of the treatment of negative infinitives in epistolary prose in late
seventeenth- and early eighteenth-century English allows us to conclude that
two systems of clausal negation do indeed co-exist in the historical sample.
However, the older, *do*-less pattern (*V* + *not*) is evidently not vigorous in the
way that the negative construction with *do*-support is. The dominance of
auxiliary-anchored clausal negation suggests that the presence of V+ *not*
options in both subordinate and main clause negation is residual rather than
productive.

The relationship of recessive rule to regularizing rule does not match the
apparent age distribution of the speakers in the sample to the extent that we
might expect. That is, although it is generally true to say that the younger
Addison's contemporaries are, the fewer the *do*-less V+ *not* forms occur in their
language, it is not true all the time. One of the complete outsiders, in both social
and chronological terms, Aphra Behn, exhibits the practice more typical of
Addison's contemporaries. Like theirs, her language demonstrates the recessive
construction's restriction to a few stereotypical verbs.

The study of the frequency and occurrence of negative infinitive clauses in
the historical sample yields no evidence that speakers appear to perceive
sufficient structural ambiguity to warrant the adoption of a construction like a
split negative infinitive. Where there is some possibility of systemic clash — that
is in the case of the *V not to* pattern — it seems that the more established the
negation system with *do*-support is in the speaker's language, the less likely the
construction is to support its interpretation as a negated matrix verb rather than
a negative infinitive. Finally, it is noteworthy that although the *V to* pattern is
the most common type of infinitive in present-day English, its negative
counterpart *V not to* occurs sporadically and infrequently in the historical
sample by comparison with the *V NP not to* pattern. It remains for a comparative survey of positive and negative infinitives to be conducted in the historical
sample in order to discover whether this difference can be accounted by some
special role of negation in complex clauses in the two varieties of English.

Notes

1. I acknowledge the work of Sinthya Solera for transcribing George Stepney's letters from microfilm of the British Library manuscript collection, and the work of Sheila Williams, who transcribed Matthew Prior's letters from the microfilm of the Longleat manuscript collection of his private letters and state papers. I am also very grateful to Jeanne Arete, my research assistant, for her construction of significant sections of the corpus including the letters of Addison, Defoe, Dryden, Swift, Pope, Lady Mary Wortley Montagu, Congreve, Aphra Behn, and Sarah Churchill, Duchess of Marlborough. I am grateful to the Earl of Harrowby for permission to use the unpublished letters of Edward Wortley. Last, but not least, I am grateful to Randi Reppen for tagging the texts.

2. For an exploration of the nature of Joseph Addison's inner circle, see Fitzmaurice (2000c).

3. In fact, in September 1704, Prior wrote a congratulatory letter to the Duchess of Marlborough on the occasion of her husband's victory at Blenheim over the 'French and Bavarians', offering her a celebratory poem to commemorate the victory, entitled 'A letter to Monsieur Boileau Despreaux; Occasion'd by the Victory at Blenheim, 1704'. Prior asked the Duchess to show the poem to Queen Anne. The Duchess was evidently unimpressed; Prior wrote on the letter: 'She sent back the letter unopen'd and said she was sure yt Mr Prior write but what he would, He could not wish well to Her and her family'. [Prior Papers (Marquess of Bath) vol 13: folio 55].

4. Rissanen (1999: 290) notes, 'Somewhat surprisingly, this construction is rare in Early Modern English and gains ground again only at the end of the eighteenth century. The most common elements appearing between the *to*-particle and the infinitive are the negative particle and adverbs of manner and degree'. The examples Rissanen offers are from More's *Confutation of Tyndale* (16th century) and Stapleton (17th century).

5. Confirmation of this claim for Behn's syntactic modernity needs to be further tested, for instance, by looking at her use of the progressive, perhaps relative clause markers, as well as pronoun usage. It may be that she is conventional and thus old-fashioned in her lexis while being quite modern in her syntax.

6. In addition to the searches reported here, I conducted a rapid search of the sample for infinitives split by adverbs of manner such as *well, heartily,* and *fast,* and of degree such as *almost, entirely,* and *perfectly.* I could find no occurrences of these adverbs in split infinitives.

7. The following table illustrates the difference in the occurrence of infinitive patterns in present-day English and in the historical sample. NB. The comparison considers variants rather than equivalents; Biber *et al.* do not consider negative infinitives. It remains to compare the incidence of positive and negative infinitives in the historical sample. The table shows the most frequent to the least frequent in each sample.

PDE (Biber *et al.*, 698)	Historical sample
V + *to*	
V + NP + *to,*	V NP not to
	[V so X as (not) to Y]
	[Adj not to]
	V not to

be V*ed to* (rare in conversation
but frequent in news and academic prose)
V + NP + bare infinitive (rare)
V + *for* + NP + *to* (rare)
V + bare infinitive (rare)

Be verb-ed not (formulaic)

for NP not to

[V Adj (for X) not to]

The square brackets indicate patterns not considered in Biber *et al.* but which occur in the historical sample.

8. Here is an example of the infinitive negative with *for* that differs from Swift's in that the core construction is not explicitly preceded by a verb. Instead, the pair of comparative clauses together function as a subject complement of the expletive *it*. 'I think it as scandalous for a Woman not to know how to use a needle, as for a Man not to know how to use a sword.' (Montagu). The balance created by the comparison is rhetorically effective; in this example, Lady Mary delivers what amounts to a homily on appropriate skills for men and women. The construction is so carefully constructed that it may be interpreted either as ironic or as serious, and thus is potentially humorous.

References

Biber, D., Johansson, S., Leech, G., Conrad, S. & Finegan, E. 1999. *The Longman Grammar of Spoken and Written English*, London: Pearson Longman.

Denison, D., 1993. *Historical English Syntax: Verbal Constructions*. London: Longman.

Ellegård, A., 1953. *The Auxiliary Do: The Establishment and Regulation of its Use in English*. Stockholm: Almqvist & Wiksell.

Fischer, O., 1992. Syntax. In *The Cambridge History of the English Language Volume II: 1066–1476*. N. Blake (ed). Cambridge: Cambridge University Press. Pp. 207–408.

Fischer, O., 1997. The grammaticalisation of infinitival *to* in English compared with German and Dutch. In *Language History and Linguistic Modelling. A Festschrift for Jacek Fisiak on his 60th Birthday*. R. Hickey and S. Puppel (eds.). Berlin: Mouton. Pp. 265–80.

Fischer, O., 2000. Grammaticalisation: unidirectional, non-reversible? The case of *to* before the infinitive in English. In *Pathways of Change: Grammaticalization Processes in older English*. O Fischer, A. Rosenbach and D. Stein (eds.). Berlin: Mouton. Pp. 149–170.

Fitzmaurice, S., 2000a, Remarks on the de-grammaticalization of infinitival *to* in present-day American English. In *Pathways of Change: Grammaticalization Processes in older English*. O. Fischer, A. Rosenbach and D. Stein (eds.). Berlin: Mouton. Pp. 171–186.

Fitzmaurice, S., 2000b, The Great Leveler: the role of the spoken media in stylistic shift from the colloquial to the conventional, *American Speech*, Vol. 75, No. 1, Spring 2000. 54–68.

Fitzmaurice, S., 2000c, *The Spectator*, the politics of social networks, and language standardisation in eighteenth-century England. In *The Development of Standard English 1300–1800*. L. Wright (ed.). Cambridge: Cambridge University Press. 195–218.

Gelderen, E. van., 1998, *For to* in the History of English. *American Journal of Germanic Language and Literature* 10.1: 45–72.

Rissanen, M., 1999, 'Syntax', in *Cambridge History of the English Language, Volume III: 1476–1776*. R. Lass (ed). Cambridge: Cambridge University Press. 187–331.

Tieken-Boon Van Ostade, I., 1987. *The Auxiliary Do in Eighteenth-century English: A Sociohistorical-linguistic Approach*. Dordrecht: Foris.

CHAPTER 13

Investigating register variation in nineteenth-century English

A multi-dimensional comparison*

Christer Geisler

Uppsala University

1. Introduction

This study investigates the development of English registers through the nineteenth century. Until recently, 19th-century English has been a largely neglected area of linguistic research (see Görlach 1995, 1999). As the basis for the study serves the CONCE corpus (A Corpus of Nineteenth-Century English) of one million words of running text (see Kytö, Rudanko & Smitterberg 2000, and Table 1b below). One important aim of the paper is to compare register variation in the 19th century to previous research on diachronic register variation (in particular Biber & Finegan 1989, 1992, 1997, and Biber 1995). A second aim is to explore relative differences and similarities between registers within a single dimension. The CONCE corpus is a multi-register corpus compiled at the universities of Uppsala and Tampere, consisting of the seven registers Drama, Trials, Parliamentary Debates, Fiction, Letters, History, and Science. The texts in the CONCE corpus have been coded using more or less the same system of text-level and reference codes as in the Helsinki Corpus. Furthermore, the registers are stratified following the extralinguistic criteria applied to the Helsinki Corpus (see Kytö 1996), partly in order to offer follow-up material for research on early Modern English.

As the corpus is divided into three time periods, Period 1 covering 1800–1830, Period 2 1850–1870, and Period 3 1870–1900, the results of the dimension score analysis as utilized in Biber & Finegan (1989, 1992, and 1997) can be compared diachonically through the nineteenth century. Some of the results of the present study suggest that some registers are clearly heterogeneous, especially when compared across the three time periods.

2.   The multi-dimensional approach

In this study, the dimension score analysis uses the sets of co-occurring grammatical features in Biber (1988:102–103, algorithms on pp.221–245). The calculation of the dimension scores (or factor scores) follows the methodology as outlined in Biber (1988:93–97) and Biber (1995:117–119). This involves the following steps: (a) tagging the corpus (see below); (b) extracting feature counts for each text sample in the corpus (these features are given in Table 1a); (c) normalizing the feature counts per 1000 words; (d) standardizing the normalized scores in (c) to a mean of 0.0 and a standard deviation of 1.0; (e) computing dimension scores for each text sample by adding up the standardized frequencies in (d) that have salient positive loadings and subtracting salient negative loadings (if any) on a dimension. For example, a dimension score for each sample on Dimension 3 is calculated by adding up the standardized scores for the features *wh*-relatives, pied piping constructions and nominalizations and subtracting the sum of the three features place adverbials, time adverbials and other adverbs (see Table 1a). The scores for periods 1 to 3 in Tables 3 through 6 represent the means of the dimension scores across each time period and register.

The interpretive labels of the four dimensions in the present study are taken over from Biber's previous studies:

Dimension 1: Involved versus informational production
Dimension 2: Narrative versus non-narrative concerns
Dimension 3: Elaborated reference versus situation-dependent reference
Dimension 5: Impersonal versus non-impersonal style

They reflect the situational, social, and cognitive functions shared by each set of co-occurring of linguistic features. The relations among registers, or their relative placement on a dimension, support these labels. In short, Biber & Finegan (1989) identify three parameters of a textual dimension: Linguistic — in being defined by sets of statistically co-occurring linguistic features; Functional — in representing situational, social and cognitive functions; Relative — in characterizing relations among different registers within a dimension.

The CONCE corpus was tagged using Conexor's EngCG-2 tagger (http://www.conexor.fi). Words given multiple tags by the EngCG-2 tagger, indicating that the tagger could not decide on a particular tag, were excluded from the algorithms. There are approximately 19,000 ambiguous tags in the

Table 1a. Linguistic features used for the calculation of dimension scores.

Dimension 1: Involved versus informational production	Dimension 2: Narrative versus non-narrative concerns	Dimension 3: Elaborated reference versus situation-dependent reference	Dimension 5: Impersonal versus non-impersonal style
Positive features:	past tense verbs	Positive features:	Positive features:
private verbs	third person pronouns	*wh*-relatives	conjuncts
Contractions	perfect aspect verbs	pied piping	agentless passives
present tense verbs	public verbs	nominalizations	*by*-passives
second person pronouns	*no*-negation		other adverbial subordinators
not-negation		Negative features:	
demonstrative pronouns	No negative features	time adverbials	
Emphatics		place adverbials	No negative features
first person pronouns		other adverbs	
pronoun *it*			
main verb *be*			
causative subordination			
discourse particles			
indefinite pronouns			
Hedges			
Amplifiers			
wh-questions			
possibility modals			
stranded prepositions			
Negative features:			
Nouns			
word length			
Prepositions			
type/token ratio			
attributive adjectives			

corpus, representing approximately 2% of the tagged corpus. No manual editing was carried out on the tagged corpus, and only features that allowed automatic extraction were included. The following features, which could not be reliably extracted using computer programs, were not included in the calculation of the dimension scores (the feature number refers to the computational algorithms in Biber 1988: Appendix II):

Table 1b. Distribution of text samples in the tagged version of CONCE.

Period		De-bates	Drama	Fiction	History	Letters	Science	Trials	Total
Period 1 (1800–1830)	Number of text samples	11	9	7	6	10	7	15	65
	Wordcount	19509	31567	41806	30795	121019	37791	62042	344529
	Average text size	1774	3507	5972	5133	12102	5399	4136	5300
Period 2 (1850–1870)	Number of text samples	11	5	7	7	13	5	11	59
	Wordcount	19256	30611	38896	30326	130777	31339	60382	341587
	Average text size	1751	6122	5557	4332	10060	6268	5489	5790
Period 3 (1870–1900)	Number of text samples	11	6	7	6	9	7	17	63
	Wordcount	19491	29983	30096	30389	90241	30305	67146	297651
	Average text size	1772	4997	4299	5065	10027	4329	3950	4725
Total text samples		33	20	21	19	32	19	43	187
Total word-count		58256	92161	110798	91510	342037	99435	189570	983767
Average text size		1765	4608	5276	4816	10689	5233	4409	5261
Number of authors per period		—	3	3	3	10	3	—	

Dimension 1: Proverb *do* (Biber's feature no. 12), *that*-deletion (feature no. 60; this feature was later included in the analysis), sentence relatives (feature no. 34), clausal coordination (feature no. 65), *wh*-clauses (feature no. 23), -*ed* WHIZ-deletions (feature no. 27).

Dimension 2: -*ing*-participial clauses (feature no. 25).

Dimension 3: Phrasal coordination (feature no. 64), *wh*-relative clauses were not split up into subject and object relatives as in Biber 1988 (features no. 31 and 32).

Dimension 4: Split auxiliaries (feature no. 63)

Dimension 5: -*ed* WHIZ-deletions (feature no. 27), -*ed* participial clauses (feature no. 26)

Since several of these features are more common in expository/written registers, their exclusion may slightly distort the dimension scores of registers such as History, Debates, and Science.

For the purposes of the present study, the corpus was divided into 187 text samples on which the statistical calculations are based. It should be noted that there are differences in the distribution of both the number of samples per time period and register, as well as the number of words per text sample (Table 1b).

The distribution of samples in Table 1b masks the fact that, for some of the registers, the number of unique authors is much smaller. In Fiction, Drama, History, and Science there are three unique authors per period; Letters contain approximately ten unique authors per time period. The CONCE samples are generally twice as long as the corresponding Helsinki Corpus samples.

Table 2 shows that all dimensions are statistically significant predictors of register differences (the F-statistic, like Chi-square, easily reaches statistical

Table 2. Statistical significance of the dimension score analysis.

Dimension	F-value	Probability	R-square (r^2)	Newman-Keuls groupings
1	111.79	<0.0001	0.788	5 groups
2	56.25	<0.0001	0.652	4 groups
3	43.57	<0.0001	0.592	3 groups
4	20.51	<0.0001	0.406	5 groups
5	68.42	<0.0001	0.695	4 groups

Note: Dimension 4, which is labeled 'overt expression of persuasion' in Biber 1988: 111, and 'overt expression of argumentation' in Biber 1995: 159, was dropped from further analysis. The dimension scores are calculated by summing up various modal features and infinitives.

significance with large sample sizes). As in Biber (1988:127), we also give R-square values for each dimension showing how much statistical variability is due to register differences: For Dimension 1, R-square equals 0.788, which means that 78.8% of the between-group variation is due to register. Table 2 also provides the statistical groupings suggested by the Newman-Keuls multiple comparison test, which is a post-hoc test comparing combinations of various group means. For example, for Dimension 3 the Newman-Keuls test indicates that there are statistically three major groups of registers (these are discussed further in Section 3.3). In addition, in order to test statistical variation of a particular register across the three time periods, Tables 3 to 6 give F-values, with their associated probabilities and R-square values, for each register on a dimension. A significant probability, with $p. < 0.05$ (for a 5% threshold), indicates that changes in a register across the three time periods are statistically significant. R-square values above 0.20 are regarded as indicating an important relationship although they may not be statistically significant (cf. Biber & Finegan 1989:498). Statistically significant probabilities of an F-value or important R-square values are italicized in Tables 3 through 6.

In this study, the dimension score analysis is also used to place a particular register relative to other registers in CONCE. For instance, CONCE contains Parliamentary debates and Trials which were originally included because they represent aspects of speech-related discourse; Parliamentary Debates were also included as specimens of political language of the time. As it turns out, only Trials emerge as typically speech-based distributing on the "oral pole" on the three major dimensions (Dimensions 1, 3, and 5). The Parliamentary debates are similar to the expository Science and History registers in several respects. This indicates that the present dimension score analysis has the additional important function of locating a particular register relative to other registers in the corpus. Register comparability is another problem when reviewing previous studies. Biber (1995) makes a distinction between specialist expository registers and others, whereas Biber & Finegan (1992) separate speech-based versus written registers, and Biber & Finegan (1989) investigate drift in essays, fiction and letters across several centuries.

3.   Analysis of dimension scores in CONCE

This section analyzes relations among the various registers in CONCE on a specific dimension. Three comparisons are made: (1) the relative placement of a register on a dimension compared with other registers; (2) multiple comparison tests of the registers to ascertain whether they form subgroups; (3) a comparison of a specific register across the three time periods in order to uncover statistically significant diachronic changes.

3.1 Dimension 1: Involved versus informational production

Dimension 1 is identified in Biber (1988: 135) as communicatively encompassing informational versus involved production. It is one of three dimensions primarily associated with an oral/literate dichotomy. Using the multidimensional technique enables us to identify important similarities and differences between hitherto unexplored registers. Figure 1 and Table 3 suggest that most registers have become slightly more involved across the three time periods. The results of F-tests of variance indicate that only changes in Parliamentary Debates and Trials are statistically significant (see Table 3 under the corresponding F-value and its associated Probability). There is no conflict between an overall statistically significant dimension and statistically non-significant dimension scores of a particular register, such as the non-significant F-value of 0.63 for Letters in Table 3. The statistically significant results on the dimensions in Table 2 show that the various registers, or groups of them, are distinct, whereas the change of a register across the three time periods may not be noticeable.

The results of a second test in Table 2, the Newman-Keuls groupings, indicate whether the seven registers are statistically different from each other or whether some registers form subgroups. The Newman-Keuls tests suggest the following clusters of registers on Dimension 1 (the registers forming a group are not statistically different from each other) : (A) Drama and Trials, (B) Letters, (C) Fiction, (D) Debates and Science, and (E) History. Note that these subgroups are apparent from Figure 1: the interpretation of the groups is that Drama and Trials form a group consisting of the most involved texts, which emphasize interpersonal and affective content, or which reflect real-time/online production: high frequencies of grammatical features such as first and second person pronouns, present tense verbs, *wh*-questions and low frequencies of nouns, prepositions, attributive adjectives. At the informational pole of Dimension 1, we find two groups formed by Debates and Science (subgroup D) and History. Letters and Fiction are two distinct groups with Letters being more involved (overall positive dimension scores) than Fiction (negative dimension scores). Informational texts typically reflect edited/planned production (Biber 1988: 131–32).

Debates and Trials are the only two registers that contain statistically significant changes across the three time periods: Table 3 shows that the probability of the F-value for Debates equals 0.0082 and for Trials the probability is less than 0.001. As a text example illustrating characteristic features of this dimension, extract (1) is from the text with the highest Dimension 1 scores, indicating a high degree of involvement.

(1) The right knee was bent in considerably, and he stood so as to rest himself upon his left leg?
— Yes, his left leg.
  When did you see the claimant again?
— I think it was two years ago last August.
  How came you to do so?
— I was driving to Alresford. I drove into the Swan Yard — the Swan Hotel — and just as I got out of the trap the claimant was coming across the yard, and he sang out, "Halloa, Powell, is that you?" and I said yes.
  He called out "Halloa, Powell, is that you?"
— Yes.
  Had you any notice of his coming, or had he any notice of your coming?
— No; I had no notice myself in the morning that he was coming.
  And he had no notice of your coming?
— No.
  And it was quite accidental meeting?
— Yes.   [Text: T3tritic]

The significant scores for Debates are due to the large increase in period 3. The main reason for the large increase is that the later Parliamentary debates are in the first person with speaker assignment, whereas the earlier ones are third person narrative accounts in the form of reported speech, as in extracts (2) and (3).

(2) (4.15.) COLONEL WARING (Down, N.): *I* had *not* the slightest intention to intervene in *this* Debate a few minutes ago, but when the hon. Member for West Belfast, who has just sat down, gave such a direct challenge to Irish Members to get up and support the Amendment of the hon. Member for South Tyrone, *I could not* refuse to accept the challenge. ...*I* have the utmost respect for the opinion of the Marquess of Salisbury; but *does* the hon. Gentleman believe that any remarks of Lord Salisbury on the question would have the slightest effect either in

inciting Ulstermen to action or in deterring them from taking what
action they think fit?   [Text: T3debpar]

(3)   Monday February 19. [PRISONS IN IRELAND.]
       Mr. W. Pole then rose to make his promised motion on the state of the
       prisons and on the prison laws of Ireland. He observed that the report of
       the commissioners who had been appointed to investigate this subject,
       sufficiently shewed the lamentable state of the prisons in Dublin. It was
       shocking to humanity, that the evils detailed in that report had so long
       been permitted to exist without any steps having been taken to remove
       them. …Mr. Foster seconded the motion.
           Mr. M. Fitzgerald had intended to take up the subject, but he was
       glad that it would now be done more effectually: particularly as the chief
       justice had made the digest, that eminent individual being no less distin-
       guished for his humanity than his legal knowledge.   [Text: T1debhan]

These two extracts are different in that the first text in (2) is in the first person
(*I had not…I could not…*), whereas the second text in (3) is entirely in the third
person (*Mr. W. Pole then rose…He observed that…*).

Table 3. Mean scores for Dimension 1 'Informational versus Involved Production'.

Period	Debates	Drama	Fiction	History	Letters	Science	Trials
Period 1	-11.37	11.79	-4.94	-22.13	2.96	-10.72	6.78
Period 2	-9.70	13.63	-1.39	-18.15	4.86	-9.29	11.25
Period 3	-4.84	15.23	-0.91	-18.17	3.62	-6.88	15.16
F-value	5.65	0.86	0.51	2.46	0.63	2.00	8.75
Probability	0.0082	0.43	0.612	0.117	0.539	0.167	0.0007
R-square	0.27	0.09	0.05	0.24	0.04	0.20	0.30

Both Trials and Debates become more involved throughout the century. It
is clear from the dimension scores that only Trials come out as a speech-based
register: it is close to Drama on several dimensions (Dimensions 1, 3, and 5).
Since the Debates in periods 1 and 2 are mainly third person accounts of past
events in Parliament, the Debates register is in fact most closely associated with
the specialist/expository registers Science and History.

    Among specialist/expository texts, the drift towards more informational
production noted by Biber & Finegan (1997) was not confirmed statistically;
all registers moved, although only slightly, towards more involved production,
as in Figure 1.

3.2 Dimension 2: Narrative versus non-narrative concerns

Dimension 2, which covers the opposition between 'Narrative and Non-narrative Concerns', is only briefly discussed in Biber & Finegan (1997:271–272), and not at all in Biber & Finegan (1989) and (1992) since they focus on Dimensions 1, 3, and 5 where the split between an oral/literate pole is most clearly seen. But Dimension 2 is of great interest for the interpretation of

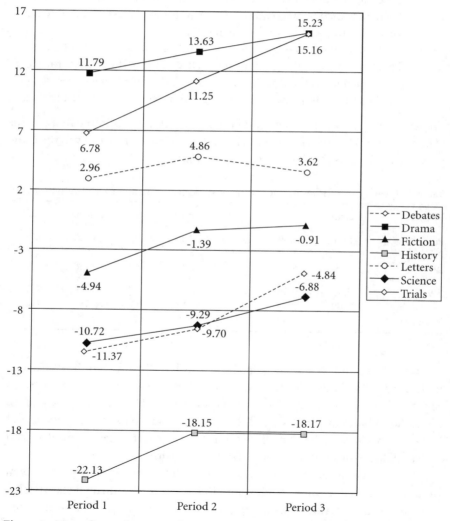

Figure 1. Mean dimension scores for Dimension 1 across three time periods.

diachronic register variation in the CONCE material. As Biber (1988:137) points out, the narrative concerns are reflected in high frequencies of past tense verbs, perfective verbs, third person pronouns, public verbs (such as *claim* and *say*), and synthetic *no*-negation, and consequently represent the marked case. However, the overall low scores on Dimension 2 only indicate that many registers are unmarked as to narrative concerns.

Table 4. Mean scores for Dimension 2 'Narrative versus Non-narrative concerns'.

Period	Debates	Drama	Fiction	History	Letters	Science	Trials
Period 1	1.30	-0.36	2.01	-1.77	-1.12	-5.24	4.20
Period 2	0.57	-1.08	2.26	0.85	-1.94	-5.45	2.24
Period 3	-3.86	-2.08	1.66	-0.31	-1.51	-5.86	4.43
F-value	*27.104*	3.044	0.18529	*4.626*	1.329	0.796	*3.286*
Probability	*<0.0001*	0.074	0.8324	*0.026*	0.280	0.468	*0.047*
R-square	*0.64*	0.26	0.02	*0.37*	0.08	0.09	*0.14*

We can group registers as to the degree of narrativeness. The Newman-Keuls groupings in Table 2 show that the registers are statistically divided into four distinct groups: (A) Trials, (B) Fiction, (C) Debates, Drama, Letters and History, and (D) Science. The group with the highest scores on the dimension is the speech-based Trials register, followed by Fiction. These two registers have positive dimension scores and can be regarded as markedly narrative. Debates have positive scores in the first two periods, but change dramatically in period 3. The narrative properties of the Debates register are most apparent in period 1. Biber & Finegan (1997) show that especially expository registers change towards less narrative style in their data.

There is a group consisting of four registers that are not statistically different from each other: Debates, History, Drama, and Letters. Lastly, the Science register stands out as clearly unmarked as to narrative concerns in a group of its own. The most striking finding is that the clearly speech-based register Trials emerges as being the most narrative. Consider extract (4) from a trial belonging to period 1 (T1trimar).

(4) [Q.]   *He* told you, also, *he* had two dreams, which announced to *him* that it was *his* duty to set fire to the Minster?

— [A.] Yes.

[Q.]   And did *he* not say that his wife had *no* objection to keep the

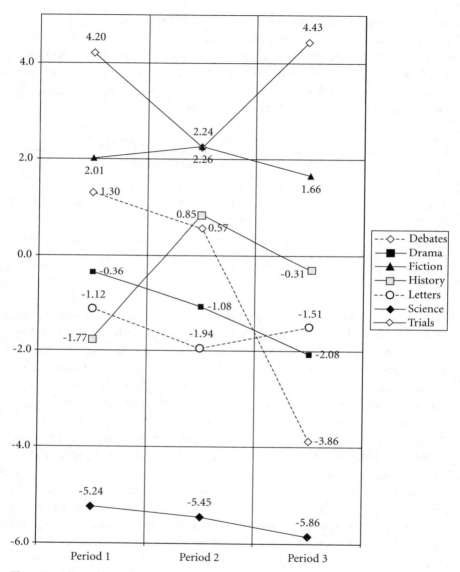

Figure 2. Mean dimension scores for Dimension 2 across three time periods.

secret, as *he* had taken a singular way to convince *her*?

[A.]   No, *he* did not say how that was.

[Q.]   But *he* told you about *his* dreams?

— [A.]   Yes.

[Q.]   You have heard the examination of the other witnesses, have you?
— [A.]   Yes.
[Q.]   *He* told you the same dreams, did *he*, as they have stated?
[A.]   Yes.
[Q.]   Did *he* not say *he* was afraid of *his* wife objecting to it?
[A.]   O, yes; *he* said *he* was afraid of *her* objecting to it, and *he* took a
         very particular way of convincing *her*; *he* stated that *he* took *her*
         wedding ring off *her* finger, and when *she* awoke, *she* made sad
         work about it, and *he* suffered *her* to work on three or four days,
         and *he* then told *her* that if *she* would keep the secret *he* was
         going to entrust *her* with, *he* would restore *her* ring.
[Q.]   Then *he* told *her*, did *he*?
— [A.]   *He* forced *her* to vow to keep it secret, and then told *her* his
         intention, and then *she* cried.

                                                                 [Text: T1trimar]

Example (4) contains numerous past tense verb forms and third person
pronouns (italicized), and *no*-negation (*no objection*). Witness depositions and
cross-examinations clearly consist of a good deal of narrativeness. Fiction is the
prototypical register with narrative concerns, as in (5) with past tense verb
forms italicized.

(5)   It *was* the beginning of October when she met Miss Wells, children, and
      luggage at the station, and fairly *was* on her way to her home. She *tried* to
      call it so, as a duty to Humfrey, but it *gave* her a pang every time, and in
      effect she *felt* far less at home than when he and Sarah *had stood* in the
      doorway to greet the arrivals. She *had purposely fixed* an hour when it
      would be dark, so that she *might* receive no painful welcome; she *wished*
      no one to greet her, she *had* rather they *were* mourning for their master.

                                                                  [Text: T2ficyon]

Among the registers there are three (marginally four) that have statistically
significant dimension scores across the three time periods: Debates, History,
and Trials change through the time periods. For History an increase in narrative
scores between period 1 and 2 may be noticed in Figure 2, for Debates there is
a clear decrease throughout all three time periods. The Trials register is more
complicated, with a substantial drop in period 2 which actually accounts for the
statistically significant result for this register. The dimension scores for period
1 and 3 are roughly identical (4.20 for period 1 versus 4.43 for period 3 in
Table 4). The Trials register contains a similar radical shift in period 2 on

Dimension 3 (see Table 5 and Figure 3). Drama also changes towards less narrative concerns; the probability of the F-value in Table 4 is above the 0.05 threshold, but the R-square value is fairly high at 0.26.

3.3 Dimension 3: Elaborate versus situation-dependent reference

The third textual dimension basically involves noun phrase elaboration. Biber (1988) interprets this dimension as expressing the opposition between 'explicit and situation-dependent reference'; in Biber & Finegan (1992) it is labeled 'Elaborated versus Situation-dependent Reference'. The grammatical features in the dimension score calculations include summing up *wh*-relatives, pied piping constructions, nominalizations and subtracting place adverbials, time adverbials, and a group of other adverbs (see Table 1a). One feature, phrasal coordination, was left out in the present study. As with Dimension 1, this dimension involves two parameters based on 'plus' features and 'minus' features. Thus, registers with high mean scores have high frequencies of *wh*-relatives, pied piping constructions, and nominalizations, in conjunction with low frequencies of place and time adverbials and other adverbs. Texts with low scores on this dimension have inverse proportions of these grammatical features: high frequencies of place and time adverbials as well as a preponderance of a group of other adverbs. Example (6) illustrates a trial with markedly frequent occurrences of place and time adverbials.

(6) [$Q.$]   Did she remain *in that parlour the whole of the day*?
— [$A.$]   Yes, she did.
[$Q.$]   Where was the Prisoner, Mr. Angus, *that day*?
— [$A.$]   Sometimes in one part of the house, and *sometimes* in another.
[$Q.$]   But was he out of the house at all *that day, on the Wednesday*?
— [$A.$]   No, he was not.
[$Q.$]   You say he was *sometimes* in one part of the house and *sometimes* in another; was he *frequently* in the parlour *that day*?
[$A.$]   He was much *in the parlour*.
[$Q.$]   Now what became of Miss Burns *at night* — did she remain *in the parlour*?
— [$A.$]   Yes, Sir.
[$Q.$]   Did she remain *there* all night as far as you know?
— [$A.$]   Yes, as far as I know.
[$Q.$]   Did you bring any thing *down stairs* for your master *at night* — any bedding?
[$A.$]   Yes, a Counterpain.   [Text: T1triang]

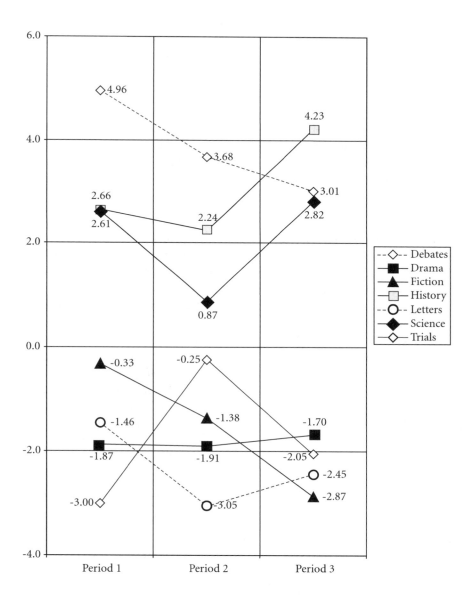

Figure 3. Mean dimension scores for Dimension 3 across three time periods.

In the CONCE data, Figure 3 shows that the registers on Dimension 3 form a clear dichotomy between expository registers (History, Debates and Science with overall positive dimension scores) and nonexpository registers (Drama, Fiction, Letters and Trials with overall negative dimension scores). The Newman-Keuls groupings in Table 2 suggest three subgroups of registers on Dimension 3: (A) Debates and History, (B) History and Science, and a large group consisting of (C) Drama, Fiction, Letters, and Trials. History is not statistically different from Debates or Science. Debates have the highest dimension score in period 1 (4.96), indicating that this register contains numerous postmodifying clauses (*wh*-relative clauses and pied piping constructions). However, although this register is marked by a statistically significant drop in referential elaboration across time, it nevertheless remains on the positive pole of the dimension with dimension scores close to those of Science in period 3, as in extract (7).

(7)   For, without entering into the question whether the exact representation of that House was altogether satisfactory, or discussing the inequalities *which* Gentlemen continually urged who thought an equal representation would be a far preferable thing, he would say that the people of this country were deeply and thoroughly attached to the present form of government *under which* they lived; and he had always considered it a condition in every reform, a condition *which* he thought had been happily complied with hitherto, that the representation of that House, the mode *in which* it was constituted, the mode *in which* the people elected their representatives, should be compatible and consistent with a monarchy and House of Lords, *which*, along with the House of Commons, were fundamental and essential parts of our form of government.

[Text: T2debhan]

Table 5. Mean scores for Dimension 3 'Elaborate versus situation-dependent reference'.

Period	Debates	Drama	Fiction	History	Letters	Science	Trials
Period 1	4.96	-1.87	-0.33	2.66	-1.46	2.61	-3.00
Period 2	3.68	-1.91	-1.38	2.24	-3.05	0.87	-0.25
Period 3	3.01	-1.70	-2.87	4.23	-2.45	2.82	-2.05
F-value	3.395	0.049	1.862	4.994	1.685	0.704	5.334
Probability	0.047	0.953	0.184	0.021	0.2032	0.509	0.088
R-square	0.18	<0.00	0.17	0.38	0.10	0.08	0.21

The dimension score analysis of the Parliamentary Debates shows that the texts in period 3 are much more involved, less narrative and referentially more situated.

The only other important change on Dimension 3 concerns History, where there is a significant increase in elaboration (from a mean dimension score of 2.66 in period 1 to 4.23 in period 3). This increase indicates that History texts have more elaborated noun phrases toward the end of the century, as in example (8).

(8)   And the course *which* he took to restore the authority of the British was, even in the opinion of his detractors, the very best *which* he could have taken. He telegraphed to Bombay for the soldiers *which* the peace with Persia had freed from duty; he telegraphed to Madras and Ceylon for any troops *which* could be spared from presidency or colony; he sent to Singapore for the regiments *which* were on their way to China to punish an aggression of the Chinese.   [Text: T2hiswal]

None of the nonexpository registers vary significantly across the time periods. As on Dimension 2, Trials jump in period 2 (with a fairly important R-square value of 0.21 in Table 5). Biber & Finegan (1989 and 1992) and Biber (1995:294) found significant changes for Fiction towards more situation-dependent reference. In CONCE as well, the mean dimension scores for Fiction drop from -0.33 in period 1 to -2.87 in period 3, but this change is not statistically significant (see Table 5).

3.4 Dimension 5: Impersonal versus non-impersonal style

Dimension 5 is the third of the dimensions representing an oral/literate pole. The dimension is labeled 'Abstract versus Non-abstract Information' in Biber (1988), and in Biber & Finegan (1997:259) 'Impersonal versus Non-impersonal Style'. The dimension scores are calculated by adding up passives, *by*-passives, conjuncts, and a group of adverbial subordinators (see Table 1a). In this study, no counts for participial clauses and WHIZ-deletions are included. As with Dimension 2, high mean scores on this dimension indicate that texts are marked with regard to abstract style. Conversely, low mean scores only show that the register is unmarked as to the degree of abstract style. Biber (1988:112–113) argues that Dimension 5 differentiates between registers with an abstract and technical focus and other registers.

Figure 4 shows that the CONCE data are divided into expository and nonexpository registers: The expository registers Science, History and Debates all have positive dimension scores and all the nonexpository registers have

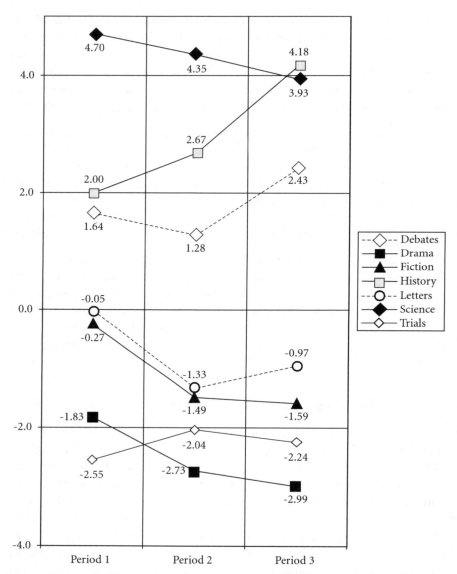

Figure 4. Mean dimension scores for Dimension 5 across three time periods.

negative dimension scores. The Newman-Keuls groupings in Table 2 reveal that there are five distinct subgroups: (A) Science, (B) History, (C) Debates, (D) Fiction and Letters, and (E) Drama and Trials. Hence, the scores for Fiction and Letters on the one hand, and Drama and Trials on the other are not statistically different. All three expository registers (Science, History, and Debates) are statistically distinct from each other. Biber & Finegan (1997: 269) also found the expository registers to be fairly heterogeneous with regard to the impersonal pole on Dimension 5 (cf. Kytö et al 2000: 91–92; Biber 1995: 133). The Science texts have the highest scores (4.70 in Table 6) representing a register that has clearly an abstract/technical focus, as in (9).

(9)   The loan will certainly have ultimately *to be repaid*; but, at the time when it *is contracted*, it acts with the same force as an export upon the country which receives it, and with that of an import to the country which gives it. In fact, the borrowing country exports its securities, which *are imported by the capitalists* who lend.   [Text: T2scigos]

Drama in period 3 is unmarked as to this dimension with few passives, conjuncts, and other adverbial subordinators, as in extract (10).

(10)   [Inez.] And let me fill them in according to my wildest imaginations — let me guess how much of what remains of that heart of yours *was given* to this stray companion, and how much to that stray companion. Ah, no, no, no, no! Let's draw a veil.
       [Sir R.] But you haven't told me anything.
       [Inez.] I will. Sincerely I have loved once. And I should like to remain constant, if constancy were not such a dream.
       [Sir R.] Is constancy a dream?
       [Inez.] What else is it? You have loved once, and yet with her consecrated image in your heart's holy of holies, you have opened its outer courts to a rabble of petticoats, drunk the wine and broken the bread with sluts, tossed off life's sacrament with any strange priestess that offered it — look at the remains of the feast! Oh, no, no, no, my dear friend! if constancy is not a dream, if faithfulness is not a shadow, where are they *to be found*?
       [Sir R.] Not in my heart. Yet I have loved once. Thank God for it!
                                                                   [Text: T3drajon]

The increases attested for Debates (from 1.64 in period 1 to 2.43 in period 3) and History (from 2.00 in period 1 to 4.18 in period 3) are not statistically significant (see Table 6 and the probabilities for Debates, 0.307, and History, 0.337). Three nonexpository registers, Drama, Fiction, and Letters, change across the three time periods (see F-values and their associated probabilities in Table 6). This finding partly corroborates the results in Biber & Finegan (1989 and 1992) of a "drift" in English registers. In CONCE, a change occurs towards a more personal/nonabstract style among several nonexpository registers.

Table 6. Mean scores for Dimension 5 'Abstract versus Nonabstract style'.

Period	Debates	Drama	Fiction	History	Letters	Science	Trials
Period 1	1.64	-1.83	-0.27	2.00	-0.05	4.70	-2.55
Period 2	1.28	-2.73	-1.49	2.67	-1.33	4.35	-2.04
Period 3	2.43	-2.99	-1.59	4.18	-0.97	3.93	-2.24
F-value	1.229	4.463	3.579	1.165	4.166	0.191	0.706
Probability	0.307	0.028	0.049	0.337	0.0257	0.828	0.499
R-square	0.07	0.34	0.28	0.13	0.22	0.02	0.03

Biber & Finegan (1989:512) found relatively little change across the centuries among letters and the change was not statistically significant, Fiction, on the other hand, changed significantly (1989:499).

4. Discussion and Conclusion

I have presented here a pilot study of seven registers of nineteenth-century English and their stylistic variation across four dimensions.

Biber & Finegan (1997:269) suggest different evolutionary paths for such registers as fiction and science, where science registers become more specialized (having a narrower readership) and fictional registers more popular (having a wider readership). Such a split is partially discernible in the CONCE material.

On Dimension 1, the expository registers (Science, Debates, and History) load on the informational end while the three nonexpository registers (Drama, Trials, Letters) come out as highly or moderately involved. On Dimension 2, the speech-related register Trials is highly narrative, followed by Fiction. Science texts are markedly non-narrative. The Debates register changes dramatically in narrative concerns, but this shift is explained by the fact that only the first two time periods contain reported speech in the third person. Indeed, it is the first person speeches in period 3 that account for the statistically significant changes on Dimensions 1 (towards involvement), 2 (less narrative), and 3 (towards less elaborated reference) (as comes forth in Kytö et al 2000:95 fn., Debates are only partly speech-related). As to the opposition between elaborated reference and situation-dependent reference on Dimension 3, the expository registers are marked by having elaborated reference. History texts become more elaborated towards the end of the century in the form of an increased use of postmodification. Drama, Letters, Fiction, and Trials are predominantly situation-dependent having fewer relative clauses and higher ratios of features such as time and place adverbials. Finally, expository and nonexpository registers are differentiated on Dimension 5. This is also the only dimension where we find a statistically significant drift in the sense that three registers (Letters, Drama, and Fiction) become progressively more personal/nonabstract.

Regardless of whether Debates are third person reported speech from the first two time periods or first person speeches from period 3, the texts are marked by frequent uses of nominal or abstract features signaling information density such as nouns, prepositions, relative clauses, and passive voice. The fact that period 3 Debates are generally first person monologues does not make them situationally involved, situation-dependent in reference, nor nonabstract. In contrast, Trials, another speech-related register, is involved, has situation-dependent referential features, and is nonabstract/personal. The witness depositions and the cross-examinations are chiefly inter-personal in that they involve fairly natural conversation in the form of question-answer dyads (despite a very formal setting). Furthermore, the subject matter in the Trials is mainly the past whereabouts and actions of individuals.

As regards subgroups of registers in CONCE, tests show that Debates pattern together with Science and/or History on three of the dimensions (Dimensions 1, 2, and 3). Drama and Trials are statistically similar on three dimensions (Dimensions 1, 3, and 5). In conjunction with the relative placement of Debates and Trials on the various dimensions, these groupings support the validity of treating Debates as an expository register, and Trials as a non-expository one.

Science is the only register that does not change to a statistically significant degree across the three time periods.

The CONCE corpus contains three speech-related registers, but only two of these registers come out on the oral pole: Trials and Drama clearly pattern towards the oral pole on Dimensions 1 (Involved), 3 (Situation-dependent reference), and 5 (Nonabstract style). On the whole, the drift among registers noted in Biber & Finegan (1997) was only partly confirmed in CONCE, whereas the relative placement of several registers on a particular dimension largely agrees with previous research. The distribution of the dimension scores also points to new insights into nineteenth century register variation. In particular, a speech-based register Trials, consisting of British trials and witness depositions, indeed "plots" on the oral end of several dimensions (Dimension 1, 3, and 5).

The present study identifies various registers and compares them to one another. Two follow-up studies treat properties of specific registers. In Geisler (2001) it is shown that the personal letters of men and women contain distinct features and that women's letter-writing changes more than men's. Geisler (to appear) investigates the sub-disciplines of the Science register, and finds that the various scientific disciplines such as chemistry, biology, and geography are in fact already distinct registers as early as the 19th century.

The main insight gained in the investigation of the 19th century data is that registers and sets of registers which share certain situational characteristics are clearly defined. As regards overall tendencies of language change during the century, the picture is less clear, primarily because of little previous research on the language of that century.

In sum, there is generally a dichotomy between expository and non-expository registers, which in some cases increases with time. In terms of gradual diachronic change, only some registers shift: the non-expository registers Drama, Fiction, and Letters become less abstract, whereas the expository History texts gradually become more narrative and use more elaborated reference.

Note

* I thank Merja Kytö for valuable comments on previous versions of this paper. The research reported here has been generously supported by travel grants from the Language Division, Uppsala University.

References

Biber, D. 1988. *Variation across speech and writing.* Cambridge: Cambridge University Press.
Biber, D. 1995. *Dimensions of register variation: A cross-linguistic comparison.* Cambridge: Cambridge University Press.
Biber, D. and Finegan, E. 1989. Drift and the evolution of English style: A history of three genres. *Language* 65: 487–517.
Biber, D. and Finegan, E. 1992. The linguistic evolution of five written and speech-based English genres from the 17th to the 20th centuries. In *History of Englishes: New methods and interpretations in historical linguistics,* M. Rissanen, O. Ihalainen, T. Nevalainen and I. Taavitsainen (eds), 688–704. Berlin: Mouton de Gruyter.
Biber, D. and Finegan, E. 1997. Diachronic relations among speech-based and written registers in English. In *To explain the present: Studies in the changing English language in*

honour of Matti Rissanen, T. Nevalainen and L. Kahlas-Tarkka (eds), 253–275. Helsinki: Société Néophilologique de Helsinki.

CONCE = A Corpus of Nineteenth-century English, being compiled by Merja Kytö (Uppsala University) and Juhani Rudanko (University of Tampere).

Geisler, C. 2001. Gender-based variation in nineteenth-century English letter-writing. Paper presented at *The Third North American Symposium on Corpus Linguistics and Language Teaching*, Boston, April 2001. To appear in *Corpus analysis: Language structure and language use*, C. Meyer and P. Leistyna (eds). Amsterdam: Rodopi.

Geisler, C. to appear. Intra-register variation in 19th-century English science texts. *New vistas into Victorian English: Studies in 19th-century morpho-syntax* (working title), M. Kytö, M. Ryden, & E. Smitterberg (eds).

Görlach, M. 1995. *New studies in the history of English.* Heidelberg: Universitätsverlag C. Winter.

Görlach, M. 1999. *English in nineteenth-century England.* Cambridge: Cambridge University Press.

Kytö, M. 1996. *Manual to the diachronic part of the Helsinki Corpus of English Texts: Coding conventions and lists of source texts.* 3rd edition. Helsinki: Department of English, University of Helsinki.

Kytö, M., Rudanko, J., and Smitterberg, E. 2000. Building a bridge between the present and the past: A corpus of 19th-century English. *ICAME Journal* 24: 85–97.

Index

In the series STUDIES IN CORPUS LINGUISTICS (SCL) the following titles have been published thus far:

1. PEARSON, Jennifer: *Terms in Context.* 1998.
2. PARTINGTON, Alan: *Patterns and Meanings. Using corpora for English language research and teaching.* 1998.
3. BOTLEY, Simon and Anthony Mark McENERY (eds.): *Corpus-based and Computational Approaches to Discourse Anaphora.* 2000.
4. HUNSTON, Susan and Gill FRANCIS: *Pattern Grammar. A corpus-driven approach to the lexical grammar of English.* 2000.
5. GHADESSY, Mohsen, Alex HENRY and Robert L. ROSEBERRY (eds.): *Small Corpus Studies and ELT. Theory and practice.* 2001.
6. TOGNINI-BONELLI, Elena: *Corpus Linguistics at Work.* 2001.
7. ALTENBERG, Bengt and Sylviane GRANGER (eds.): *Lexis in Contrast. Corpus-based approaches.* 2002.
8. STENSTRÖM, Anna-Brita, Gisle ANDERSEN and Ingrid Kristine HASUND: *Trends in Teenage Talk. Corpus compilation, analysis and findings.* 2002.
9. REPPEN, Randi, Susan M. FITZMAURICE and Douglas BIBER (eds.): *TUsing Corpora to Explore Linguistic Variation.* 2002.
10. AIJMER, Karin: *English Discourse Particles. Evidence from a corpus.* 2002.
11. BARNBROOK, Geoff: *Defining Language. A local grammar of definition sentences.* 2002.